ANGRY WHITE MALE

ANGRY WHITE MALE

HOW THE DONALD TRUMP PHENOMENON IS CHANGING AMERICA–AND WHAT WE CAN ALL DO TO SAVE THE MIDDLE CLASS

WAYNE ALLYN ROOT

FOREWORD BY **ROGER STONE**

Skyhorse Publishing

Psalms 7:11 (KJV) *God judgeth the righteous, and God is angry with the wicked every day.*

Skyhorse Publishing books may be purchased in bulk at special discounts for sales promotion, corporate gifts, fund-raising, or educational purposes. Special editions can also be created to specifications. For details, contact the Special Sales Department, Skyhorse Publishing, 307 West 36th Street, 11th Floor, New York, NY 10018 or info@skyhorsepublishing.com.

Skyhorse˚ and Skyhorse Publishing˚ are registered trademarks of Skyhorse Publishing, Inc.˚, a Delaware corporation.

Visit our website at www.skyhorsepublishing.com.

10 9 8 7 6 5 4 3 2 1

Library of Congress Cataloging-in-Publication Data is available on file.

Cover design by Brian Peterson
Cover photo credit: Alexander Miller

Print ISBN: 978-1-5107-1842-5
Ebook ISBN: 978-1-5107-1843-2

Printed in the United States of America

This book is dedicated to my father David Root and my immigrant grandfather Simon Reis. They were true-blue American patriots and small businessmen. They taught me right from wrong. They taught me about God and country. They taught me what made America great and exceptional: capitalism, competition, mobility, and opportunity. Because of their wisdom and counsel, I clearly see what is happening to America and the great American middle class today. We are under attack. We are being targeted, intimidated, and persecuted. We have every right to be angry. This is our story.

And, of course, this book is also dedicated to the man who can save the middle class and make America great again—my hero, inspiration, and the next president of the United States, Donald J. Trump.

"It's so clear what's happening in America. If you can't see it, you're either blind or you are part of the problem."

—Wayne Allyn Root

Author's Note

I dare you. I double dare you. Because of the provocative title, and my high-profile conservative credentials, I'm certain vicious and biased liberal "hit men and women" will try to spin this book as "racist." It's not. I dare you to find a racist word in this book. You won't. This book doesn't attack any racial, religious, ethnic, or sexual orientation group. What it does is defend a group that is being targeted, attacked, intimidated and persecuted—the great American middle class. I titled it *Angry White Male* because the current American middle class happens to be predominantly white. I am an angry white male defending it. But I'm also defending the millions of middle-class women and religious and ethnic minorities who are also part of America's middle class. I guess Obama, Hillary, and liberals just consider them expendable, "collateral damage." This book points out the reverse racism and hypocrisy aimed at America's middle class. We are under attack. We are marked for extinction. *We* are the victims of racism. It's time to stand up in self-defense.

Additional note: Any product or endorsement I make in this book is for companies and products that I use and believe in—the sponsors of my radio show.

Contents

Foreword by Roger Stone

Wayne Allyn Root has written "The Handbook of the Trump Revolution."

Wayne Allyn Root is an acquired taste. Brash, combative, outspoken, and self-created American businessman, politician, television and radio personality, author, television producer, and political pundit—he is an unabashed advocate for smaller government and American sovereignty. Wayne, who often signs his emails with his initials "WAR," is probably the most famous celebrity you've never heard of (until now). In fact, Wayne has a large body of bestselling books, hit television shows, and reverberating political commentary to his credit.

Let's just say Wayne Allyn Root is a man who understands the odds. Root's media career began in New York City on WNBC radio (now WFAN) in the early 1980s. He moved onto NBC's *The Source* radio network, syndicated around the country in over one hundred markets, as a sports talk host.

A free market advocate, Root is a shrewd analyst of market trends, Wall Street, and Vegas gambling odds—a rare combination. This has allowed the optimistic and gregarious conservative to make and lose many fortunes. Wayne is a man who knows how to hustle and knows how to make a buck. That the Obama IRS targeted Wayne for his outspoken opposition to our current president is undeniable. The prolific author and political commentator has undergone vigorous audits and harassments by the Internal Revenue Service yet the stalwart Root has refused to buckle under to the obvious political pressure. Like Donald Trump, Wayne is relentless and unstoppable.

Deeply tanned with a wide smile and perfect gleaming white teeth, and always perfectly coiffed, Wayne Allyn Root gives off the air of a Hollywood movie star, or a TV newsman, but he is neither. Dogged in his advocacy for economic growth and opportunity and smaller, less intrusive government, Wayne has gladly taken the slings and arrows of the liberal elite who seek to mock him because they cannot rebut his ideas.

There is something about Wayne that is perfectly American. Perhaps it's his sunny optimism, or his steadfast belief in the bedrock principles of this country.

In 2008, disgusted with the free spending and Wall Street bailouts by establishment Republicans, Wayne bolted the party of Lincoln to launch his candidacy for the Libertarian party nomination for president. The ever-ebullient Root would have been a much stronger candidate than former Congressman Barr—Barr posed as a libertarian just long enough to grab that party's presidential nomination, although he was required to take Root as his vice presidential running mate in order to garner the delegate votes necessary for nomination. The better man was on the lower half of the ticket.

Undaunted, Root has continued to pummel Obama over his job-killing economic policies, disastrous foreign policies, and the mountain of debts in borrowing that his administration is bequeathing us.

The unflappable Root has now reinvented himself yet again. He was one of the first figures in America to see the potential for the presidential candidacy of Donald J. Trump, and has been a constant presence on cable television and talk radio, defending the New York billionaire and his controversial platform on cutting taxes, regulations, and the size of government; repealing Obamacare; securing the border; reforming trade policies to save the American middle class; and rebuilding America's military strength.

Even worse for the Democrats, Wayne has emerged as one of the most effective critics of Hillary Clinton and her entire record of incompetence, corruption, and lies. Root's skewering of the former first couple has been relentless and effective. That could be why he has come under constant attack by liberal cable television icons like Jon Stewart, Rachel Maddow, and Bill Maher.

Always controversial and never willing to be quiet in the face of wrong-headed government policies, anything Wayne Allyn Root writes is worth reading. In fact, Wayne has an annoying habit of being ahead of the curve in gauging the public's disgust with the failed policies of the two-party duopoly and the neo-cons who have driven us to endless wars, while bankrupting the nation.

Wayne was among the first to recognize the inherent danger of radical Islam, as well as the unchecked flood of illegal immigrants who are sucking dry the American system, while perpetrating a crime wave against the American people. Wayne calls it as he sees it—unvarnished, blunt, and plainspoken. Another Trump-like attribute.

Now in *Angry White Male*, Root provides a manifesto for Donald Trump's silent majority, and outlines how immigrants and non-Americans flood here by the millions to sign up for America's generous taxpayer-financed welfare state.

Wayne is the quintessential "Angry White Male."

Roger Stone
New York City
June 2016

Introduction

Bill Maher and the Apology

In the middle of writing this book Bill Maher asked me to be the "sacrificial conservative guest" on his HBO show *Real Time with Bill Maher*. On the show I was asked about Obama's visit to Japan. I was asked if Obama should have visited Hiroshima—the site of our nuclear attacks that ended World War II. I was asked, "Was it appropriate for Obama to visit?"

This gets to the very core of this book . . . to the core of why I'm an "Angry White Male." As I said to host Bill Maher on the show, I'm not a fan of apologies, especially if you're apologizing for responding to something terrible the other guy did. Japan bombed Pearl Harbor. They started the war; we merely ended it. They committed terrible atrocities against our soldiers and American POWs throughout the war.

My father, David Root, served in the South Pacific. He fought at Okinawa, the bloodiest battle of World War II. He saw firsthand the atrocities of the Japanese.

Our nuclear bombs didn't just take lives, they saved lives. Ironically, probably more Japanese than American lives. Experts estimated the invasion of Japan would have cost at least one million lives. One of them might have been my father's.

So my answer to Bill Maher was that I'm not a fan of even *the appearance* of apologizing for those atomic bombs, unless of course Japan's prime minister is willing to come to Hawaii to apologize to the American victims of Pearl Harbor.

I pointed out that that is a negotiation that only a President Donald Trump could win.

But I found the response from Bill Maher's liberal viewers interesting. I received death threats . . . and people wishing me a "long slow painful death." Some lectured me on all the apologies we owe to Japanese survivors, American Indians, and, of course, African American slaves.

I suddenly realized it's time for Obama's victims—middle-class America (which is predominantly white)—to speak up. Here is my answer to liberals across the country.

You're 100 percent right—apologies are sometimes necessary.

Obama and his socialist cabal should apologize to every middle-class American for the harm they've done to the US economy . . . upward mobility . . . middle-class jobs (there are none) . . . and the American Dream (it's dead).

They've created an unimaginable DISASTER. They've destroyed the greatest nation . . . greatest economy . . . greatest economic system (capitalism) . . . and greatest middle class in world history.

We are living in an Obama Great Depression.

Obama should also apologize for adding well over $10 trillion to the national debt (by the time he leaves office), which could lead to a severe debt crisis and the eventual collapse of the US economy, but at a minimum will certainly cripple the quality of life for our children and grandchildren.

Obama should also apologize for the lies and fraud of Obamacare. He lied when he said, "If you like your insurance, you can keep your insurance." Really? I lost mine. So did millions of other Americans. We are owed an apology.

Obama should also apologize for the disastrous effects of Obamacare, which has doubled and tripled premiums, copays, deductibles, and prescription costs; killed quality high-wage middle-class jobs; and made it almost impossible to start or run a successful small business.

But in the case of Obamacare, apologies alone won't do. The architects of Obamacare are owed a prison sentence for committing the biggest fraud in American history.

Obama should apologize for the vicious IRS attacks— trying to persecute people for their political and religious beliefs. Or didn't you know the IRS was ordered to go after conservative, Tea Party, Christian, and pro-Israel groups? I was one of the victims. Where's my apology?

Obama should apologize for cutting $2.6 billion for veterans, while adding $4.5 billion to the budget for the importing of Syrian migrants into the United States. Every veteran in America is owed an apology.

Obama should apologize for demanding in his last budget as president that Congress allocate almost $18,000 for every illegal alien child or teen that enters America. That's $3,000 more than an American-born senior citizen gets for

Social Security, even though they paid into the system. Every American-born senior citizen is owed an apology.

Obama should apologize for the disastrous economy he has created with his radical leftist agenda.

Obama and his buddies in the Democratic Party should apologize for what they've done to Detroit, Chicago, Baltimore, Memphis, New Orleans, and every other urban city run 100 percent by Democrats for the past fifty-plus years that are now all bankrupt, choked by debt, dominated by abandoned homes, shrinking population, streetlights out, violent crime, murder, and hopelessness. They've been under 100 percent Democratic rule. What's the excuse?

Obama should apologize for demoralizing every business owner in America by saying, "You didn't build that."

And Hillary should apologize for saying "Businesses don't create jobs, government does."[1]

As soon as Obama, Hillary, their socialist cabal, and every guilt-ridden white liberal apologizes for all that . . .

Then and only then should we worry about things done seventy, one hundred, and two hundred years ago. I wasn't there for any of the things liberals want us to apologize for. Since I bear no responsibility, I don't see what I have to apologize for.

But Obama, Hillary, and their liberal friends should apologize for what they just did to the great American middle class. That group is predominantly white, but there are many millions of other Americans of all races caught up in the attack. I guess they are just considered the victims of unintended consequences.

They should also apologize to every small businessman and woman in America. Every business I personally own and every friend I have who owns a small business is in trouble, struggling to overcome the burdens of business under Obama: dramatically increased taxes, regulations, energy costs (because of the fraud of "green energy"), health care costs, legal bills, and IRS attacks. The liberal policies of Obama's administration have damaged and demoralized every small business owner and job creator in this country.

There are twenty-eight million small business owners in America. Over 85 percent happen to be owned by non-Hispanic white Americans, according to CNBC.[2]

Hence the reason there are so many angry white males. But that still means millions of small business owners are women, black, Hispanic, Asian, or Native American. They have every right to be angry, too.

Where is our apology?

Obama, Hillary, Bernie, their socialist cabal, and the guilt-ridden white elite liberals ruining this great country called America are not about to apologize. As a matter of fact, they have no intention of resting until America is no longer exceptional, the American Dream is dead, and we, the middle class (but not them), are leading crappy lives of equality (i.e., shared misery).

Why *won't* they apologize? Because this destruction of America is not happening due to ignorance or ineptitude. Instead, it is part of a conscious, coordinated plan to destroy this country. You probably didn't know that this plan to "bring down America" is actually taught in our ultra-liberal univer-sities. Obama learned it at Columbia. How do I know? I was Obama's college classmate, I learned the plan as well, and in this book I'll expose it to all of you.

I'm an angry white male. This is my story.

Part I

I'm an
Angry White Male

1

I Am an S.O.B.

Every author, no matter how fair and impartial he might try to be, comes with his own life experiences and point of view. So before we get into the meat of this book, let me give you a little background on me.

I am the perfect Angry White Male because I was born into the perfect (and classic) white middle-class life. I can't speak to the black experience, or Hispanic experience, or any other kind of experience. Because I was born white. This book is my story and my experience. It isn't better or inferior to anyone else's. But it's mine.

I am an S.O.B.—son of a butcher. I'm also a G.O.B.—grandson of a butcher. My father and grandfather were special people. They represented the greatness of America, the salt-of-the-earth drive, ambition, morality, patriotism, work ethic, faith in God, and love of family and country.

They both aimed for the American Dream. My grandfather found it. He turned his four-man butcher store into a big success. My father struggled—his two-man butcher store achieved only mediocre success. Yet my dad was happy, loved America, and believed he had achieved his version of the American Dream. Despite never making any serious money, my dad fulfilled the only real dream he had: to be his own boss.

The important point here is that they both had a shot—and that's what makes America great. In America, anyone can become an owner—of their own home, business, life. It may not be pretty. It may not be perfect. But it's yours. Owning a business, even a small one, is a little piece of heaven. And what has made America great for centuries was that through hard work, ambition, tenacity, and personal responsibility, anyone could build what my father and grandfather did. Sorry Obama, but "we DID build it."

A small businessman in my father's and grandfather's day was no Kennedy or Rockefeller or J. P. Morgan—no mogul, no billionaire. But he or she could move up in class, be their own boss, and stake a claim to a better life and a better future for their kids. My grandparents and parents could pay their bills, buy a new car every four years, go on annual vacations, pay for their children's college, and live a great middle-class life. You didn't need to be a millionaire or billionaire to live a great life in the old America.

My grandfather and father both did well, to varying degrees. They both died satisfied. They both believed their kids and grandkids would do better than they did. They knew America was exceptional. They knew firsthand the American Dream was real. They knew firsthand the streets were paved with gold.

Here's the crucial question: why would anyone want to purposely aim to "fundamentally change" that?

Obama admitted publicly that was his goal. And little by little, that life enjoyed by my father and grandfather is gone.

Today, owning a small business is a struggle. Paying the bills is a struggle. Paying the *legal* bills is a struggle. Paying the taxes is a struggle. Paying the landlord is a struggle. Filling out the IRS tax returns is a struggle.

The cost of regulations makes it almost impossible to start a business or keep a business running. Between high income taxes, payroll taxes, property taxes, workers' compensation bills, legal bills, energy bills, skyrocketing health care bills, incorporation fees, minimum wage laws for employees, the threat of lawsuits, IRS audits, government regulations—it never ends, and nowadays it rarely ends *well*.

Later in this book you'll hear the statistics about the dramatic decline of small business and the death of business start-ups (the lifeblood of middle-class job creation). What I'm talking about isn't an opinion. What's happening is a fact.

Today, anyone who starts or owns a business is targeted, persecuted, and marked for extinction by both Democrats looking to tax, spend, and redistribute us to death; and Republicans looking to keep us "small" and struggling to give the advantage to their big business donors. We get creamed by both sides and on both ends. The hits just keep on coming!

If anyone would know, it's me. I am a small businessman. Except for an eighteen-month period when I was a national television anchorman, I've never worked for anyone in my life. I've always been a small business owner, independent contractor, and "One-Man Army."

I've never taken a check from the government in my life. I've never worked for the government. I've never done business with the government. I've never had a "safe" weekly paycheck from a big corporation. I've never had a pension. No company has paid my health insurance. My income has always been based on performance—i.e., commission. I am the "Last of the Mohicans." I'm capitalism *squared*. I'm the American Dream on steroids. I'm Willie Loman (from *Death of a Salesman*) come to real life and updated for 2016. I don't depend on anyone but me. I eat what I kill. I'm a real-life Renaissance man. Sadly, there aren't too many like me left anymore.

But that's not a mistake or coincidence. It's a purposeful plan. Small businessmen, performance-based and commission-based salesmen, and independent contractors are being systematically driven to extinction.

While the GOP is no friend of mine and rarely does anything to help me succeed, the Democrats are my sworn enemy. They are out to *destroy* me. Could it be a coincidence that everything Obama believes in, everything he's done— every goal, every policy—is aimed directly at me and Americans just like me?

- He's raised my income taxes.
- He's raised my payroll taxes.
- He's raised my Obamacare taxes.
- He's raised my capital gains taxes.
- He's dramatically raised taxes on dividends and bank interest.
- He's limited my tax deductions.
- He's limited my exemptions.
- He's phased out my child credits.

- He's ruined the quality of my health care and dramatically raised my insurance premiums.
- He's added draconian regulations.
- He's dramatically raised my legal and accounting bills because of the new complicated taxes and regulations.
- He's dramatically raised my energy bills with his climate change and green energy obsession. To educate those who are ignorant or delusional, fossil fuels are dirt cheap. "Alternative energy" is sky high. Pretty simple stuff.
- He's tried to hurt the tax advantages of Subchapter S companies.
- He's tried to eliminate or drastically restrict the use of independent contractor status (ask Uber).
- He's made life almost impossible with rampant use of tax liens by the IRS. Once the IRS places a lien on you or your business, your credit is ruined, all funding from lenders dries up, and you are effectively prevented from earning a living.
- He's hit small business with Obamacare rules, overtime rules, and minimum wage raises.
- He wants to eliminate the cap on FICA (Social Security taxes). I could not survive that one.
- He wants to eliminate my lifesaving deductions for business expenses, mortgage deduction, and charitable donations. (I could not survive that either.)
- He's passed laws making it almost impossible to choose to leave America and do business or banking overseas.

- He wants to pass TPP, which would kill middle-class jobs by the millions and place all of us under foreign laws.
- He's aimed IRS tax audits at small business.
- He's passed new laws allowing the IRS to seize your passport if you owe $50,000 or more, so you are no longer free to leave the country. How scary is that? Any successful small businessman could easily ring up a $50,000 tax bill after only sixty days of being late for payroll taxes. We're all in grave danger. Think about this: without a passport you can no longer take a business trip overseas. So the IRS has taken away your right to earn a living.
- He's passed laws that make it all but impossible for small business owners to set aside money for retirement.
- He's handed over the country to lawyers and class action lawsuits.
- He's passed Dodd-Frank regulations that make it almost impossible to raise money anymore for a small business.
- He's passed draconian banking laws that make it impossible for small business owners like me to ever qualify for a mortgage on an expensive home. So I can never again qualify to own the very home I live in right now.
- He's made the Environmental Protection Agency (EPA) king and tyrant ruler of America, imposing draconian regulations and fines on small businesses, farmers, ranchers, landowners, and anyone with a puddle on their property.

- Of course, this same out-of-control EPA has put coal out of business—and with it, hundreds of thousands of high-paying middle-class jobs.
- He even tried to badly hurt businesses by attempting to ban us from using criminal background checks on potential employees. Can you imagine flying blind when you interview murderers, rapists, and financial scammers for a job? Then if you hire them to interact with your customers and something goes wrong, you get sued. *That* should be good for your business!
- And get this one: Obama tried to impose 442 different taxes that were never passed by the Republican Congress, or all of us would already be out of business.[1]

What a list.

What a madman. How much worse could it get if we had a pure communist tyrant out of the old Soviet Union in charge? It's like a personal attack directed straight at my life by the Obama administration. And there's a new attack every day. *Literally.*

Is anything I do *not* under attack? There is no point even trying to debate: Obama, Hillary, Bernie, and their socialist cabal clearly want to wipe small business owners, landowners, property owners, farmers, ranchers, any and all salesmen, and independent contractors off the face of the earth.

And all of those groups just happen to include about twenty-eight million Americans just like me—predominantly white, small business owners or independent contractors.

CNBC estimates this group is 85 percent white. Most of us vote Republican and are supportive of conservative policies, candidates, and causes. Most of us are homeowners. Most of us are high-income earners. Most of us are churchgoers. Most of us are married with children. Every bill, policy, and tax I listed above is aimed to cripple us.

So this is clearly no coincidence. *It's crystal clear.* Our way of life is under attack. Obama and his socialist cabal hate us for our work ethic, success, and ownership. They want to take it all away, punish us, and redistribute our income and assets. They want us to live in misery. They want us to be serfs: dependent on only big government and big business for our survival. They want us poor, broke, helpless, and hopeless— with nowhere else to turn. So they need to slowly bankrupt us and dry up our money.

That is the life Obama, Hillary, Bernie, and their socialist cabal are trying to kill in the name of guilt, equality, fairness, social justice, and, of course, revenge and reparations.

But, again, let me stress that the GOP establishment is not much better. They fight for their biggest donors only. The rest of us don't matter because we have no lobbyists, or DC law firms, or million-dollar checks for the politicians.

The middle class made America great, not the other way around. It wasn't the rich elites, academics, politicians, or bureaucrats. Small business was (and still is) the economic engine of the greatest economy in world history. Capitalism, social mobility, and the economic and individual freedoms guaranteed by the US Constitution have lifted more people out of poverty than all other political systems in world history *combined*. They are the very foundation of the American Dream. The middle class is quite simply the class that produces almost everything.

Today, the middle class is being targeted, persecuted, and systematically wiped out. I, and millions of others like me, are angry about it. Hence the title of this book, *Angry White Male.*

This group isn't the super wealthy "1 percent." But they are the "top 10 percent," who pay over 70 percent of the taxes in America.[2]

And they are the "top 20 percent," who pay 92.9 percent of the taxes.

And they certainly are the "top 40 percent," who pay 106 percent of the taxes. Yes, the correct figure is 106 percent.[3]

Like I said, we pay just about everything (and then some).

The middle class and small business owners built America with our blood, sweat, and tears. Our ambition, sacrifice, and courage to risk our own money in pursuit of the American Dream provides virtually all the trillions of dollars in taxes. Without us, the taxes we pay, and the jobs we create, there is no government. We pay for the government agencies, programs, and bureaucrats. We pay for the public works projects, highways, schools, hospitals, and airports. We pay for the welfare state.

Yes, Mr. Obama, *we did build it.*

Big government politicians like Obama should be praising and celebrating us, not denigrating us. Politicians and government bureaucrats survive and prosper because of us, not the other way around.

My vision as a conservative and capitalist has always been to provide opportunity and lift everyone up regardless of race, sex, or social status. My vision of equality is everyone doing well, independent of government. The leftist's vision of equality is to make everyone equally miserable, poor, hopeless, helpless, and dependent on government. By destroying the middle class, power and control is centralized in the hands of the elite, privileged, political class and the super wealthy who fund them.

By the way, this is how most societies have functioned throughout history. Think about the dark days of kings, aristocracy, and serfs. Think *Downton Abbey*. Think *Braveheart*.

What's standing in the way of an elitist, aristocratic, serf society is an independent middle class that doesn't need or want government's help. For the progressive elites, that's a big problem. The middle class gets in the way of big government's control. That's why liberals believe the middle class must be eliminated and along with it the capitalist economy that fosters independence, rewards ambition and personal responsibility, and provides upward mobility to achieve the American Dream.

So you see, it isn't about black or white. It's about a leftist vision of tearing people down, instead of lifting them up. Never forget: the tools being used are social justice, guilt, revenge, reparations, and redistribution . . . versus empowerment and personal responsibility. And, of course, an open border that allows in millions of foreigners who have no understanding of, or love for, capitalism or economic freedom. They're interested only in survival. And they demand high taxes on the middle class to pay for their survival.

America itself is central to this plan. America is the beacon, the shining light on the hill. America is the proof for millions of "serfs" trapped under the rule of tyrants the world over that freedom exists, that the individual can triumph. America gives hope to the masses that one day they can be free, happy, and wealthy.

Therefore, in the eyes of these leftist tyrants, the ideals of America must be stamped out. Ironically, guilty white liberals chose a black American to do the dirty deed. They were smart. They knew that because of guilt and a fear of being called "racist," white America would allow Obama to do things no white liberal could ever get away with. It's truly ironic that the man whose slogan was "HOPE" is well on his way to snuffing out the very last hope for mankind.

What has been done to the predominantly white middle class in the past eight years is unimaginable and mind-numbing. You need to face the truth before you can act on it. Taking action is the only way to reverse fear and desperation. Complaining doesn't help. Only taking action will set you free.

That action starts with putting a plan in place to protect yourself and save our nation. The great news is this book will present that plan and provide you with options.

I hope you're now starting to understand why I believe we have every right to be Angry White Males. Our livelihoods are being taken away. Our freedom and future as productive members of society hangs in the balance.

2

Angry White Male

The definition of a racist: "Anyone winning an argument with a liberal."

In many ways, *Angry White Male* is an autobiography. This book is my story, my testimony to being an angry white male. The things I believe in are under attack: God, country, American exceptionalism, capitalism, Judeo-Christian values, and the great American middle class.

As I've noted previously, this book is not an indictment of or attack on anyone who is not a white male. This book is simply making the case for self-defense of the great American middle class, which Pew Research has shown to be predominantly white. Pew broke the middle class up into four distinct groups basically representing upper middle class, middle class, working middle class, and the anxious, struggling, trying-to-hang-on class. Pew reports the first group is 79 percent white, the second group is 75 percent white, the third group is 73 percent white, and the fourth group is 56 percent white.[1]

My defense of the middle class is not only that of white Americans. It is also the defense of millions of ethnic minorities who have sacrificed and worked hard to achieve the

American Dream of being part of the middle class. They are also under attack, and I am defending them, too.

This book takes a detailed look at what's happening to an entire group of good people: law-abiding, tax-paying, hardworking middle-class citizens, most of whom happen to be white. We're being targeted, intimidated, persecuted, demonized, silenced, financially brutalized, annihilated— literally wiped off the map.

Let's look closer at why the "progressive" political, media, and big business elites have targeted the American middle class for extinction.

First, it's happening to self-medicate wealthy white liberals who feel guilt, embarrassment, and self-hatred about the power, money, and connections they inherited. It's open season on middle-class white males so these spoiled brat, lucky sperm club, white liberals can feel better about themselves.

Second, it's happening in the name of a mental illness called liberalism, whose adherents believe they are the intellectual elite who know what is best for the masses. And to control the masses they must make them all dependent on government, run by the elite, to survive. As I'll show throughout the book, in order to achieve that goal, guilty white liberals have to destroy the middle class. They know that can only be done by destroying America's foundations of God, country, patriotism, capitalism, American exceptionalism, individual responsibility, economic mobility, and the very existence of the American Dream.

Third, it's happening because bankers, Wall Street, and the very wealthy are more comfortable with us as dependent serfs than as potential upwardly mobile middle-class competitors. They don't care about white or black. They only care about the color green—money. They are greedy. They want the whole ball of wax. They want all the chips on the table. They don't like true capitalism. They favor *crony capitalism*. They want open borders, not because they care about bringing foreigners into America in order to elect Democrats. They just want cheap labor so they can get richer.

They want government contracts, government investments, and tons of quantitative easing (QE, Federal Reserve money printing). Because it all goes to them.

They also like government regulations and high taxes. Why? Because the more regulations, the better it is for them. They have armies of lawyers, accountants, lobbyists, and compliance officers. They can afford to navigate the thousands of pages of onerous regulations.

They don't care about high taxes. They have tax lawyers and tax shelters. All these rules, regulations, and taxes kill the little guy, the middle class, small business. This kills the competition. These big boys don't want any of us to be able to compete with them. They want a society that favors giant multinational companies and puts little guys out of business. Look around, it's happening every day. Small stores struggle to compete with Wal-Mart; small restaurants struggle to compete with national chains; small hardware or food stores struggle to compete with big box stores. And every new government tax or regulation makes the struggle just that much harder and more unfair.

Clearly, liberals and big business crony capitalists can never be honest about their goals. If so, we would kick them out of power. Instead, they look us in the eye and lie, saying the actions they are taking to destroy the middle class are only about achieving equality, fairness, and "social justice."

Are you starting to get the picture? We're screwed. We're the target. The super wealthy and politically connected elites are against us. They're all looking out for their own selfish interests. And we, the predominantly white middle class, are not in their best interests. So we're being targeted. Their laser gun sights are aimed right at us.

So you're damn right I'm angry. And every one of you, regardless of ethnic background, has every right to be angry. This may be my personal angry white male story, but it also belongs to tens of millions of angry middle-class Americans of all ethnic backgrounds.

We didn't attack first; we're responding in self-defense. Our backs have been put against the wall, and we have no choice but to stand up for ourselves and our children before we are legislated out of existence, penniless, powerless, and, of course, afraid to speak for fear of being shouted down and immediately labeled "racist."

3

#ObamaWorstPresidentEver

The very definition of an angry white male is someone willing to state the truth no matter how politically incorrect. Even more specifically, it is someone willing to state the politically incorrect truth about our nation's first black president. The truth is . . . he SUCKS. He's horrible. He's terrible. He is the God-awful worst. None of that has anything whatsoever to do with the color of his skin. It has to do with only one thing: *facts*.

Despite eight long years of lies and propaganda from government and the mainstream media, it's time to call Obama exactly what he is:

#OBAMAWORSTPRESIDENTEVER.

The problem is that there are two Americas. Obama's America is filled with poor people, illegal aliens, and people addicted to welfare, food stamps, Obamacare, and hundreds of other government programs. Oh, and let's not forget all the academicians and people who work for the government.

Obama's voters have no part in the private sector (where all the jobs and tax monies come from). Their lives are tied to government checks and government payrolls. They have their hands perpetually out. Obama's voters sign *the back* of checks.

Obama's voters think the economy looks peachy keen. Nothing has changed. As long as their government checks keep on coming, they don't notice anything wrong with the economy. And why should they? For them, everything is fine. It's easy to live in denial when you're living on OPM (other people's money).

But for the rest of America—aka middle-class America and small business owners—it's a very different story. For Americans who sign *the front* of checks and spend their lives paying taxes *into* the system, America is a mess, the economy is a disaster, there are no jobs. For that group, the conclusion is pretty simple and straightforward: #OBAMAWORSTPRESIDENTEVER.

These two groups come from different worlds. Some might say different planets. You might even say "Republicans are from Mars, and Democrats are from UrANUS."

As if on cue, to prove my point, the latest job report came out while I was writing this book. Under Obama, I'm used to "good jobs reports" that show 200,000 crappy part-time low-wage jobs being created in any given month. Those same "good reports" forget to mention that the 200,000 new crappy part-time jobs are mitigated by 300,000 Americans giving up and dropping out of the workforce that month. The unemployment rate keeps dropping not because Americans are getting jobs but because they have given up looking for work anymore.

And the reason we've had some "job growth" under Obama is because Obamacare has created a dysfunctional economy where three part-time jobs are needed for a middle-class family to make less than one good job used to pay. So those 200,000 jobs per month being reported are total B.S. Everyone needs three jobs to just live a miserable life.

But the jobs report that came out in June 2016 was far worse. It is so bad that the Obama frauds can't even cover it up with fake stats. Things are so bad, even the cover-up is no longer possible. The jig is up!

The results announced in June were pure DISASTER.[1]

Experts predicted 160,000 new jobs for May 2016. The actual total: 38,000. The "whisper (best case scenario) number" had been 200,000 new jobs. Instead, the number was far closer to zero than either 160,000 or 200,000. It was the worst jobs number since September 2010.

But it was worse than it looked because the Labor Department also revised downward the previous two months' jobs reports by 59,000 less jobs.

Even worse, the number of working-age Americans *not* working went up to a modern record of 94.7 million. Why? Because a mass exodus of 664,000 workers gave up trying to find a job and left the job market in one month (May).[2]

Six hundred sixty-four thousand is the population of Washington, DC. The equivalent of the entire population of Washington, DC, just left the US workforce in one month![3]

Instead of working and contributing to the economy by paying taxes, where are these people going? To welfare, food stamps, disability, Social Security, Medicare, Medicaid, and free Obamacare. Most of them will never work again because it just isn't worth it anymore. A family is better off on welfare, food stamps, housing allowances, and free Obamacare.

Don't forget the free Obama phones. If the same family were working, they might make less money and owe taxes and have to pay for their own health care. It pays better to live off government.

And who gets the bill for these millions of Americans who will never work again, forever trapped in poverty and government dependency? The American middle class. We're *screwed.*

It's important to note this is happening at the same time gross domestic product (GDP) is close to zero. Zero economic growth, of course, is why there are zero new jobs. Sounds like an "Obama Great Depression" to me. And if these numbers don't constitute a Great Depression, I'm afraid to ask, "What does?"

Keep in mind that, even with good jobs reports under Obama, it's been all part-time, low-wage jobs. I call it "the Obama Illegal Immigrant Economy." The only jobs are mowing lawns, cleaning toilets, or washing dishes.

Don't believe me? Then how do you explain that of the one million net jobs gained by women since 2007, the entire net gain went to "foreigners." That statistic is provided by Obama's own Labor Department.[4]

Foreigners (people not born in the United States) had the *entire* net gain. Among native-born American women there was a net loss of 143,000 jobs during that period. The Obama economy is in free fall.

But wait, the news gets worse. Layoffs are up 24 percent in 2016 versus 2015. Rail traffic is down fourteen months in a row. Shipping traffic is down. Retail sales are down.

Manufacturing is down. Unsold inventories are piling up. Commercial bankruptcies are soaring.[5]

So without further ado, here are the facts of the Obama economy. These facts prove three things beyond a shadow of a doubt:

1. The US economy under Obama is in terrible decline, crisis, and on the verge of collapse.
2. The American middle class—which happens to be predominantly white—has been slaughtered by the liberal policies of Obama.
3. There is no doubt: #OBAMAWORSTPRESIDENT EVER

Look at the nine charts on ZeroHedge.com, my favorite economic website.[6]

- Student loan debt—dramatically up.
- Food stamp use—dramatically up.
- Federal debt—dramatically up; by the time Obama leaves office, up more than all other presidents in history COMBINED.
- Federal Reserve money printing—dramatically up, to keep the economy artificially afloat.
- Health insurance costs—dramatically up (and going much higher).
- Labor force participation rate—down dramatically.
- Workers' share of economy—down dramatically.
- Median family income—down dramatically.
- Homeownership—down dramatically.

The Obama Economy Is in Free Fall

Here is a powerful list of shocking, damning, specific facts about the Obama economy:

Gross domestic product (GDP) is the only real determinant of economic growth. Barack Obama is the only president in the history of America to preside over seven straight years of GDP growth under 3 percent.[7]

The year 2016 is off to a pace that virtually guarantees this will be the eighth straight year with GDP under 3 percent. If so, Obama will become the only president in America's history to never produce a single year of 3 percent or higher GDP.[8]

The longest previous streak of under 3 percent GDP in the history of America was four years (1930 to 1933) during the depths of the Great Depression.[9]

From 1790 to 2000, America's economy averaged GDP growth of 3.79 percent. Obama's eight years are on pace to average GDP of 1.55 percent—substantially less than half of our country's average economic growth for 210 years.[10]

For the first time in American history, more businesses are being destroyed each day than are being created.[11]

More Americans now receive entitlements than work full-time.[12]

Thirteen of the twenty-three Obamacare State Co-Op Exchanges have failed (gone bust and broke). The remaining ten have losses of over $200 million per year.[13]

In this Obama economy, 40 percent of American workers now earn less (adjusted for inflation) than a full-time minimum wage worker in 1968.[14]

Twenty percent of US families don't have a single member who is employed.[15]

A record numbers of Americans are not in the workforce (over 94 million).[16]

More young Americans now live with their parents than at any time since Great Depression.[17]

Forty-three percent of the twenty-two million student loan borrowers aren't making any loan payments.[18]

Two-thirds of Americans don't have $500 for an emergency bill.[19]

Food stamp use under Obama is up by 43 percent.[20]

The number of new food stamp recipients under Obama is three times higher than new job recipients (13,298,000 added to food stamp rolls versus 4,276,000 new jobs since January 2009).[21]

#OBAMAWORSTPRESIDENTEVER

But here's the *truly* amazing thing . . .

Hillary Clinton openly brags she is running for Obama's third term.[22]

She wants to extend and expand his presidency. She wants to support and *protect* his legacy. She wants us to vote for more of the same. Amazing.

I guess that makes her . . .

#HILLARYWORSTPRESIDENTIALCANDIDATE EVER

As I've said repeatedly, nothing I'm writing is a condemnation of any racial, religious, ethnic, or sexual orientation group. This book is merely an act of self-defense. There is no question what is happening. There is no question the target is the predominantly white middle class.

But the perpetrators aren't black or minority. As a matter of fact, most of them are guilt-ridden white liberals like Hillary Clinton, Bernie Sanders, Harry Reid, Nancy Pelosi, John Kerry, Debbie Wasserman Schultz, Elizabeth Warren, and Joe Biden.

To succeed in their goal of destroying the middle class and the American Dream they can't allow the middle class to understand what is really happening to them. They can't allow the middle class to understand there is an actual plan and they are the target. So this is where the lies, slander, and cover-up begin.

4

Rachel Maddow—
Angry White Liberal

Wow, this book just keeps writing itself!

I had barely finished writing the Introduction about my Bill Maher experience when out of the blue comes a six-minute diatribe about me from Rachel Maddow to open her MSNBC show. Instantly, I thought, "There's another chapter."

Ms. Maddow is the polar opposite of me. She is the reason I'm writing this book. She is the classic "Angry White Liberal." She hates me and people like me with such passion, it's frightening. How do I know? Just watch her talk about me on her TV show. This was the third time in two years Rachel has led off her show with a diatribe about me.[1]

Keep in mind Rachel's television time is valuable "real estate." A minute on national TV is valuable like beachfront property. No one wastes five to ten minutes talking about someone or something to start their national TV show unless it's damn important. I must be damn important to Rachel, or damn effective, or damn annoying, or all of the above. I've clearly got the attention of liberal icons like Maddow. What I'm doing and saying is resonating loud and clear, and they are scared stiff. The left has aimed its cannons at me for a reason: what I'm doing and saying is clearly *working!*

So effective conservatives like me must be slandered and discredited. This strategy is right out of the playbook of Marxist legend Saul Alinsky. As I'll detail later, Obama studied Alinsky. So did Hillary. I'm sure Rachel Maddow learned from him, too.

When Rachel talks about me, she quivers. She looks like a volcano about to explode. She taps her pen with nervous energy and is clearly obsessed. I take it as a gigantic compliment. Thank you, Rachel. It's quite an honor when radical liberals like you clearly see me as one of the most hated conservatives in America. It's an honor to know you obsess about me all the time. It's an honor to know you get a "shiver running down your leg" when thinking about me. No TV host in the world opens three shows with five- to ten-minute diatribes about Wayne Allyn Root unless I'm a threat to your plan, to your philosophy, to everything you believe in.

Liberals must divide and slander to conquer. That's the Saul Alinsky way. The issue they use to divide and slander is always money. Conservatives, as I pointed out in the last chapter, understand money; they want to earn it and enjoy it. We don't see money as a sin. We don't see success as a slur or embarrassment.

Liberals have a very different relationship with money. They don't understand it or how it is made. They think money grows on trees. Or comes from government. They have a distaste for anyone who makes it.

That's why instead of appreciating a successful businessman like me and calling me CEO, or entrepreneur, or small businessman, or author, or international business speaker (which all describe what I do), Maddow called me "a get-rich-quick guy." This is how angry white liberals see and portray anyone who is successful in business. They sneer at us. They smear us. They denigrate us. They slander us. They look down on us. We are just like money to them: *dirty.*

Many Democrats have no clue the economy is in terrible decline, crisis, and near-collapse. To quote Ronald Reagan, "It isn't so much that liberals are ignorant [in this case about money and the economy]. It's just that they know so many things that aren't so."

After reading the last chapter, you now understand what Obama's liberal anti-business policies have done to America, the economy, and the formerly great American middle class. They haven't lifted anyone out of poverty. Just the opposite— these policies have added three times more Americans to the food stamp rolls than the job rolls.

We've been decimated, annihilated, targeted for extinction, and it's working. This is a theme I've been harping on for eight long years of the Obama presidency. Every prediction and warning I've released has come true. My predictions have been uncannily accurate. Each economic fact makes me look smarter. Liberals like Maddow have no choice; they can't point to the results so they're only weapon is to distract the masses from the truth. They've got to discredit anyone telling the truth about the economy. They must smear, denigrate, and slander truth tellers like me.

As if on cue, the morning after Rachel Maddow's rant against me, the disastrous job report I reported on in the last chapter came out.[2]

It was suddenly clear that the emperor (Obama) had no clothes—and no leg to stand on. The results are right in front of everyone's eyes: decline, crisis, and economic free fall.

That's why angry liberals like Rachel Maddow need to distract you. I have spent eight long years talking about the economy and middle-class jobs. Ninety-nine percent of my commentaries and 99 percent of my TV and radio appearances are about the economy and how close we are to disaster and collapse because of liberal policies designed to *purposely* destroy capitalism and American exceptionalism. Their goal is to destroy America's middle class and make them dependent on government. And, sadly, I've been proven correct for eight long years as the decline deepens and accelerates.

Let me state it again. As sorry as I am to say it: *I was right.*

Of course, angry white liberals have to close their eyes to the facts or everything they believe in will be discredited. So Maddow and her liberal cohorts must distract you. Hence, when it comes to me, she ignores the many books and hundreds of editorials I've written about the economy and my economic predictions, and instead focuses on one story I wrote about my days at Columbia University with my college classmate, Obama. Then she uses that one story out of hundreds to falsely label me as a "conspiracy theorist."

Interesting phrase. In this case, it's simply a mean-spirited, distorted way to say that I don't drink the Obama Kool-Aid. I ask questions, I investigate, I search for the truth. To liberals, anyone who asks questions, seeks truth, or questions motives for what a politician does is a "conspiracy theorist." Worse, since the president happens to be black, I'm also labeled a "racist."

To compound matters, Maddow even distorted what I said. What is true is that as a Class of '83 Columbia graduate (the same as Obama) I've been asked by the media if I knew Obama at Columbia. I've always answered honestly that I didn't know him, never saw him, never heard of him, never met a single classmate who ever saw him or knew him. I simply told the truth. What I never said—ever—is that he didn't go there. Never. But she reported on her national TV show that I am a "conspiracy theorist" who says Obama never went to Columbia.

What I am is a commonsense citizen and taxpayer asking questions about the most powerful man in the world. Questions the mainstream media—led by guilt-ridden white liberals like Rachel Maddow—have never asked of a black president for fear of being called a "racist."

Unless you're blind, deaf, or really dumb, it's clear that Obama's story at Columbia smells rotten. There's something wrong with the narrative. The words to describe Obama's time at Columbia are suspicious, mysterious, strange, weird, and just plain rotten. And to top it off, his college records have been sealed for all eight years of his presidency.

So when asked about my classmate, I answered honestly. Then I asked questions anyone with a brain would ask about the man whose finger rests on the nuclear button. Questions like . . .

Why did I never see or hear of Barack Obama at Columbia, even though I knew virtually every other political science major?

How come I've asked so many of my fellow classmates and none of them admits ever knowing him or even seeing him at Columbia?

How come Professor Henry Graff, perhaps the most honored professor in Columbia history, and Columbia's "Presidential Historian," says no one named Barack Obama ever took one of his classes?

How did Obama get into Columbia with poor grades from a very average college (Occidental)? Students like that are never accepted for transfer into Columbia.

Why are his college records sealed? What is he hiding?

When I was asked by the media what I thought Obama was hiding, I again answered honestly. I said to the media, "My educated guess is he got into Columbia by committing fraud: by posing as a foreign exchange student from Indonesia (where Obama was raised as a boy). Columbia loves diversity. That lie would have catapulted Obama to the front of the line. Now he's embarrassed to admit he committed fraud by being an American posing as a foreigner. Just an educated guess. But a damn good one. Even several of my liberal pro-Obama Columbia classmates have told me they suspect I've hit the nail on the head.

I think asking questions of a president is the duty not only of journalists but of all citizens. That is especially true when the media—filled with biased, corrupted, angry white liberals like Rachel Maddow—have abdicated that duty.

Funny how angry white liberals spew hatred, sling names, and ask questions all the time. But no one calls them "conspiracy theorists." Doesn't Obama calling conservatives like me racists, hatemongers, radicals, or extremists make him a "conspiracy theorist"?

If Hillary blames her never-ending criminal problems on a "vast right wing conspiracy," doesn't that make her a "conspiracy theorist"? Even Wikipedia defines the phrase "vast wing conspiracy" as a conspiracy theory created by Hillary Clinton.[3]

When Hillary likens Trump to nuclear war, Hitler, and the Holocaust, doesn't that make her a "conspiracy theorist"?[4]

If Senate Majority Leader Harry Reid says he "heard" Mitt Romney didn't pay taxes for ten years, he's not called a "birther" or "taxer" or labeled a "conspiracy theorist." Even after everything Reid said was proven a lie and he *admitted* he made it up just to win the election for Obama, the media never labeled or called him a nasty name.[5]

The angry white liberals of the world like Rachel Maddow control the media, so they get to lie, slander, libel, ask questions, and assign the name "conspiracy theorist" without ever being labeled or maligned themselves.

They do it to distract the masses from the truth. And that truth is that Obama really is a bad guy who is purposely overwhelming the system and bringing down the economy with the goal of "fundamentally changing America." Those were his words. Either that or he's a stupid, clueless, ignorant idiot who is trying to help the economy, but failing every step of the way. I believe he's a very bright man who knows exactly what he's doing.

I'm no "conspiracy theorist" for asking important questions and pointing out the truth. Or for merely wondering why Obama won't release his college records. Prove me wrong, Mr. Obama. Make me look foolish. Rachel, beg Obama to do it. Tell your hero he can destroy me with one simple step. It's so easy. I challenge you Mr. President: *release your college records.*

But he won't. Because he can't. Because the emperor has no clothes.

Obama has a deep, dark secret that could destroy his legacy buried in those college records. That's my guess. No different than Harry Reid's guess about Mitt Romney's taxes. The only difference is Romney proved Reid a fool and a liar. Obama has never unsealed his college records.

And he never will.

But angry white liberals like Rachel will never admit the truth. They want to outlaw the truth. They would ban free speech and free thought if they could.

Since they can't, they slander and libel people like me to destroy their political opposition. And even worse, they do it to distract the American people from the truth—that the disastrous liberal, anti-business policies of Obama, Hillary, and their liberal cronies have destroyed the economy.

Angry white males like me want to expose the truth. Angry white liberals like Rachel Maddow are scared to death of the truth. Like Jack Nicholson said in the movie *A Few Good Men,* "You can't handle the truth."[6]

5

The Roots of This Disaster

Obama and I at Columbia

The decline of America, the economy, and the predominantly white middle class under Obama isn't due to mistake, ignorance, or incompetence at the hands of a "community organizer." It's a purposeful, brilliant plan hatched at Columbia University to destroy capitalism, American exceptionalism, Judeo-Christian values, and the American Dream. At its root, this plan is about destroying the predominantly white middle class and small business owners. Because as a great bank robber once said, "That's where the money is."

I am Obama's classmate, Class of '83, Columbia University. Columbia was and is a radical leftist Ivy League college at the corner of Marx Street and Lenin Avenue. The professors taught us many things—some good, many bad. But the worst thing we learned at Columbia was a hatred for America. We were taught to be guilty for "white privilege" . . . to be guilty for the racism and discrimination of America . . . to be guilty for poverty caused by white people and our greed . . . to be guilty for how women, blacks, minorities, and gays were held down in America. It was all "the white man's fault."

We were also taught a plan to change it all, or as Obama says today, "to fundamentally change America." The plan was called Cloward-Piven.[1] It was named after a Columbia hus-band-and-wife professor team. The plan was brilliant in its simplicity. The plan was to "overwhelm the system" so that the US economy would collapse. This was how we could kill capitalism once and for all. Then we could start over.

How do you do that? By putting as many Americans as possible "on the dole." Crush the middle class, make them dependent on government, get everyone you can on welfare and food stamps, and then crush the budget with spending, entitlements, and debt. The country and economy eventually collapse under the weight of everyone getting checks from the government. You've "overwhelmed the system."

Now that the economy is dead, and the people are poor and starving and desperate to feed their families, there is com-plete panic. *Now you've got them.* They'll buy *any* promise at this point. They just want hope. They just want to save their children. So now you offer them a new start with socialism (to replace the old capitalist system). Of course, you blame capitalism for all their problems. You're offering something new and fresh. You're offering a second chance. You're offer-ing to pay for everything in return for total government con-trol. "You'll never have to worry again. We'll take care of you." And, of course, you're also offering lots of "free stuff" to a starving populace. How could they say no?

Any of this sound familiar? To one degree or another, this is exactly what's been happening to America under the last eight years of Obama.

Obama is a smart man. He added a couple of new wrinkles. He super-charged the system. How could you overwhelm the system even faster? First, you pass Obamacare. That is the world's biggest tax increase and redistribution plan. You pile the spending and debt up even faster to overwhelm the system, all under the guise of helping the sick. *Brilliant.*

The second new wrinkle is to purposely leave the border open for eight years. You dismantle any and all border enforcement.[2] You order border agents to "stand down."[3] You create a twenty-four-hour hotline for illegal aliens to call to complain about poor treatment by border agents.[4] You spend millions of dollars of taxpayer money to provide free lawyers and free legal representation to every illegal child.[5] You shield almost every illegal alien criminal from deportation,[6] and you spend millions of taxpayer dollars to advertise in Mexico that even illegal aliens qualify for food stamps in America, so tell your friends and relatives in America to ask. "Spread the word."[7]

This has all really happened under Obama. It's hard to even believe.

So Obama came up with a more powerful partner to Cloward-Piven. He allowed in millions of foreigners—both legal and illegal—to overwhelm the system much faster. You might say he wanted to "explode the system."

But Columbia University wasn't unique. This philosophy was taught at many Ivy League and elite universities by radical leftist professors with contempt for America and "those rich white people who control the system." The brightest students at the elite colleges all learned how to "fundamentally change America." They learned how to channel Fidel Castro.

Remember when Rudy Giuliani said he thought "Obama doesn't love America," and it set off a media firestorm?[8] The media literally wanted to tar and feather poor Rudy. But who are these members of the media? I met many of them at Columbia. Many, if not most, of my classmates wound up in the mainstream media. That explains everything.

The same biased-leftist media members who ripped Rudy Giuliani to shreds for stating the obvious were the same students thirty years earlier in class at Columbia with me on the day Ronald Reagan was shot. Guess what their reaction was back then? They *cheered* the assassination attempt on President Ronald Reagan. They clapped, high-fived, and hugged—celebrated like it was New Year's. Today, when I read about my former classmates in our Columbia college alumni magazine, they are almost all either in the media or lawyers in the Obama administration creating regulations on business. This explains *everything.*

Today, they no doubt support students at California state university system campuses who voted to remove the American flag. Nothing has changed. Once a radical America hater, always a radical America hater.[9]

Naturally, that same biased-leftist media (mostly made up of my Columbia classmates and those from other Ivy League schools) decided to play "gotcha" with the 2016 Republican presidential candidates. They asked them, "Do you agree that Obama doesn't love America?" As usual, GOP candidates panicked and ran away from Giuliani's statement, which is precisely why Donald Trump became the GOP Presidential nominee. We were waiting for a candidate who would not run for cover when the media attacked, who played on offense, who would hit back—HARD. Trump fit the bill.

But the point here is that I know my Columbia classmates like the back of my hand. I understand what makes them tick. Thirty-plus years ago, they were at least honest in their beliefs. They called themselves communists, Marxists, socialists, and even Bolsheviks. They liked being called "radical." They bragged that they hated America and wanted to bring the system down.

And here's the really important part. Even though almost everyone at Columbia was white, they all hated white people (or at least they gave that impression, in order to look cool). They were all guilty about their "white privilege." They talked nonstop about their goal to bring down the "white power structure" of America. Of course, they were all so guilty because they were rich, spoiled brats who'd had everything handed to them on a silver platter from the day they were born. Pathetic liberalism is almost always about guilt. They were guilty about being born white and rich.

The result was a hatred for America, white people, rich people (i.e., their own parents), and anyone in power (99 percent of whom happened to be white). And a love for all things radical and Marxist in nature. In other words, they all loved and respected a revolutionary communist like Fidel Castro. I heard this leftist nonsense every hour of every day.

So now you understand my classmates. Now you understand what makes the media tick. They're mostly white, guilt-ridden, spoiled-brat, indoctrinated Ivy League leftist radicals.

Now that we understand them, I'll show you how to beat them at their own game. Here is the perfect answer anytime a member of the biased media asks a Republican candidate, "Do you think Obama loves America?"

The answer is, "I believe Obama loves America . . . the same way Castro has loved Cuba for the past half century. And I believe Obama loves America the same way Hugo Chavez loved Venezuela, the same way Stalin loved Russia, the same way Ho Chi Minh loved North Vietnam, the same way Pol Pot loved Cambodia, and the same way the socialist presidents of insolvent, bankrupt, European Union countries like Greece, Spain, Portugal, Italy, and even France today love their country. Or didn't you know the Jobs Minister of France recently whispered in front of an open microphone, "France is totally bankrupt"?[10]

I'm sure Obama loves America the same way those socialist geniuses all loved their countries and their people. Yet they managed to destroy their countries and economies. That's what socialism, communism, or Marxism (whatever you want to name it) does: it destroys everyone and everything it touches. Ask the people of Detroit now living in an abandoned city.[11]

It's not a matter of patriotism. Obama may love America. I'm sure Fidel Castro would say, "I'm the biggest Cuban patriot that has ever lived." Castro loves his people, and he will love Cuba until his dying breath.

But look at the results. Castro's country lies in ruins. The Cuban people own nothing, not even their own thoughts or free speech. Disagree, protest, speak out publicly and the Castro brothers send you to prison to rot or die. People living in the country that Fidel Castro loves so much have spent the last half-century escaping through shark infested waters in boats made of spit, glue, and rubber tires. The Cuban people were willing to die to get away from the man who loves his country to death.

In all socialist countries, "the state" takes care of you. "The state" knows what's best. "The state" tells you what to think. In each and every case, all that love (and smothering state control) ruins your life.

So "does Obama love America?" Perhaps, but it's clear his version of love is similar to the husband who beats his wife, all the while proclaiming "I love you, honey—this is for your own good."

That's exactly what Republican candidates need to say when the media asks, "Does Obama love America?" That's the perfect answer. Watch the media turn ash white and look sick to their stomachs. I know how my Columbia classmates think.

No one can prove whether Obama loves America or hates America. This is how the media defeats Republicans.

We can't prove Obama hates America, so saying it allows the media to make us look foolish.

But what I do know is that Obama is destroying America. I can prove that. The facts are all over this book. I do know Obama is very much like Castro.

The people I trust who have dealt with Castro—the parents and grandparents of my friends in the Cuban community—all say Obama is Fidel Castro all over again. They've seen firsthand the lies, corruption, fraud, propaganda, massive taxation and regulation, the tyrant saying with such sincerity that he loves his country and is here to "save" it. They've heard Castro say that everything he did was for "the good of the people." They recognize another Castro when they see him—and Cubans who lived under Castro are *certain* Obama is Castro. By the way, so is Hillary. Remember, she has stated she is running for a third term of Obama.

It's not just Castro. Every socialist tin-pot dictator is the same. They all channel Saul Alinsky. Everything they say is the opposite of the truth. Everything they say is to deceive and distract. Everything they do is to bribe the poor with "free stuff," stolen from the predominantly white middle class and business owners. The politically correct name is "income redistribution." But it's theft. It's the central tenet of communism and Karl Marx's "Communist Manifesto."[12]

Rip off your opposition to make them poor and redistribute the stolen loot to the dependent poor, buying their loyalty and votes. That's socialism . . . that's Castro . . . and that's Obama . . . that's Hillary . . . that's Bernie.

I have one more recommendation to Republican candidates when asked "gotcha" questions by the biased media. When asked what you think of Giuliani's comments, or Trump's comments, or Wayne Root's comments, or any other comment they think will trip you up because they believe your only choice is to agree or disagree with that comment or opinion, you can put them in a corner. Throw it all back at them. Tell them you'll answer only when they've asked Democratic presidential candidates if they agree with Obama's comments that Muslim terrorists have "legitimate grievances"?[13]

Ask them if Democratic candidates agree with Obama that "Islamic" and "terrorist" can't be used in the same sentence? Ask them if they agree that illegal aliens given amnesty should collect up to $24,000 in income tax credits even though they paid no taxes?[14]

Do they agree that $10 trillion in new debt added by Obama could destroy our economy and our children's future?[15]

Tell them you'll answer their questions only when you hear Democratic candidates for office answer those questions.

I'm a chess master at understanding Obama and all my Columbia classmates in the media. I understand how to turn the tables on them.

It's time to fight fire with fire. It's time to stop bringing a knife to a gun fight. This is war. This is a battle for the very survival of America, American exceptionalism, small business, capitalism, free enterprise, and free speech. And, of course, what really matters for the purposes of this book is the survival of the great American middle class that is targeted and under attack.

Sure, Obama loves America, just like those socialist and communist tyrants loved their country. That is, as long as they own it, control it, and can fundamentally change it. But you'll notice it never ends well. They always ruin the citizens' lives. They always destroy the middle class. They always destroy the children's future. They always turn prosperity to poverty. "Equality" always leads to shared misery. History always repeats.

It's time to speak up now before America is gone. It's time to stand up to evil. It's time to stand up to bullies. It's time to take back America from the tyrants who claim to love it . . . *to death*.

That's why you needed a crash course in "Columbia University Radical Thinking 101." Guess what? You're now an expert.

6

The Attack

Let's look at some of the ways we're being targeted, intimidated, and persecuted. The evidence is out in the open.
Look at the Obama IRS scandal. Just look at the groups who
Obama and his socialist cabal chose to target and persecute:
conservative groups, Tea Party groups, Christian groups,
Jewish groups, pro-Israel groups, pro-Constitution groups,
pro-life groups, donors to conservative causes or candidates,
and any Obama critic (like me) brave enough to appear in the
media to report the raw truth.[1]

I was one of the victims of this over-the-top attack on
political opponents and critics of the president. I saw the
attack up close and personal. And I have proof it was a political
targeting and persecution based on my conservative political
views. "What proof?" you might ask. How about comments
about my conservative political views and appearances on
Fox News and conservative talk radio written on the pages of
my actual IRS tax returns by the IRS agent who was auditing
them? How about the front of my tax returns marked "Sensitive Case." Really? What was "sensitive" about it? I didn't realize the political views of an American citizen made their tax
returns "sensitive"?

How about one of the top IRS officials in the country
demanding my tax audit case be immediately closed? Why

was a top IRS official involved? Why the rush? Well, the date may have been important. My case was hurriedly ordered closed the day before IRS official Lois Lerner testified in front of Congress, claiming Fifth Amendment privilege on the grounds it could incriminate her. I wrote about all this and published the proof at TheBlaze.com and Fox News.[2]

This IRS scandal went far beyond me. I was a very small cog in a gigantic criminal conspiracy. It involved both religious and political persecution. It was the worst witch-hunt in US history. Yet the media has been doing a good job of making it disappear.

But there it is. The specific "hit list" of groups chosen for targeting, persecution, and attack has just been released and is one of the reasons for writing book. That "hit list" could be renamed "Angry White Male." Everything being attacked was what the predominantly white middle class of America believes in: God, country, family, capitalism, conservatism, Israel, Judeo-Christian values, and the US Constitution.

What do you suppose the reaction would have been from liberals, the mainstream media, and Obama if the shoe had been on the other foot? Can you imagine if it were disclosed that a white Republican president named Reagan, Bush, Romney, or Trump used the IRS to persecute black Americans, the NAACP, the ACLU, civil rights groups, black charities, Hispanic pro–illegal immigration groups, Muslim groups, atheist groups, liberal groups, and liberal critics of the president.

Can you even imagine the reaction?

I think the country would have been burned to the ground. We'd have seen riots and unrest; "million-man marches" on Washington, DC; the impeachment of the IRS commissioner; top IRS and presidential aides sent to prison; and many conservatives run out of DC on a third rail, just ahead of a tar-and-feathering. I have no doubt the Republican president of the United States would have been removed from office.

But in a country where the media and college professors are almost 100 percent white guilty liberals, there was no uproar. There was only a massive cover-up. The fact is that the mainstream media gave a local New Jersey traffic scandal involving a Republican governor (Chris Christie) seventeen times more coverage in a twenty-four-hour period than they gave to the IRS scandal during the previous six *months*.[3]

This IRS scandal is the canary in the coal mine. It exposed the blueprint for the liberal agenda to destroy the predominantly white middle class, for wiping angry white, straight, Christian, pro-Israel, pro-Constitution males off the face of the earth; for making us penniless, powerless, and too intimidated to speak out about what's happening. The blueprint is that the government leads the attack and the liberal media covers it up.

If we don't fight back, it will only get worse. If bullies are allowed to get away with beating, intimidating, or stealing, it always gets worse, much worse. They get emboldened. They start to believe they can get away with anything. They start to believe the rules don't apply to them. And the things they do get progressively more extreme, radical, and dangerous.

I'm reasonable and fair. I believe in compromise. Many of us compromised on the liberal agenda for gay rights and gay marriage, but instead of being satisfied, liberals demanded transgender bathrooms and little boys "self-identifying" as little girls, so they can use girls' bathrooms, locker rooms, and showers. It never ends with the left. Give them an inch, they demand a mile. So it's time to fight back. *It's time to defend every inch.*

This is not a racial, black-and-white "Obama issue." It's a liberal/progressive "we know what's best for you" issue—and if you don't agree, we'll fine you, prosecute you, force you out of business, or sic the weight of the US government on you or your business. Yes, Obama was the ringleader, but the vast majority of the attackers are pathetic, white, guilty liberals.

Hillary's publicly stated goal is to protect and expand Obama's legacy. There will be no difference between Obama's agenda and Hillary, Bernie, or any other Democrat. Liberals are at war with God, country, Constitution, American exceptionalism, capitalism, the great American middle class, and, of course, their ultimate whipping boy: straight white males.

Angry white males can be the "soccer moms" of the 2016 election, meaning it's time for us to get involved and make a difference. My goal is to make it hip and cool to be an angry white male. My goal is to wake up my fellow angry white males, to mobilize, to focus on the mission. *To defend every inch.*

And I want to expand the tent to white females and all other members (of any race) of the under-attack American middle class. If you're black, Hispanic, or Asian and you own a small business or work for one, you're under attack, too.

If you're a Christian, you're under attack.

If you're a Jew who loves Israel, you're under attack.

If you're hardworking and pay into the system, you're under attack. That includes private-sector workers, cops, and, yes, union members, too. You're all under attack.

This is a battle for the survival of "the makers" versus "the takers." It just so happens that "the makers" (i.e., taxpayers) are the predominantly white middle class. We're mad as hell and we're not going to take it anymore. We must fight back or lose our country and everything we believe in. Our goal is not racism or superiority. Our goal is fairness and equality, whether white or black, male or female, straight or gay. We don't want to be superior over anyone; we just want to be treated equally, too.

The problem is that our enemies on the left have no interest in "fairness," equality, or free speech. They mouth those words, but it's a lie. Their goal is silencing us, banning our opinions, and labeling us as "racists" for telling the politically incorrect truth. Their goal is to keep us dependent and under their thumb. And to achieve that, progressive icon Saul Alinsky taught progressives that "the ends justify the means."

Want proof? Look no further than bans on free speech and conservative speakers at college campuses across America. Study the actions of Obama's Gestapo (aka the IRS) for proof. See Obama's use of the Securities and Exchange Commission to punish ratings agencies that dared to downgrade the credit rating of the United States.[4]

Study the lies and misrepresentations used to sell the fraud called Obamacare. These people have no interest in fairness. They consider themselves superior. They want their way or the highway. They want mind control. They want us under their thumb. They are classic bullies.

Watch what happens when we give an inch on gun control. If we give them gun registration or background checks, they'll move straight to gun confiscation. Compromise to the political left means you agree with them. There is no middle ground. There is only fraud, lies, slander, and name calling. Give them an inch, and they'll always try to take a mile. So we're not going to give an inch anymore.

The goal of the left has never been equality. It is adherence and total loyalty to their "superior" philosophy. They want us to become second-class citizens. They want to ban our free speech and violate our rights. They want us poor, helpless, and dependent on the government so we don't have the money or power to fight back. They want shared misery (except for themselves, of course). They want revenge and reparations.

Today, reparations have camouflaged names: high taxes, onerous regulations, Obamacare, climate change, IRS attacks, expanded welfare spending, and food stamps. These are all forms of reparations. They take money from the people who earn it and redistribute it to the favored groups of the left.

We have no choice but to stand up for our own self-defense. We must no longer stand by as our rights and hard-earned income and assets are ripped away. We can no longer worry about political correctness or offending someone. The left doesn't care about offending or persecuting us. While we're worried about offending them, they're destroying us. While we're worrying about words, they're using actions: executive actions, legislation, and targeting by powerful government agencies to destroy us. It's time to say, "We've had enough—and we're not going to take it anymore."

Let the revolution begin.

7

Size Matters

At a young age, I was taught by my parents that "two wrongs don't make a right." Black Americans had a right to be angry at the way they were treated one hundred years ago, fifty years ago, maybe even twenty-five years ago. It was a logical reaction to racism and discrimination. Were blacks "racist" for being angry at the horrible way they were treated, especially by their own government? Were they "racist" for trying to gain back their freedom, dignity, free speech, or civil rights? Of course not. The only true racists are people treating you badly, based solely on race, religion, or the color of your skin. Today, people like me pointing out injustice aren't "racists." We're the good guys. Black people were right to complain, to be angry, to protest—*back then.*

But today it is white males and the predominantly white middle class getting the short end of the stick. We and our parents didn't march for civil rights, fight for equality, and stand up against racial inequality so the pendulum could be reversed and swung *against* us, so our children would lose jobs or admission to college because they're white. How wrong. How absurd.

If it's "racism" for government or business to allow discrimination against black people based solely on the color of their skin, then it's just as racist for government or business to discriminate against white people or purposely give jobs to black people based solely on the color of their skin.

Liberals will try their best to paint me as a racist for writing this book, for telling this story, and, worst of all, for standing up and telling the truth. But as I already wrote, the definition of a racist is *anyone winning an argument with a liberal.*

The truth is that I don't have a racist bone in my body. Never have, never will. I was raised in a predominantly black town. I attended an almost all-black public middle and high school. Ironically, I was the minority at those schools. I don't want America to be run for white people or for black people. I don't want employment laws or housing laws to be biased in favor of white people or in favor of black people. I don't want America to go back to "the good old days." I recognize and acknowledge there were no "good old days" for black Americans.

But I also don't condone the America of today practicing reverse racism and violating my civil rights and those of my children. I want the playing fields in America to be tilted toward Americans. Not white Americans, not black Americans. *All Americans.*

That's the true definition of fairness and equality. Hurting one group to help another, or hurting one group to gain revenge for what happened to another many decades ago, isn't fairness or equality. It's just racism and discrimination all over again, but this time aimed at a different group.

Barack Obama, Hillary Clinton, Bernie Sanders, and the mostly pathetic, guilt-ridden, white liberal leadership of the

Democratic Party have set race relations, fairness, equality, and social justice back a hundred years, and we are beginning to see an angry reaction to systemic reverse racism and overt discrimination against the predominantly white American middle class. Two wrongs do not make a right. What's happening is clear as a bell—and it's wrong.

It's time to hit back. It's time to fight for every inch. That's why I believe 2016 will be . . .

The Year of the Angry White Male.

And that's why I believe Donald Trump will be the next president of the United States. Trump is the reaction to the pendulum swinging way too far. Trump is the reaction to the wrongs of today. Trump is the reaction to reverse racism. Trump is the reaction to out-of-control political correctness. Trump is the reaction to hypocrisy. Trump is the reaction to a corrupt, out-of-control federal government. Trump is the reaction to the fraud and cover-up by the predominantly white, guilt-ridden liberal media. Trump is the ultimate "angry white male." Trump will win because angry white males have become the "soccer moms" of the 2016 election. We are finally standing up.

Trump will win because it's time to fight back; it's time to defend every inch. *Trump will win because size matters.*

Proof That Angry White Males Have Every Right to Be Angry

This destruction, this annihilation, this conspiracy to destroy the middle class is real. The murder of the middle class is not a theory. It's not an opinion. It's not a figment of my imagination. It's a proven fact. During the time I was writing this book, three studies were published backing up what I'm saying. Sometimes, timing isn't important—*it's everything.*

Study 1: Pew Research Proves Death of Middle Class

A definitive study was released by the nonpartisan Pew Research Center.[1]

Yes, Pew is the same research group mentioned earlier who studied and identified the dominant percentage of whites versus minorities among the middle class.

Pew's latest research reports that between 1999 and 2014 more than four-fifths of America's metro areas have experienced income declines. Pew's figures reveal a steady erosion of America's middle class.

The steepest declines were seen in industrial towns. It is no coincidence that these job and income losses came from the predominantly white working and middle class.

But the trend isn't just seen in the Midwest or among working class, blue-collar whites. The same trend and the same declines can be found among college-educated white-collar Americans. Pew Research found that even in areas of high-tech reinvention such as Austin, Texas, and Raleigh, North Carolina, incomes are falling and the middle class is shrinking.

Pew found that even in the suburbs of Denver, Colorado, where over six hundred thousand new residents have arrived since 2000, heavily weighted toward college degrees, median household income (adjusted for inflation) fell from $83,000 in 1999 to under $76,000 in 2014.

This clearly shows the murder of the middle class. The rich are getting richer, while the poor are taken care of by the government and paid for by middle-class taxpayers. The savaged middle class is being taxed and regulated so heavily to pay for the poor that eventually there will be no more middle-class jobs, no more middle-class families. Our incomes are down, our jobs are disappearing, our bills are escalating, our health care costs are exploding (thanks to Obamacare), and our taxes are dramatically higher. For America's middle class, this is a disaster of epic proportions.

So now you know why we're angry. We have every reason to be angry. We've been targeted for extinction.

Study 2: Economic Innovation Group Proves There Are No Middle-Class Jobs

The second study was a look at job creation in America. I've argued for all eight years of the Obama presidency that his policies are destroying "Main Street." Yes, Wall Street has been flying, and Silicon Valley has been flying, and the suburbs of Washington, DC, are enjoying record income and home price appreciation. But outside of those few places, the economy is D-E-A-D. There are no business start-ups or jobs being created outside of Silicon Valley; Manhattan; Washington, DC; Boston; and Austin. The rest of the country is starving and barren. That's been my argument for eight long years. Historically, the key to America's economic success has not been big business or high tech or government. It's always been small business and start-ups. And today, they are being taxed and legislated out of business, which is why there are no new high-quality middle-class jobs being created.

Sure enough, a new study out by the bipartisan Economic Innovation Group, based on data from the Census Bureau, has shown just that.[2]

They report a frightening nationwide slowdown in start-ups and job creation. What few start-ups are happening are located in a few big cities and nowhere else—to be exact, Silicon Valley, Manhattan, and Austin, Texas. That's it. Just twenty counties have produced half the new business start-ups in America. Just a handful of big cities are producing the extremely limited growth we have, and it's not even good growth. Even these few areas are merely "treading water," the study reports. But the rest of America, in particular rural America, has dropped off a cliff. This is very bad news.

The report says exactly what I've been arguing for eight long years: small business is being killed by big business. No one opens a bodega or hardware store or health food store or clothing store anymore because they can't compete with big box retailers. And no one opens a manufacturing plant because all those jobs have been shipped offshore by big business. The little guy is dead. That means entrepreneurship, outside of a handful of well-funded technology start-ups, is dead. That means mobility and opportunity is dead. And that means job creation is dead because business start-ups of two hundred or fewer employees have historically created the bulk of high-quality middle-class jobs. And Obama's oppressive liberal/progressive policies are responsible for killing those start-ups; they are NO MORE.

We're in big trouble, folks. And guess who lives in all these vast swaths of rural areas: middle-class white people. Outside of New York or San Francisco or Austin or DC, middle-class white people have no future. They have no way out of their crappy circumstances. No mobility. No opportunity to do better than their parents. This is the murder of the predominantly white middle and working class. And it's the reason for angry white males. It's also the reason for the Donald Trump phenomenon. Read the exact conclusion of the *Washington Post* story about this study:

"Polling suggests it is one of the driving forces in the political unrest among working-class Americans—particularly rural white men—who have flocked to Republican Donald Trump's presidential campaign this year."[3]

Study 3: The Center for Immigration Studies Proves Illegal Immigrants Are Coming to America for the Welfare

There is a third part to *Angry White Male*. First is the murder of the middle class. Second is the death of small business and job creation. The third part is about native-born Americans being overrun by an invasion of foreigners, in particular illegal aliens.

While this "murder of the middle class" is happening due to liberal policies of tax, spend, regulate, and sue, the reality is that our wide-open borders are an even bigger problem. America is literally being invaded, and the liberal and political elite are not only doing nothing to stop it, they are encouraging it.

Of course, those of us who want to stop this invasion are called racists. The media, big business, and big government politicians (even establishment Republicans like Jeb Bush) claim these illegals are coming here "out of love." Well, the facts are in. It is indeed out of love—a love of welfare and government checks!

Immigrants, in particular illegal immigrants, aren't coming for a love of America's ideals. Most are coming here to collect welfare. And who pays for this massive transfer of wealth? Yes, the predominantly white middle class, the working and taxpaying people of America. The angry white male.

Not only do illegals get tons of "free stuff," but they take our jobs, they hold down our wages, they overwhelm and bankrupt our schools and health care system, and they explode the national debt. They are even assigned civil rights lawyers. And get this one: they get "earned income tax credit" checks from the IRS even though they are here illegally. This is madness.

To make it worse, the guilt-ridden white liberal politicians and media lie. They tell us it's not happening. They say the border is fine. They say there is no problem. They say illegals are not flowing over the border. They say immigrants are a net positive for America. They say all this while illegals collect record-setting government entitlements, while Obama budgets $17,000 per illegal child—more than a life-long American-born worker gets from Social Security after a lifetime of hard work and paying into the system. To pay for it all, Obama cut billions from veterans to hand those same billions to illegal aliens. But folks, there's no problem, nothing to see, move along.

No more arguing or debating. Illegals flow across that border for one primary reason: *a love of our generous welfare system*. The proof is now in. Keep in mind these statistics were provided by our own federal government. Illegal immigrants collect more in welfare benefits than native-born Americans. See the facts. We are letting people flood across the border to bankrupt our country, to overwhelm our economic system, to create shortages and economic crises for native-born Americans. As Donald Trump would say, "How stupid can we be?"[4]

Where does the money come from to pay for all this? It comes primarily from the predominantly white middle class.

Not only are these millions of illegals taking away American jobs, they are also suppressing middle-class wages by supplementing their low incomes with welfare benefits. To add insult to injury, those benefits are paid for with higher taxes on the middle class, much higher health insurance costs on the middle class, much higher property taxes on the middle class, much higher sales taxes on the middle class, and a much higher national debt, which will be paid back by even higher taxes on the children and grandchildren of the American middle class.

Is it any wonder I'm an Angry White Male?

It is a national disgrace and disaster. But one thing it's not is a coincidence, bad luck, or bad timing. This is all part of a plan targeting the predominantly white middle class. Liberals claim it is about social justice. In truth, it is about filling the country with foreigners who are dependent on welfare from big government, and therefore can always be counted on to reliably vote Democrat for higher taxes, bigger welfare checks, and even bigger government.

It's all part of a plan to create a vicious cycle. Government taxes and regulations make it difficult to survive. Government makes it difficult to run a business. Government makes us poorer. Government makes us dependent. All of this means we don't have money to make political contributions anymore. I've personally cut my contributions to GOP candidates dramatically. But we all know that in politics, money is power, money is victory. Then to double the pain, government purposely keeps the border wide open to invite in foreigners who want bigger government and more welfare from cradle to grave. Government also makes it easier for them to vote without ID. Then both legal and many illegal immigrants exercise this massive conflict of interest by voting reliably for more welfare checks and higher taxes. All at the expense of the dying middle class.

To write this, to report this, isn't racism. This is simply the truth about what is happening to America and the predominantly white middle class. It doesn't make any group "bad." It's not an attack on Hispanics. It's not an attack on foreigners. I'm simply reporting the facts. This is happening. This is a purposeful plan. I don't even blame the people who are accepting this welfare. They are just accepting what is being offered. The blame goes to pathetic, guilt-ridden white liberals and their cronies in the liberal media, big business, and political establishment.

Their goal is to fundamentally change America by overwhelming the system and changing the ethnic demographics of the electorate away from the predominantly white middle class. And *it's working*.

This is no mirage. This isn't guesswork. It's not my opinion. It's real, it's happening. It's the reason for the angry white male phenomenon. And it's the very foundation of the Donald Trump phenomenon. Trump leaped past the deepest GOP field in history—sixteen governors, senators, and superstar politicians—based on a promise to build a wall, secure the border, and enforce immigration laws.

Now you understand why Trump won the GOP nomination. Now you understand why angry white males (and many others) are angry. We have every right to be. The cannons are being aimed right at us. It's time to fight back in self-defense.

P.S. Long term, even more dangerous to the primarily Hispanic illegals coming to collect free things is the government-endorsed and -aided policy of flooding America with Muslim immigrants, legal and illegal. Unlike other immigrant groups, few Muslims have indicated any interest in accepting American values and assimilating themselves into the great American melting pot. As demonstrated throughout Europe, this is a group focused on establishing separate communities with their own laws and values, biding their time until they can impose their values on the rest of us. It even has a name. Spreading Islam through colonization is a "jihad" (the religious duty of Muslims to maintain and spread their religion). America is being invaded, not by military force, but by the policies of the radical left. Their goal is to fill this nation with foreigners who have no understanding or interest in American exceptionalism, American values, culture, freedom, or personal responsibility. They want white males to become foreigners in our own land. But enough. More on this later in the book.

How Bad Is the Economy?

How bad is the US economy in 2016? I would argue that we are living in a fantasy land. We are fed propaganda, lies, and distortions on a daily basis by the Obama administration and the biased leftist mainstream media that covers up for their buddies in the Democratic Party. It's one big happy family, telling one gigantic lie. The reality is that our entire economy is now based on distortion. It's all based on government spending and Federal Reserve money printing. But both of those create trillions of dollars in debt, which all has to be paid back by the middle class—you and I. Just the interest on the debt would overwhelm the entire budget and drive America into bankruptcy and crisis if interest rates ever rose back to just the historically low rates of the early 2000s (instead of today's artificially suppressed rates of zero).

If not for Fed money printing, the stock market wouldn't be at all-time highs. Based on the true economic decline going on in America today, stocks could very well have crashed to a record low, or been on a long, steady decline. If that happened, older Americans would be wiped out. They'd have no way to retire. They'd have trouble paying for food and rent. Even worse, government employee pension funds would be broke, with no possibility of paying pensions to millions of government employees. Worse yet, publicly traded companies would have far lower stock prices, thereby forcing them to either close their doors or lay off much of their workforce. With this combination of older Americans without any money to spend, government employees left broke without their pensions, and big business laying off millions of workers, think of the effect on consumer spending and retail sales. We'd be in total collapse right now. Hence, the Fed printing presses never rest.

But it gets worse. We don't see an Obama Great Depression with our naked eyes because it's all covered up (or should I say "papered up") with government checks. We'd see tent cities and food lines if it weren't for welfare, food stamps, housing allowances, free meals at school, free Obamacare, free Obama phones, earned income tax credits (another form of welfare), aid to dependent children, and even free contraception. The government pays for everything. The entire economy runs on "free stuff." But take all that free stuff away and watch what happens.

The result would be rioting, unrest, violence, and economic collapse like America has never experienced in history. It would look like Venezuela today, where over a decade of rule by socialist leaders Chavez and Maduro has turned Venezuela from the economic envy of South America to pure disaster, with mass poverty, violence, rioting, food shortages, looting, and, worst of all, toilet paper shortages. The people are jobless, starving, *and* can't wipe their butts. That's what happens when you eventually run out of "other people's money." You literally hit zero in the bank.

There is no more middle class in Venezuela. Like our neighbor Mexico, there is only a tiny elite class of super-rich living in guard-gated compounds protected by armed guards, and everyone else lives in equality (pure misery). The middle class and small business are gone.

That's the future for America's predominantly white middle class if Hillary Clinton (or any other Democrat) extends Obama's legacy. His policies are the same as Venezuela's: big government, big spending, big entitlements, big unions, tons of "free stuff," and free health care. Eventually, the money runs out when you run out of suckers. Venezuela is already there. We are next.

What makes this downright frightening is that if Hillary or another liberal/progressive is elected to a third Obama term to continue his disastrous policies, the results are going to be dramatically worse than 1929. The Great Obama Depression will become the Greatest Depression *ever*.

Why? Simple. Because it gets worse every day. The debt is exploding. The Fed printing is breaking the presses! The taxes are so high, no one I know can keep up with their taxes, so the IRS is putting tax liens on Americans at a frightening and shocking pace, which in turn ruins their credit, thereby destroying their ability to earn a living. And the vicious cycle continues.

But the biggest problem of all is that the first Great Depression had *none* of the problems and obligations we are now facing:

In 1929:

- America did not have $19 trillion in debt and trillions more in unfunded liabilities. Many economists claim the true national debt is in the range of $119 trillion to $219 trillion, once we add in unfunded liabilities and government employee pensions. Everyone "in the know" knows this can never be paid back.

- Most of our states were financially solvent. That is not the case today. Far too many states are basically bankrupt, insolvent, and dependent on the federal government to survive. Exhibit A is California, our Greece.

- We had far fewer government employees living off taxpayers. Today, we have a mind-boggling twenty-two million government employees, with many earning over $100,000 annually. Today, 77,000 federal employees earn more than the governors of their states. Today, the average federal employee is compensated over $120,000 annually. Worse, a tremendous number of government employees retire at age fifty with substantial pensions for *life*. That means just one government employee could have a $5 to 10 million golden parachute. Just one. Multiply that by millions of government retirees. Protected by their unions and the politicians they own, government employee pensions are strangling the US economy. Even FDR said he could not imagine allowing public employees to unionize. Now we know why.

- Social Security, Medicare, and Medicaid didn't exist. The federal government had no such obligations that today threaten to consume the entire federal budget within a decade. Today, illegal aliens demand and receive Medicaid, Obamacare, and a Social Security card. It's pure madness. And, of course, as a "bonus" don't forget we're a much older country now, with Baby Boomers all heading for retirement. And we live much longer, too. So who will pay these Social Security and Medicare bills? Uh-oh.

- There was no such thing as "entitlements." The federal government offered no such things as welfare, food stamps, aid to dependent children, English as a second language programs, or so-called earned income tax credits for people here illegally, who "earned" absolutely nothing. Who will pay for all this as economy worsens, debt worsens, and much of the middle class runs out of money, or retires?

- Americans didn't consider it the responsibility of government to pay for breakfast and lunch for students—*let alone illegal immigrants.* But wait, it gets much worse. Today, many if not most public schools send students home for the weekend with two days of free meals because those same helpless parents who couldn't make breakfast for their own children can't be expected to provide food over the weekend.

- We didn't offer unemployment payments for years on end, let alone the ability to join the disability rolls for life, based on a declaration of mental illness or back pain (two ailments that cannot be disproven). Why do you think today there are ninety-four million working-age Americans not working, while at the same time there are over a hundred million Americans on entitlements? Those two lists are the same general size because they are the same people. One-third of the population is too young or too old to work. One-third of the population no longer cares to work. They think sitting home, sleeping late, watching soap operas, and collecting government checks is "earning a living." And who pays for it? The middle class. We are the one-third left to support the two-thirds who don't or can't earn a dime. Good luck with that.

- We didn't have millions of illegal immigrants and their children collecting billions of dollars in entitlements from US taxpayers. Illegals not only collect many different welfare checks, but collect dramatically higher amounts than native-born Americans. Only America would be dumb enough to let people in illegally, then reward them with more money than it gives to its own law-abiding citizens. As Trump says, "Boy, are we dumb!" I recited the stats earlier in this book.

- All legal immigrants wanted was the right to work. My grandparents from Russia and Germany received no government benefits. They worked day and night to provide for their family and become American citizens. It was sink or swim. My grandfather, Louis Root, died in the poor ward of a Brooklyn hospital, leaving behind seven children with no paycheck. I'm proud to say they all went to work and never collected one dollar of government aid. That's why America survived the *first* Great Depression. How will we survive this one? Today, one in five households doesn't have a single person working under their roof. And still the illegal immigrants continue to pour over the border, bringing more mouths to feed.

- We had citizens with a strong work ethic, all motivated to earn the American Dream for their children and grandchildren. Today, the hungry, motivated citizens and entrepreneurs of the world are in China, India, Mexico, and other countries where you work or starve. Here, everyone—legal, illegal, native-born—wants cradle-to-grave support from government.

- Don't forget, we once had an education system that was the envy of the world. Today, our public school system is a national disgrace, creating generations dependent on government. The difference? Today, teachers' unions are in charge, instead of parents. And today, almost every home of every poor or minority child has no father present. Tell me how this is going to work out.

- And we had cheap, plentiful oil. Today, Obama blocks offshore drilling, while canceling the Keystone pipeline. More and more, radical environmentalists are trying to shut down fracking, which is the form of energy production that is fueling (excuse the pun) our plentiful energy. If Hillary is elected president, I believe our energy prices will skyrocket, too, thereby badly wounding the middle class even further. This could be the final straw for America.

So I've made my point: We are in a world of trouble, hurt, and economic crisis. But it's all "papered over" by government spending and fake money printing. But the bill will soon come due. I see signs everywhere that it is unraveling right now. There are signs of economic collapse everywhere—as long as you read alternative media, not the lies of the mainstream media.

Right now, who pays the bills for this papering over of poverty and misery? The predominantly white middle class—in the form of higher taxes, higher health care costs, higher everything.

But if this giant Ponzi scheme ever collapses all the way and, like Humpty Dumpty, breaks into a thousand pieces that can never be put back together again, it's the children and grandchildren of the middle class who will pay the ultimate price—a lifetime of Venezuela-like, or Cuba-like, or Greece-like poverty and misery. They will never forgive us or understand how we let this happen.

The solution is actually quite simple: cut government, cut spending, cut entitlements, cut foreign aid, cut taxes, dramatically reduce government employee compensation and pensions, stop the wars, encourage drilling, balance the budget, reform the Fed, term-limit politicians, restore school choice, dramatically reduce the power of teachers' unions, and back the dollar with a gold standard. And, of course, elect Donald Trump president to build the wall, secure the border, and end sanctuary cities. Or like so many other great empires of history, America and the great American middle class may never recover from the Obama Great Depression—or the Hillary Greatest Depression of All Time. But more on all this later.

Obamafraud

The Perfect $17 Trillion Trojan Horse

Obama wanted to accelerate his "overwhelm the system" plan from our old Columbia days. Well, this is certainly how you do it.

Obama, supported by the mainstream media, perpetrated the world's biggest Ponzi scheme. It's crippling the US economy, bankrupting the predominantly white middle class, and driving up the national debt. It is known as Obamacare.

I call it by a more accurate name: **Obamafraud.**

We've been scammed. We've been lied to and defrauded. While exploding health insurance premiums for small business and middle-class Americans, bringing the economy to a virtual standstill, Obamacare exchanges and co-ops are going bankrupt, costing taxpayers billions!

So far, thirteen of the twenty-three Obamacare State Co-Op Exchanges have failed (gone bust and broke). The remaining ten have losses of over $200 million per year. The $1.24 billion of federal start-up money used to start them all is most probably gone forever. It will never be repaid.[1]

But what should matter to you is that the Obamacare exchanges even went bust in Vermont and Hawaii. If Obamacare has run through every federal dollar in small, ultra-liberal states like Hawaii and Vermont, what hope is there for the rest of the nation?[2]

But on a personal level, the story is even worse. Like millions of Americans, my health care premiums have skyrocketed from $500 per month to well over $1,700. For Obama voters, I'll keep it simple: that means my rates have more than *tripled* because of Obamafraud.

But that's only the start. My copays have doubled, my deductible is massive, and my family's prescriptions are barely covered. One recent emergency room visit cost a copay of $500, plus $2,500 in other uncovered costs. That's *with* insurance that costs over $1,700 per month.

Obama calls me "rich." I earn a high income and my family is healthy, yet these health care costs are draining my budget and crowding out all other expenses. In response, my family is cutting spending dramatically. Do you have any idea what this means? Multiply this disaster happening to millions of middle-class families, and it's clear why the economy is in free fall, why gross domestic product (GDP) is near zero, and why jobs will be lost by the millions.

Let's examine the *real* story of Obamafraud, the world's biggest scam and Ponzi scheme that the mainstream media calls a "success."

Obama and the media claim millions of new signups. They call that "a great achievement." Really? Let's apply the Obamafraud story to the private sector.

Assume you own a car company and offer fifty people who don't have cars free cars, and 20 percent take you up on it. Is that "a great achievement"? Obama offered free or greatly discounted health insurance, and a few million people are taking him up on it. WOW! He's like *Moses!*

What if you ban the style of cars that fifty car lovers are already driving and then offer free replacement cars and they take them. Is that "a great achievement"? Obama banned the insurance policies of millions of Americans, then told them they had to get a new one (or face penalties). Is a combination of people accepting free stuff—and other people getting new Obama-approved insurance policies because Obama took their old policies away—"a great achievement?" WOW. Obama is so talented!

What about the cost? Nothing to see here! If you spend $1 billion of other people's money on an auto factory, then sell $1 million worth of cars, is that a "success"? That's exactly what Obama did. He spent and lost a few billion dollars of other people's money building a defective website, then fixed it, then hired thousands of overpaid bureaucrats and IRS employees to oversee it all, then spent billions more on wasted taxpayer loans to co-ops that are all going bankrupt.

Who pays for it? YOU—with higher premiums, higher taxes, and massive new national debt. Obama has wasted billions of dollars of other people's money. WOW, what a talented man.

But wait, it gets worse. What if each of the fifty people who love cars spent $25,000 on their old cars. But now, after Obama banned the old style, they need to spend $50,000 each on new cars. They'd *never* waste $50,000 unless they were forced at gunpoint. In the private sector example, they'd be forced at gunpoint by mafia thugs. But in real life, Obama just uses the IRS and government thugs to force you to buy something you don't want or need.

We were forced to throw away perfectly good $25,000 cars. Now we're broke and heavily in debt because you made us spend—at gunpoint—$50,000 on a new car we never wanted or needed. What "a great achievement."

But wait, there's *more!*

While you made everyone (at gunpoint) buy new cars, you also ruined the entire auto industry because no one can make money. So many carmakers (like doctors) have decided to retire or go out of business. So now, people are walking around with "the right" to free cars, but there are no cars for them.

That's exactly what Obama did. He forced people to sign up for free health care, but doctors are leaving in droves. They want nothing to do with Obamacare. So you've got "free health care." Hooray! Unfortunately, there's no one to provide it. You'll be stuck in long lines for years to get your "free stuff." Is that "a great achievement"?

Obama gave away free cars to poor people who never owned a car, and his Kool-Aid-drinking defenders call that "an achievement" because they took a free car. WOW, Obama has some magical powers of persuasion!

Then he banned the average middle-class American's health insurance policy. They were forced at gunpoint to buy a new one. Now he claims "success" because they did so—all because he ruined their perfectly good old policy.

And to pay for it all, he's charging middle-class Americans double or triple. By the time they add in deductibles and copays, they may be paying quadruple. They pay because they have no choice; there's a gun to their heads. But they are left with no money, so they stop buying other things. So the economy is crippled. This is the vicious cycle of Obamafraud.

Worst of all, Obama has badly damaged the *quality* of the US health care system. Doctors are leaving in droves, while millions of new patients are being added to the system.[3] The result will be gridlock and bankruptcy.

Or haven't you heard that the United Kingdom's government-run health care system is insolvent and on the verge of collapse and bankruptcy?[4]

By 2020, the United Kingdom will be forced to close 20 percent of its hospitals. At this moment, patients wait up to eight hours for ambulances. British doctors call the government-run system "worse than communist China."

Now Obama has brought this train wreck to America. It costs far more but delivers nothing but misery, disaster, and bankruptcy.

Since it cost the taxpayer billions, Obama's definition of "success" must be called *debt*. We pay for all this by piling up massive national debt that will someday soon turn America into Greece. And it's all achieved through extortion and media cover-up. It's organized crime sanctioned by government.

Obamacare isn't a "success" or a "great achievement." It's a con job. A scam. A Ponzi scheme. It is at the heart of the plan to overwhelm the US economy, collapse capitalism, and bury the predominantly white middle class—the perfect Trojan horse. US Senator Jeff Sessions studied Obamacare and, using the government's own accounting measurements, came to the shocking conclusion it will cause $17 trillion in new debt. The US economy cannot survive $17 trillion in unfunded obligations!

This new debt will force us to our knees, begging government to save us. To feed the beast of big government, taxes will have to be increased to unimaginable levels. Obamacare, the Trojan horse that Obama "gifted" to the American people as a promise to save us, is actually here to destroy us.

For those who hate America, the beauty of this Trojan horse is that it keeps adding to the debt, destroying all that is great about this country, long after Obama is gone. Hillary and Bernie both are anxious to expand it. *They both promised during the 2016 campaign to spend even more!*

Our children and grandchildren won't even remember Obama's name, but he will have changed their lives and the economic system they live under. In a bit of health care irony, Obamacare is like herpes—the gift that keeps on giving.

In a book called *Angry White Male*, I think it's important to point out that all this spending, all these new taxes, all these regulations, all this debt won't be overwhelming poor people. They have nothing to lose. They have no income. They have no assets. So there's nothing to take from them. But they will enthusiastically support this massive program because it gives them something for nothing.

And the super-wealthy? They, of course, can afford it, but probably won't have to pay for it because they have the lawyers, accountants, and politicians to protect their wealth.

So who gets the bill? You and I, the predominantly white middle class. The group Obama, Hillary, and their white guilt-ridden liberal friends hate so much.

Remember, we're always the targets. The goal is to drain our income with a combination of new draconian taxes and regulations, as well as a dramatic increase in the costs of health insurance to pay for millions of loyal Democrat voters to get it free.

This is why I call it Obamafraud. This is pure fraud and highway robbery. This is how you destroy a generation of angry white males. You bury them in taxes, spending, debt, and massive health care costs. Everyone involved should be sent to prison for life. This is a fraud that makes Bernie Madoff look like a minor league pickpocket.

11

The Conspiracy against
Angry White Males

"Politics is the art of looking for trouble, finding it everywhere, diagnosing it incorrectly, and applying the wrong remedies."

—Groucho Marx

Ultra-liberal Democrats and the mainstream media (I know, I repeat myself) cannot understand why white voters, particularly white men, are so angry. Well, I'm going to share with you the raw, politically incorrect truth. It's an indictment of a president and system practicing reverse racism and overt discrimination—in plain sight for all to see.

First, there is no doubt that blacks, minorities, and people of color had it rough for many decades. Women, especially in the workplace, had the system tilted against them. *We get it.* And during the past hundred years, especially the last sixty, the vast majority of us fought hard to eliminate it.

No one can deny the terrible things done to blacks: slavery; discrimination in jobs and housing; poll taxes; and "Whites Only" signs in front of bathrooms, pools, water fountains, and restaurant counters. The list of wrongs and grievances is long and real.

But that was then, and this is now. And two wrongs don't make a right. The sorry truth is that the pendulum has swung way too far in the other direction. It has gotten to a point where virtually every action, law, and utterance out of our nation's first black president's mouth is intended to denigrate or damage the predominantly white middle class. *Or haven't you noticed?*

Let me start with the obvious.

Suicide

Studies and polls show blacks and people of color are relatively happy and unchanged in their satisfaction level for decades. Yet under Obama, America is in the middle of a massive suicide epidemic. Who is committing all this suicide? *White middle-aged Americans.*[1]

In other words, the white middle class and "angry white males" are so unhappy they are killing themselves. We should be worried about "White Lives Matter." But, of course, then we would be called "racist."

Is the liberal view it's "all in our heads"? Or could something actually be wrong? Do liberals think an entire race has suffered a dramatic increase in depression and suicide because life is so easy and great for white people? Because we have such fantastic advantages? Because great jobs, perfect relationships, and wealth just appear out of thin air or fall out of trees for white people?

Or could this depression, anger, and suicide be the result of no jobs or only menial, crappy, low-wage jobs; or a dramatic drop in our incomes and assets; or dramatic increases in taxes, health insurance, electric bills, grocery bills, and college bills— all of which has made it virtually impossible to provide for our families. The fact is that our own government is destroying the middle class and killing the American Dream of upward mobility. The predominantly white middle class has been sacrificed to give welfare and free health care to everyone else. And to add insult to injury, "everyone else" doesn't just mean other, less fortunate fellow citizens who most of us want to help; it also means every illegal alien who can walk across the border, many of whom hate us and the whole concept of America. Result? We're killing ourselves. That *might* have something to do with it.

In other words, for your typical middle-class American, life sucks. Under Obama and the political elites, the quality of middle-class life has been gutted, and the American Dream of upward mobility is dead. And who makes up this great American middle class? Predominantly white people.

Ironically, the crux of the liberal argument is that white people have all the money, power, and high-paying jobs and own all the businesses. Yet when laws and policies are passed to redistribute their money to those who are poor and dependent, liberal politicians, intellectuals, and the media refuse to admit these policies are nothing more than reverse racism and discrimination.

These policies are a sign of ignorance and stupidity, especially as to how an economy works. A study of every socialist country in world history shows that "fairness, equality, and social justice" leads to devastating widespread poverty and shared misery. Venezuela is the most recent example that big government tax-and-spend policies lead to economic collapse, food shortages, and no toilet paper. Hotels ask guests to BYOTP—"bring your own toilet paper."[2]

Gotta love big government, huh? It doesn't just kill spirit, or kill people, it even kills toilet paper!

The only thing every country basing its economy on diversity, social justice, and affirmative action has succeeded in is making the powerful, political elites filthy rich and making *everyone* else poor. Liberal (i.e., socialist) policies lead to economic disaster. No one is lifted up, everyone is torn down, and the middle class, not the wealthy, are the ones who suffer. Sound like what is happening right now in America?

Obama and his progressive crony elites in the media and Congress have spent almost eight years conducting a massive, radical experiment basing our economy on "diversity, equality, and social justice." The result? Obama has succeeded in destroying America's middle class, just like every other country that ever tried to legislate equality. And that middle class happens to be overwhelmingly white.

Was it worth it? Did income redistribution—that is, taking money and jobs away from small business and the overwhelmingly white middle class with massive taxes and regulations, onerous Obamacare, and climate change costs— and all the spending on entitlements and debt, actually benefit black Americans? You tell me. The fact is our first black president has overseen the greatest inequality in history:

Black unemployment is now *double* that of white unemployment.

Poverty is back to 1960s levels, while welfare, food stamps, and disability have hit all-time record highs.

Black violence and murder rates in inner city urban areas are spiraling out of control. Predominantly black cities like Chicago, Detroit, and Baltimore are not only bankrupt, they're war zones. Violence on inner city streets has risen to unprecedented levels. Who are the victims? *Black Americans.*

Obama has spent more, handed out more entitlements, more welfare, more food stamps, and now more debt than any president in history. Yet the economy is miserable and the only true measurement of economic growth—gross domestic product (GDP)—is near zero.

Obama is the *only* president to ever preside over seven straight years of GDP under 3 percent. Not even Herbert Hoover or FDR in the depths of the Great Depression produced an economic record as miserable and pathetic as Obama. It's an economic record of futility, which, like Joe DiMaggio's fifty-six-game hitting streak, will never be matched!

The result: 63 percent of Americans can't come up with $500 in case of an emergency.[3]

The wealth gap between white and black Americans is wider today than in the 1960s when the "war on poverty" began.[4]

Amazingly, along with driving white *and* black Americans into bankruptcy and poverty, Obama will have added a world-record $10 trillion to the debt (by the time he leaves office). That's money that has to be paid back by the middle class for decades to come, thereby guaranteeing a shrinking middle class in crisis long after Obama is gone.

And you wonder why we're angry?

Obama's success in fundamentally changing America looks exactly like the situation in every communist, socialist, and third-world country—inequality, massive poverty, shared misery, and no middle class. Thank you, Obama: you've turned America into a third-world mess.

Sadly, Obama had a golden opportunity to be a leader and make America a truly color-blind nation. I believe it is a major reason so many Americans voted for him and is what even those of us who didn't support him had great hope he would do. Instead, he's produced the worst race relations since the 1960s.[5]

Now, let's go a step deeper. Let's examine specific Obama policies that are clearly aimed right at the heart of white America. You wonder why white America is angry? Liberals can't understand why white America is outraged, shocked, and feels betrayed, denigrated, and discriminated? Here it is.

Hiring Employees in the Private Sector

How many Americans are aware that the Obama administration sued major corporations to ban them from using criminal background checks on black job applicants? The Equal Employment Opportunity Commission (EEOC) had the anti-white, outright racist audacity to argue that criminal background checks for whites are perfectly acceptable, but corporations should be banned from checking on the criminal records of blacks. Why? Because, they argued, black males are so likely to have a criminal record, they would never be hired. So business owners have no right to know the background of the person they're hiring to handle money and deal with valued customers? According to Obama, drug dealers, pimps, and rapists should wait on your female customers.

Is this a purposeful attempt to hurt the predominantly white American middle class? You decide. But it sure looks like it.

Hiring of Government Employees

Not content to strike out with his order in the private sector, President Obama signed an Executive Order in December of 2015 to "ban the box."[6]

This means federal agencies can no longer ask prospective job applicants about their criminal history. Amazingly, what this means is government employees paid with your taxpayer money (often at a higher rate than a similar job in the private sector) will now include convicted criminals. The government is using your taxes to pay convicted criminals to oversee your life.

Wait, it gets better. Government employees at agencies like the IRS, the National Security Agency (NSA), and Social Security have access to highly confidential financial information that can be stolen and sold to thieves and frauds (or people looking to blackmail politicians into voting for bigger government). Doesn't it make sense that an applicant's criminal background should at least be considered?

Is this a purposeful attempt to hurt the predominantly white American middle class? You decide. But it sure looks like it.

Housing

Are you aware that the Obama administration has told land-lords they have no right to reject a potential tenant based on a criminal record? Property owners are now obligated by law to rent to known murderers, rapists, drug dealers, pimps, carjackers, and home-invasion robbers. The administration admitted that this law is to protect criminals because they happen to be predominantly black. As always, Obama's Housing and Urban Development (HUD) department plays the race card by saying if you refuse to rent to criminals, you're "racist" because this disproportionately affects African Americans.[7]

Once again, this book isn't about race, but it is about reverse racism. I'm merely responding in self-defense.

Is this a purposeful attempt to hurt the predominantly white American middle class? You decide. But it sure looks like it.

Neighborhoods

How many Americans realize that Obama's HUD agency is forcing cities and towns across America to build high-density, low-income housing in middle class and wealthy white neighborhoods? Why? A liberal Mexican American activist at a famous economic event called FreedomFest aimed a question at Donald Trump that explains what we're facing. Clearly angry at Trump's promise to build a wall at the Mexican border, he asked Trump, *"Why don't you want to build a wall around your inner cities to protect your citizens from American criminals?"*

The factual answer to that question is we already have. It's called "suburbs." America has experienced a "white (and every other racial group with the economic ability) flight" away from inner cities to suburbs for decades. It's why Detroit lost over half its population. Decent, law-abiding people of all races with good jobs tend to run away from crime—especially once they start a family.

But to Obama and his liberal friends, this isn't "fair." People don't have a right to be mobile, send their kids to better schools, or avoid crime. Obama wants everyone to live in shared equality (i.e., misery). Now he's found a way to accomplish that. If he can't find a way to force you to live in poor, crime-ridden, inner city neighborhoods, he'll just create them in your neighborhood!

As a bonus, this policy erodes personal responsibility and capitalism by eliminating the necessity to study hard, work hard, or be disciplined to move from a poor neighborhood to a nice middle-class one.

But wait, it gets better; it's part of a socialist's wish list. This policy not only creates fairness and equality by putting poor people into wealthy neighborhoods without working for it; it also destroys the property values of middle-class, predominantly white homeowners. In the short run, the poor may be lifted up; in the longer run, everyone else is brought down. For liberals, that's "equality."

Look at it from the point of view of a middle-class American. You've worked long and hard so your kids can live in a safe neighborhood, only to see Obama force low-income housing on your block, drive your home value down, and infest your nice, safe neighborhood with crime, muggings, robberies, carjackings, drugs, and prostitution. *Nice!*

Again, while Obama and liberals keep wanting to make this a racial issue, it's not. Like whites, black middle-class Americans have followed the same route. For the most part, middle-class blacks have left the inner cities. They move to suburbs to escape crime, filth, drugs, and poverty and to give their kids a chance at success.

But Obama wants there to be no escape. He's bringing the devil to you. To your neighborhood, your block, perhaps next door. He's putting drug dealers on your corner.

Is this a purposeful attempt to hurt the predominantly white American middle class? You decide. But it sure looks like it.

Health Care

It is a fact that Obamacare's main purpose is to redistribute wealth. Small business owners (primarily white) and middle-class Americans (primarily white) have been devastated by massive increases in health care costs: insurance premiums, copays, deductibles, cost of prescription drugs, and loss of coverage. Who has gained? Poor Americans who were handed free insurance coverage. It has been a direct transfer of wealth disguised as a health care program. Poor and

nonworking Americans were handed a massive new entitlement program: "welfare in the form of free medical." As with
every government program, middle-class Americans (predominantly white) got the bill.

*Is this a purposeful attempt to hurt the predominantly white
American middle class? You decide. But it sure looks like it.*

Economy

Obama has passed the most dramatic tax increases along with
the most onerous business regulations in history. Who were
they aimed at? Predominantly white small business owners and
middle-class Americans. We know how he feels about business
owners. Remember when he said, "You didn't build that."

*Is this a purposeful attempt to hurt the predominantly white
American middle class? You decide. But it sure looks like it.*

Immigration

Obama has left the borders wide open, allowing hundreds
of thousands of illegal immigrants to pour into America, all
of whom expect cradle-to-grave entitlements. Don't forget,
Obama has also fast-tracked the importation of about one
million Muslims into America during his two terms.[8]

Well over 90 percent of these new Muslim immigrants
are on food stamps, while almost 70 percent are on welfare.
These stats are according to Obama's own Labor Department.[9]

We are fed lie after lie after lie about illegal immigration by Obama, Hillary, government bureaucrats, and, of

course, the mainstream media. We are told that illegals are not flowing across the border. In a presidential debate, Hillary claimed there is no border problem. Wrong. Record numbers of illegals are coming across in 2016. As I write this book, the number of illegal aliens crossing the border is at an all-time record pace: 40 percent higher than the record set in 2014 and double the number in 2015.[10]

More illegals cross the border into Texas than babies born to native-born mothers in Texas each week.[11]

We are told that illegals are not costing America anything. We are told they are a "net gain." What a big fat lie. Earlier in the book I proved that illegal immigrants cost hundreds of billions of dollars in welfare, food stamps, Medicaid, and other entitlements—far more than native-born Americans, both percentage-wise and dollar-wise.

We're told it's not "either/or." We're told America can afford to take care of American citizens *and* illegal immigrants. Another big fat lie. Obama just cut $2.6 billion from veterans, while allocating $4.5 billion to the importation and relocation of Syrian migrants. So why would a US president choose to cut money from vets in favor of fast-tracking Syrian migrants into our country? Why is that more important than taking care of veterans?[12]

So I guess it is "either/or." Vets, who happen to be in the predominantly white middle class, are getting shafted to pay for Muslim immigration. Perhaps the hundreds of billions spent on all other illegal immigrants is the reason there were no funds for VA hospitals and courageous heroes were put on fictitious waiting lists to die. Those heroes happened to be predominantly white middle-class citizens.

In Obama's last budget as president, he demands nearly $18,000 for every illegal child or teenager from Central America who enters the country in 2016 (he expects over 75,000).[13]

That's $3,000 more than the average American senior citizen collects on Social Security, even though they were legally born in America, worked their entire lives, and paid into the system. So native-born Americans are getting out monies they already put in, and *still* they get less than someone who comes here illegally.

Keep in mind that many (if not most) of these children and teens might very well collect welfare for life. What does that cost the middle class? If you can't see that this is a purposeful attack on the predominantly white middle class, you're blind, deaf, or very dumb.

We are told that illegals aren't criminals. Another big fat lie. One out of every five illegals has a criminal record (not including the crime of coming into the country). Illegals committed almost half a million crimes in Texas alone, just in the past four years. Half a million crimes—in one state.[14]

Multiply that number across the country and tell me the cost to society in police, courts, public defenders, prosecutors, and prison costs? What is the cost to the victims? How about the Americans murdered at the hands of illegals? That's a pretty damn steep cost.

Here's the most remarkable stat of all: 30 percent of all criminals in federal, state, and local prisons in the United States are illegal immigrants.[15]

This isn't happening by mistake or coincidence. The Obama administration is currently arguing in front of the US Supreme Court that Obama has the power to use executive action to instantly award Social Security to millions of immigrants illegally in the United States.[16]

Now let's move on to legal immigrants. Obama is purposely importing immigrants legally into the country who fit the parameters of his plan to "fundamentally change America." From 2009 to 2013, the Obama administration issued twice as many green cards to immigrants from Muslim nations as European nations—680,000 green cards for Muslims versus 270,000 for Europeans.[17]

Why is Obama choosing this ratio? Because this is how you "fundamentally change America," "overwhelm the system," and destroy capitalism, replacing it with socialism for a citizenry dependent on government entitlements to survive. The bonus is bringing in unskilled, uneducated, and dependent immigrants who will forever more vote Democrat to keep the freebies coming.

Don't get me wrong. Obama doesn't discriminate. Every immigrant who needs welfare is welcome: Muslim, Mexican, Central American. Cubans are in a special class. All they have to do is get over the border and they are immediately met with a so-called "Welcome Wagon" that gives them instant cash, Social Security cards, food stamps, and Medicaid.[18]

As the country, health care, and school systems are all overwhelmed by massive costs for illegal immigration, and the debt rises to unimaginable levels, who pays for it all? American taxpayers. And who are they? The small business owners and middle-class Americans who spend their lives paying into the system and take almost nothing out.

Is this a purposeful attempt to hurt the predominantly white American middle class? You decide. But it sure looks like it.

Why doesn't someone stand up and say it's time to stop flooding the country with even more poor and unskilled immigrants, legal and illegal, and spend those billions upon billions of tax dollars now being given to them to improve America's inner cities and the lives of American citizens? Oh, guess what? Someone has. His name is Donald Trump!

The Silicon Valley Jobs Scam

Middle-class Americans don't realize the immigration scam isn't just about working stiffs. The cannon is aimed squarely at college-educated white-collar Americans, too. It's called H-1B visas. This is precisely why college grads with massive student loan debt are living in all-time record numbers in their parents' basement. This is why the icons of Silicon Valley are freaking out about the possible election of Donald Trump. These greedy and guilty white billionaires want to keep importing hundreds of thousands of low-wage foreigners to fill their jobs, instead of higher-paid American workers.[19]

The sad truth about Silicon Valley is that they fear Trump because they don't want to pay real wages to American white-collar college grads. Guest worker programs have devastated the predominantly white middle and upper classes. We've been replaced by desperate foreigners willing to work for slave wages to get to (and stay in) America. They can never ask for a raise for fear of losing their H-1B visa.

You want to know why we are angry white males? The H-1B program has resulted in massive job losses and a decade of wage deflation. The media paints illegals as victims just looking for a better life for their families. Well, here we're talking about American white-collar young adults who played by all the rules, graduated from good colleges, studied high technology, amassed massive student debt, and are being victimized by cheap legal foreign labor. They played by the rules and got screwed. Who's the victim now?

Is this a purposeful attempt to hurt the predominantly white American middle class? You decide. But it sure looks like it.

Education

The public school system has been ruined by teachers' unions, common core, and bleeding-heart liberal ideology. The school system is so bad, especially in America's larger cities, that parents who have any hope for their children's success spend their last dime on private schools, parochial schools, or homeschooling.

That means business owners and taxpayers like myself are forced to pay *double taxation*. I'm paying obscene, unaffordable property taxes to pay for public schools that I can't send my own kids to. At the same time, I'm forced to pay $15,000 to $20,000 per child for alternative education.

So business owners and middle-class taxpayers who pay into the system (made up of predominantly white taxpayers) are bled dry to give their children a proper education, while we're also forced to pay for a terrible free education for the children of the poor, who pay no taxes and pay nothing into the system. Since they pay nothing for it, it is easy for the vested political and corrupt union interests to get them to vote for higher and higher education spending even with that system continually failing even their children. So is it any wonder the goal of liberals like Obama and Hillary is to keep poor people poor and let more and more poor and unskilled people into America, so that eventually their votes outnumber native-born, hardworking, employed Americans.

Is this a purposeful attempt to hurt the predominantly white American middle class? You decide. But it sure looks like it.

Currency

This is the most absurd example of all. Do you know what a president does when his policies have so badly damaged the economy, ruined health care, killed all decent middle-class jobs, destroyed GDP, and run up $9 trillion in new debt, resulting in black unemployment being *double* that of white and causing black violent crime to run wild in Democrat-ruled, black-dominated cities?

Obama attempts to appease the masses of oblivious voters by changing the faces and images on the front and back of five-, ten-, and twenty-dollar bills to celebrate "social justice and diversity." It's called BREAD AND CIRCUS. And it's now clear that "we are Rome" in the days just before the fall. Like Nero, Obama, his ignorant Kool-Aid-drinking socialist cabal, and the biased progressive media are fiddling while America burns.

Obama has no clue how to turn around the economy or create jobs for black (or white) Americans, so he changes the faces on the currency to distract the masses. This is "feel-good," politically correct B.S. I'm sorry, folks, but putting a heroic black woman like Harriet Tubman on the twenty-dollar bill (and she is an American hero) won't create a single job or raise the GDP above zero. Putting Martin Luther King on the back of the five-dollar bill won't help a stagnant economy.

Just like everywhere else it's been tried, the reality is that Obama and his socialist cabal have proven an economy cannot be run based on diversity and social justice. Basing *our currency* on diversity and social justice won't help either. It's just BREAD AND CIRCUS to keep the masses from unrest and rioting.

Keep in mind that Obama's treasurer, Jack Lew, ordered the mint to make the changes on currency a "priority." He also disclosed there was "great pressure" to showcase "diversity" on our money. Really? *From who?*

Who thinks in the middle of an Obama Great Depression the priority is putting images of civil rights leaders on our dollar, instead of making it a priority to create jobs and improve GDP? Insanity, ignorance, and reverse racism abounds. All of it is aimed at the predominantly white middle class.

So much of what Obama and the liberals are doing, and the media is dutifully reporting, is simply a distraction, waste

of resources, and pacifier so we won't notice how far worse
things have gotten under Obama and his liberal policies.

I've saved perhaps the best for last.

Don't Offend Criminals

Not only is Obama demanding criminal backgrounds not
be considered in hiring, but he no longer wants them to be
called *criminals*. This is a new directive sent out to colleges
by the Obama administration. The term "criminal" might
offend. Along with this directive came a pamphlet referring
to convicted criminals as "justice-involved individuals." You
can't make this up. Obama thinks a criminal is just someone
"involved with justice." We can't allow a rapist to be offended
by calling him a rapist because names hurt! So now the person that raped your older daughter can go to work at your
younger daughter's university without fear of being identified as or called a rapist. At worst, it might become known
he is someone "involved with justice." But then, in Obama's
world, it wasn't their fault; a racist white society must have
forced them to commit the crime. So from now on, just to be
fair, no one should ever again be called racist. They are just
"race-involved individuals."

*Is this a purposeful attempt to hurt the predominantly white
American middle class? You decide. But it sure looks like it.*

Allow Criminals and Violent Felons to Vote

Amazingly, Virginia Governor Terry McAuliffe just gave voting rights to two hundred thousand Virginia felons.[20]

McAuliffe is a lifelong best friend of the Clintons. This wasn't even subtle. There was no attempt to hide or disguise this as a gift to his close friend Hillary. The governor of Virginia just added two hundred thousand low-life dirtbags to the voter rolls in Virginia to try to steal the election for his buddy Hillary.

These people are tone deaf to hardworking, law-abiding, taxpaying Americans. Entrenched liberal politicians like McAuliffe have spent so much time around typical Democrat voters that they have forgotten what real Americans think of murderers, rapists, carjackers, home-invasion robbers, pimps, and drug dealers.

Democrat Governor McAuliffe's new law applies to every convicted felon . . . even violent felons . . . even felons from other states now living in Virginia. It doesn't just allow them to vote; this new law allows them to run for office, serve on a jury, and become a notary public.

Murder *victims* don't get to serve on juries, vote, or run for office ever again, but now *their murderers* do. Now, a woman raped by a serial rapist might one day see her rapist sitting on a jury, running for office, or serving the state as a notary public. Keep in mind, this law doesn't care if the criminal was a serial rapist or multiple murderer; it doesn't care whether they've committed new crimes after their initial conviction; and it doesn't care if they've paid back their victims. This law allows a victim who still has $250,000 in medical bills to see the person that shot, stabbed, raped, or bankrupted them voting or running for office.[21]

This is the thinking of today's Democratic Party. These are the lengths to which they'll go to steal elections.

Willie Horton

But I'm a "lemons to lemonade" kind of guy. I'm a positive thinker. This is more than just a travesty of justice. This is more than just the ruination of America. This is opportunity knocking. This is a gift there for the taking. The Democrats have handed Donald Trump the perfect TV ad to win the 2016 Presidential election.

Lee Atwater, the famous Republican advertising whiz who destroyed 1988 Democrat presidential candidate Michael Dukakis with the Willie Horton TV commercial, must be looking down from heaven with an ear to ear smile.

Governor McAuliffe just handed the election to the Donald Trump and the GOP *if this is handled correctly.* This is Willie Horton, Part Deux.

It's like shooting fish in a barrel.

Find mugshots of the murderers who just got voting rights. Find mugshots of the rapists who just got voting rights. Mix in a few drug dealers and pimps. Then channel the great Lee Atwater. Get to work creating the most devastating TV commercials in modern political history.

What a tragic monumental mistake Democrats just made. Not just any Democrat—the best friend, ally, and chief fundraiser of the Clintons.

I can see the TV ads now. Picture this:

SCREEN IMAGE: Image of Virginia DEMOCRAT Governor Terry McAuliffe . . .

ANNOUNCER: Hillary and Bill's best friend and chief fund-raiser just gave a gift to the Clintons. He just gave voting rights to scum . . . dirtbags . . . murderers . . . the worst of the worst criminals in Virginia—so they can register Democrat and vote for Hillary.

SCREEN IMAGE: Mugshots of the most heinous criminals, with crimes listed under their faces.

ANNOUNCER: Think about that. They murdered people . . . they raped people . . . they carjacked people . . . they invaded homes and terrorized people . . . they sold drugs . . . they beat people almost to death . . . they pimped and beat young girls.

Their victims will never again feel safe again.

But the murderer, rapist, or thug who sold drugs to children is out on street—and voting for Hillary.

This is the length to which Democrats will go to win elections.

But wait, there's more. Not only can they vote; they can serve on a jury, become a notary public, and run for office.

SCREEN IMAGE: Mugshot of murderer . . . now with a "VOTE FOR ME" ribbon across bottom of screen.

Someday your rapist may run for office.

Someday your child's drug dealer may serve on a jury.

Someday you'll need a notary public—and your mother's murderer will be notarizing your signature.

SCREEN IMAGE: Hillary at Congressional hearing saying, "What difference does it make?"

This is the depth of depravity of Hillary Clinton and her allies.

Democrats—the party of murderers, rapists, and drug dealers. Hillary is right at home.

VOTE FOR DONALD TRUMP TO MAKE AMERICA GREAT AGAIN.

Folks, it really is this bad. Yes, we are angry. And we have every right and reason to be. Sadly, it's a full-scale attack coming from all directions and it's getting worse.

12

Diversity—The War on Excellence

It's important to hear a commencement speech given by Michelle Obama to City College graduates in New York City this past June. Michelle told the graduates she chose to give the commencement speech at City College because of all the colleges in America, City College asked her to speak about "diversity."

In her speech, she directed a comment toward Donald Trump when she added that "some folks" don't value the diversity that City College embodies. "They seem to view our diversity as a threat to be contained rather than as a resource to be tapped. They tell us to be afraid of those who are different, to be suspicious of those with whom we disagree."[1]

I'm sorry, Mrs. Obama, but you have it all wrong—just as wrong as when your husband told business owners, "You didn't build it."

Of course we built it. Our taxes paid for every single thing President Obama and every government official takes credit for. Government builds nothing without our hard-earned tax dollars. So actually, Mr. Obama, "It is you who didn't build it."

Mrs. Obama is wrong for exactly the same reason. Diversity doesn't deserve credit for success in life any more than government deserves credit for building anything. *How absurd.*

Success comes from brains, talent, energy, creativity, chutzpah, and work ethic. I'm hiring an employee for those traits whether he's black, white, Hispanic, male, female, straight, gay, or somewhere in between. I'm not hiring them for their "diversity." I'm hiring them for their talent and skills. Great employees succeed because of their talents and attributes, not the color of their skin.

Anyone who hires or doesn't hire employees based on the color of their skin is a racist. But that applies as much to those who deny employment to whites, just as much as those who deny employment to blacks or other minorities. In today's world, any business person who hires based on skin color rather than talent and skills will soon be out of business.

Only government and academia can afford to hire people because of "diversity." Because both have the ability to force taxpayers at gunpoint to hand over basically unlimited money, they are able to fail and fail badly. In the business world, we can't do that.

Government extorts money like the mafia. I can't force a client to pay for something they don't want, or at a price they refuse to pay. I am limited by competition, but not government. Government and academia can hire incompetent morons; pay them obscene salaries, benefits, and pensions; and bleed billions, tens of billions, or hundreds of billions but never run out of money and then demand a huge budget increase for next year with the absurd claim the only reason they are failing so badly is that they need even more money. And they do this with a straight face.

Government can hire too many employees, then claim they failed because they need to hire more. Government can fail miserably at educating children, then ask for more money to do it right "this time." Taxes give government a license to steal. Of course, government pays no taxes on the money they bring in. What a scam.

Mrs. Obama can afford to spend tens of millions on vacations across the globe. In her big government world, her friends can waste a billion taxpayer dollars building a crappy Obamacare website that doesn't work, then waste a billion more to fix it. In her world, government can afford to add $10 trillion to the national debt on stupid ideas that never work . . . and billions more on "stimulus programs" that waste every cent . . . and billions more on bailing out Wall Street companies and banks and unions (all run by big political donors) . . . and billions more on "bridges to nowhere" . . . and billions more on a hundred failed green energy companies that lose every taxpayer dollar "invested" in them by the Obama government.

This obsession with diversity, social justice, equality, fairness, and "environmental consciousness" only works because Michelle and Barack are doing it all with OPM (other peoples' money).

In my world, I can't afford to base my businesses on diversity. When you run a small business, every penny counts. I can't afford losses. I can't afford to give a job to someone because of the color of their skin, their gender, or because they're Muslim.

I can only afford to hire someone who is the best quali-
fied for the job. If that person happens to be white, I don't
care. They get the job. If they happen to be black, I don't care.
They get the job. When you run a small business, jobs are
based on performance, not race.

For years I was CEO of a company with a hundred salesmen. For most of those years the top salesman was African
American. I hired him because he was a talented salesman
and communicator. I treated him great, not because he was
black but because he was my leading salesman. In business,
it's all about green, not black or white. In the real world (as
opposed to the fantasy world of government), we hire only
based on talent. We couldn't care less about the color of your
skin, or whether you're a man or woman, Christian or Muslim. If you can sell, you've got the job.

Mrs. Obama is lucky she has taxpayer money to back
up her "diverse" choices for hiring and spending. Then again,
let's all remember that Mr. and Mrs. Obama's government has
lost over $10 trillion (by the time he leaves office). That will
be more than all the debt created by every president in US
history combined.

*Diversity may be working out for the Obamas . . . not so
much for the rest of us.*

Before we look at the idiocy of running a company based
on "diversity" here in my hometown of Las Vegas, let's look
at how a company should be run—based on profitability, not
diversity.

Sheldon Adelson is a brilliant CEO and business visionary. His company, Las Vegas Sands, is a casino-sector superstar. The company is very financially healthy. Las Vegas Sands had net income of $1.97 billion in 2015. And overall cash flow of $1.05 billion.[2]

The company had $2.18 billion cash on hand to end 2015.[3]

Sheldon Adelson himself is worth over $20 billion. From everything I know, his company hires based on performance, with the most qualified people getting the job. Not surprisingly, Sheldon is a Republican and high-profile critic of Obama.

Steve Wynn is the CEO of Wynn Resorts here in Las Vegas. He is also a billionaire. His company, Wynn Resorts, is financially very healthy.[4]

After a bad year in Macau, Wynn Resorts still reported a profit of $87.2 million. It holds $2.3 billion cash in hand.[5]

From everything I know, his company hires based on performance. Steve Wynn is also a Republican and high-profile critic of Obama.

Then there's Caesars Entertainment, competitors of Adelson and Wynn. For many years Caesars was run by CEO Gary Loveman, a Democrat supporter and contributor.[6]

Not surprisingly, he was a former Harvard professor. Caesars prides itself on basing their hiring on "diversity." It seems to be all they talk about in their press releases.

In 2016, Caesars won an unprecedented ninth consecutive "perfect corporate equity index rating" from the Human

Rights Campaign Foundation. This group scores business based on lesbian, gay, bisexual, and transgender workplace policies. Caesars has also won numerous other awards for diversity from African American organizations.

Caesars is also "perfect" when it comes to climate change and environmental consciousness. They are the only entertainment or gaming company in America to win the prestigious "Climate Leadership Award." How nice. Caesars keeps the air clean around its casinos. Bravo.

There's one thing Caesars doesn't excel in: making money. Their obsession with diversity, bisexual rights, and climate change has led to economic disaster. They lost $2.8 billion in 2014. That was an *improvement* from the year before. You know a company is in big trouble when losing $2.8 billion is an improvement.[7]

In the fourth quarter of 2015, Caesars *only* lost another $76 million. They called that "a big improvement."[8]

In the first quarter of 2016, Caesars lost another $308 million. *For the quarter.*[9]

Caesars corporate debt hit $24 billion. And they recently filed for bankruptcy protection.

Caesars endured media headlines like . . .

"Debt-Ridden Caesars Buried in Financial Woes."[10]

"Sorting out Caesars: How the Company Slid into Distress."[11]

"Caesars Stock Plummeting Amid Debt Troubles."[12]

"Why Caesars Entertainment Has a Massive $24 Billion Debt."[13]

"Caesars: A Private Equity Gamble in Vegas Gone Wrong."[14]

Maybe if Caesars had hired the best employees, regardless of race, gender, or transgender . . . maybe if they'd had their attention focused on looking out for their shareholders and jobs of all their employees, instead of diversity awards or climate change awards . . . instead of aiming for "diversity" . . . maybe they wouldn't be $24 billion in debt and in bankruptcy court as we speak.

I know this much. Gary Loveman and President Obama both suffer from the same problems—and both produced the same results. Both hail from Harvard, both may be book smart, but they are also arrogant and think they know better than everyone else. Most importantly, they clearly value diversity over performance. The results in both cases are massive debt resulting in crisis, failure, and bankruptcy.

This obsession with diversity, social justice, and reckless disregard for piling up debt has destroyed both their economies and left both Caesars and the US economy on the verge of collapse. I guess you can say Caesar's employees will be equal—broke and unemployed.

There's a valuable lesson in there for all of us. It's the whole reason I wrote this book. Political correctness and an obsession with "equality, diversity, and social justice" are dangerous to any economy. Yes, they are nice ideas. They feel warm and cuddly. So do rainbows, puppies, and unicorns. But try out any of them in the business world some time. See if a rainbow makes you money selling New York City real estate. Good luck bringing a puppy to work on Wall Street. See if hiring "diverse" casino employees attracts high-roller gamblers. These naïve liberal ideas are a recipe for wrecking the US economy. But then that's precisely what Obama and his socialist cabal want, right?

Ah, now it all makes sense.

13

The Wall—

The Ultimate Liberal Hypocrisy

If we want to save America and the great American middle class, nothing is more important than building the wall on the Mexican border. This is such a no-brainer, it shouldn't even be up for debate. How can anyone disagree with protecting America from foreign invaders? To disagree, you'd have to want to "fundamentally change America"; you'd have to want to "overwhelm the system" with spending, welfare, entitlements, and debt; you'd have to want to change the demographics of the American electorate from native-born Americans to gigantic numbers of newly arrived foreigners who don't care about capitalism or American exceptionalism; you'd have to want ISIS and other terrorist cells to cross freely into America. *Who in their right mind would want all of that?*

Ah, yes. Obama, Hillary, Bernie, and their socialist friends in the Democratic Party. That explains it all.

Look at how ridiculous and truly hypocritical this is.

It's All Part of the Plan

Remember, nothing happening to America is happening by mistake. This is a purposeful plan, the greatest conspiracy in world history. And the fact is that an open border may be one of the most deadly weapons.

Exhibit A is that the illegal immigrant crisis at our southern border is a purposeful attempt to create a crisis, overwhelm the system, and force the American people to make a dreadfully bad decision under duress.

Americans have huge hearts. That's why we lead the world in charitable giving. There is no close second. Obama knows this, which is why he talks incessantly about emotional stories of one particular immigrant, immigrant family, or immigrant child. He is playing on our heartstrings portraying all immigrants, even illegal ones, as women, children, and families begging for help, begging to live "the American Dream."

He conveniently leaves out the stories about illegal aliens murdering, assaulting, robbing, and raping. He leaves out the epidemic of illegals driving drunk and killing innocent Americans. He leaves out the crisis illegals are causing in schools and hospital emergency rooms. He leaves out the fact that over one-third of our prison beds are filled with illegal alien felons. He leaves out the cost for police, courts, prisons, and welfare. This is all part of the Cloward-Piven plan we learned at Columbia to "overwhelm the system."

Obama is purposely creating an immigration crisis, whether it be illegal immigrant children coming by the thousands from Central America, or Syrian and Muslim migrants and refugees. Obama and Hillary's goal is not just to allow millions more in, but to grant amnesty and citizenship to the millions of illegal aliens already here.

He wants us to approve billions in new spending. Will he use that money to "solve" the crisis? NO! He'll use it to pay for lawyers for each of them (to prevent deportation), and hand them billions in welfare, food stamps, aid to dependent children, education, and, of course, free meals at school—all paid for by the predominantly white American middle class. Don't forget that Democrat politicians across America want to give illegal aliens either free college or inexpensive in-state tuition, while middle-class kids born in America pay full freight.

It's a two-for-one plan. This is how you create a permanent, loyal Democratic voter bloc, at the same time you bankrupt the middle class, leaving them dependent on government. Once the middle class is desperate, broke, and scared to death, they'll accept government checks. At that point they are far more likely to vote Democrat to keep the checks coming. *Brilliant.*

As you know, this is a purposeful plan right out of the Cloward-Piven playbook. My classmates vowed to someday put this plan into effect to overwhelm the system, collapse capitalism, crash the US economy, and force America to its knees. With Obama in the lead, they are doing it.

From that position of crisis, weakness, and panic, they vowed to "fundamentally change the country." Recognize the plan? It's happening right now.

So how do we fight back? Obama and his socialist cabal are liars, frauds, and hypocrites. Yes, they want to help the poor and downtrodden—but only with *your* money.

Yes, they want to house the world's homeless—but only in *your* neighborhood.

Yes, they want to let in the world's poverty-stricken immigrants—but only into *your* backyard.

None of this "dirty work" ever touches their mansions, yachts, private jets, private schools, or, God forbid, their precious children.

Last I checked, Sasha and Malia won't go to school with illegal immigrant classmates with lice, scabies, measles, and tuberculosis. Last I checked, illegals with gang tattoos from head to toe won't be mugging old ladies or dealing crack in front of the Georgetown mansions of lobbyists, lawyers, and politicians like Hillary Clinton.

Or . . .

Maybe they will.

I have an idea.

It's time we counter these liberal, elite hypocrites and fight them to our last breath. First, we must elect Trump, build the wall, secure the border, and end sanctuary cities.

Then, we must make it impossible for illegals to collect welfare and as hard as possible to get a job or earn money, leaving them no option but to return to their home countries. The last thing any Republican should do is support any form of amnesty.

In the meantime, let's demand the hordes of illegal immigrants, motherless children, and tattooed gangbangers awaiting court dates or deportation be housed in the fashionable Washington, DC, suburbs where our politicians live. If

Obama and his socialist cabal want illegals in this country, let them live with and care for them.

Why are we sending this needy horde of illegal immigrants to struggling middle-class neighborhoods that can't afford them? Let's send them to Beverly Hills, Brentwood, the Upper East Side of Manhattan, Scarsdale, Great Neck, Westwood, Palo Alto, Napa, Atherton, Menlo Park, Carmel, and don't forget the ritziest neighborhoods in Boston and Chicago.

These rich enclaves have the money and resources; let them care for them. Give them jobs at the Ralph Lauren store on Rodeo Drive. Or the Armani store on Madison Avenue. Or at Saks Fifth Avenue. Rachel Maddow can hire one or two as the booker for her MSNBC show.

Perhaps Hillary can get one of these illegals a six hundred thousand dollar minimal work job at NBC, like she got for her daughter, Chelsea.[1]

While we're at it, let's demand they be bussed to elite private schools; start with Sidwell Friends School, where Sasha and Malia attended.

There's the ticket. It's time to turn the tables. Let the wealthy liberals who support Obama and weep for illegal immigrants practice what they preach. Tell them if they want open borders and illegal immigration so badly, YOU TAKE THEM. It's time to send the illegal crisis to the doors of Beverly Hills, Manhattan, and Georgetown. Let's see how long they keep voting for open borders, amnesty, and sanctuary cities, if those illegals wind up living in their neighborhoods.

Liberals are exactly alike when it comes to climate change and illegal immigration. HYPOCRITES. They give long speeches about global warming and climate change, accept major environmental awards, then head back home in a private jet. They use more fossil fuel on that one trip than a typical middle-class American uses in a decade. And they give great speeches about the poor, barefoot, desperate, innocent illegal immigrant children. But their kids live in 100 percent white neighborhoods, play only with children of privilege, dine only at fancy restaurants, and attend elite private schools.

Funny how what they believe is only good for the rest of us, not for them.

The Pope

Even the pope is a bleeding-heart liberal hypocrite. He had the nerve to recently butt into American politics. That has to be the biggest mistake in the history of the Catholic Church. The pope actually attacked Donald Trump and said, "Anyone who wants to build a wall is not a Christian." Really? The pope is now taking stands against US politicians?[2]

If I were Donald Trump, I'd have several responses. The first response would be "THANK YOU. Americans aren't like any other people in the world. We are mavericks, self-reliant, rugged individualists. We march to the beat of a different drummer. We don't like government telling us what to do, let alone foreign governments or leaders like the pope. As a matter of fact, rather than taking orders from an outsider, we tend to do the opposite of what a foreign leader tells us to do. *Or don't you remember King George?"*

But the big issue here is the blatant hypocrisy. Hypocrites deserve a little embarrassment and humiliation—even religious ones. It turns out the pope is a hypocrite of the highest order.

The pope lectures Donald Trump about building a wall. But guess who has the biggest, baddest, highest wall ever built? *The Vatican.*[3]

The pope is surrounded by a giant wall and an army of border guards. Popes who live in glass houses shouldn't throw stones.

Donald Trump should channel Ronald Reagan and announce publicly and loudly:

"POPE FRANCIS, TEAR DOWN YOUR WALL."

If he doesn't want to be a hypocrite, the pope should tear down the Vatican's walls and allow unlimited immigration. Why doesn't the pope fill St. Peter's Square with tents and Porta-Potties? Where is the compassion and humanity at the Vatican?

I know I'm about to be called not only a racist, but mean-spirited, greedy, and un-Christian as well. It turns out the pope has a huge conflict of interest. There are millions of Catholic Hispanics in America, many of them here illegally. Let's be honest. They put money in his collection plates, even more than they could in their home countries. The pope is undoubtedly a nice man who means well. But it's always about the money, for churches as much as government or business.

Without donations, the church ceases to exist. Every religious leader knows parishioners will drop more money in the collection plate if they like him, if he praises them, if he defends them, if he condemns a wall between America and Mexico. But neither the pope nor the Catholic Church will get the bill for taking care of all these hordes of illegal aliens. That goes to you and me—the taxpayers.

So here's what Donald should announce publicly and loudly:

"I'll compromise, Pope Francis. I won't build a wall if you agree to pay the bill for millions of illegals, thereby removing the burden from US taxpayers."

Pope Francis lectures America about illegal immigration without a thought as to how to pay for it, without a thought as to the pain and misery that the higher taxes necessary to support millions of illegal immigrants cause to his native-born American parishioners, or the job losses and lower wages they inflict upon his native-born American parishioners.

While we're at it, where is this pope's pledge to care for and compensate the children whose parents have been murdered by the illegal immigrants he embraces and encourages to come to America?

Perhaps it's a big mistake. Perhaps Pope Francis just never noticed the big wall around his own home. Perhaps he just doesn't understand that America is the most generous nation in world history. Perhaps he's so ignorant of economics that he doesn't realize capitalism has allowed our citizens to accumulate enough wealth to donate billions of dollars to the Catholic Church.

Perhaps the pope has good intentions. But, as the saying goes, "The road to hell is paved with good intentions."

Donald Trump's parting message to Pope Francis should be:

"Before you lecture us about compassion, charity, and opening our homes to illegal immigrants, tear down your own wall and start paying the bill for illegal immigration. Then we can talk."

Gated Liberals

I'm not done skewering the idiots and hypocrites who are against building the wall. There are still other walls to examine. I know many liberals who live in guard-gated communities. *Isn't that a wall?* What about those who live in doorman-protected luxury high-rise buildings? *Aren't those walls?* You want America to let everyone in. Why don't you start by tearing down your own walls?

Israel

Walls work. Ask Israel. They built a wall to prevent Muslim terrorists from crossing into Israel. Critics were skeptical. But it has worked to perfection. Before the wall, thousands of illegal migrants and potential terrorists crossed the border into Israel. To be exact, 10,440 were caught in 2012, 17,298 in 2011, and 14,715 in 2010. But in the first year after the wall was built, thirty-six people were caught. *Thirty-six.*[4]

Is it any surprise that terrorism has also dropped dramatically? The Israeli Ministry of Foreign Affairs and the Israel Security Agency report that in 2002, there were 452 fatalities from terrorist attacks. Before the completion of the main section of the wall in July 2003 from the beginning of the Second Intifada, seventy-three Palestinian suicide bombings were carried out from the West Bank, killing 293 Israelis and injuring over 1,900. After the completion of the main section of the wall through the end of 2006, there were only twelve attacks from the West Bank, killing sixty-four and wounding 445. In 2010, terrorist attacks declined to *nine!*[5]

Why is none of this reported in the mainstream media? Walls not only work, they work to *perfection.*

Cost

The argument from liberals often involves cost. They cite an estimated cost of $12 billion. "Where will we get the money?" they ask. Well, before Obama gave it back—with *interest*—we could have used the $150 billion of Iran's money we were holding to build the wall, pay the victims of Iran's terrorism ($8 billion) and still had $130 billion left to apply to the national debt. As Donald Trump would say, "America is stupid!" We had plenty of money to do it and Obama gave it away.

Second, when liberals want money for any stupid or wasteful or self-destructive idea, they always find it. When Obama needed $4.5 billion for one year's worth of importing Syrian refugees into the United States, he found it. I'm sure if it's ever needed to build the wall, Donald Trump will find the money, too. But my educated guess is that Trump will find a way to make Mexico pay for the wall. And like the famous Wollman Ice Skating Rink in New York, he'll bring it in under budget.

Won't that be wonderful!

14

More Hypocrisy in Obama's America

What if white conservatives treated Obama the way liberals treat Trump?

Leftists are correct when they say there are two very different Americas. There's one where free speech is not allowed for conservatives, especially white male conservatives who can never criticize President Barack Obama without being called a "racist" or accused of being a KKK member.

Then there's the America where leftist protestors can run roughshod over the rights of Donald Trump and his supporters, without being called out or blamed, or facing consequences for their rude, hateful, violent actions.

While I was writing this book (in late spring of 2016), Trump rallies were being interrupted by violent protestors. Trump supporters were attacked leaving his events—pelted with eggs, spit upon, cursed at, and in some cases punched in the face and bloodied. The worst unrest occurred outside a San Jose, California, rally.[1]

San Jose is a "sanctuary city" where illegals are protected by police. The Democrat mayor actually blamed Trump when the unrest got out of control and several Trump supporters were attacked and beaten. He said Trump's words "ignited the violence." According to liberals, free speech is no longer allowed in America. According to liberal politicians like the San Jose mayor, illegal aliens are welcomed in his town but Trump supporters are not. The police chief admits he did nothing. He said it was more important for police to "hold their lines" than stop individual attacks. So he let Trump supporters be beaten right in front of police, who did nothing. He also said he didn't want his officers to respond because "it might have incited more violence."[2]

In Obama's America, the biased liberal media gets to frame it as "Trump's fault" if he is attacked by violent protestors . . . or if his supporters are beaten and bloodied outside his events by protestors waving Mexican flags . . . or if he refuses to apologize for standing up for his own rights . . . or if his supporters fight back in self-defense.

The media paints Trump (the victim of organized attacks by paid protestors) as "the bad guy" for being attacked. If a conservative Republican candidate is a punching bag and doesn't defend himself, he loses the election. If he responds in self-defense, it's all his fault. That's one hell of a rigged game. Heads you win. Tails we lose.

For just a moment, imagine if Barack Obama were ever under the same attack as Donald Trump is right now. What if conservatives joked openly about the assassination of President Obama? Every day unhinged liberals are calling for the murder of Trump all over the Internet.[3]

A *New York Times* columnist joked about it out loud.[4]

A Vox.com editor was suspended for sending out Tweets encouraging rioting at Trump events.[5]

Black rappers released a song called "F*CK TRUMP," calling for riots and the assassination of Trump if he is elected president. The media celebrated the song's release. The rappers sang the song in front of twenty thousand at a famous youth music festival.[6]

There were even twelve separate tweets by liberal journalists celebrating the death of Supreme Court Justice Antonin Scalia.[7]

Can you imagine the outrage if a white conservative journalist tried to joke about the assassination of Obama? Leftists do it daily. The media says nothing.

What if a white country singer threatened to murder Obama? Or a white rock 'n' roll group threatened violent riots across the country if Obama were elected?

What if white conservatives stood outside Obama events with signs laced with filthy curse words and cursed out everyone trying to enter? A black police officer recently described the anti-Trump protestors as "the most evil and hateful people ever."[8]

What if white conservatives infiltrated the crowd at Obama events and in the middle of his speech tried to shout him down? Would the media say that's their right to free speech? What about the rights of the attendees who have waited in line for hours to hear their candidate speak? Do their rights matter?

What if white conservatives went to Obama events, with the intent of starting fights with Obama's supporters? Would the media blame Obama's supporters for responding in self-defense? Would the media blame Obama for how individual supporters choose to act at his events?

What if a right-wing billionaire hired and paid protestors to disrupt Hillary's events? Would the media blame Hillary? What dirty names would the media call that conservative billionaire? Would they blame it on "racism"? Leftist billionaire George Soros is doing it every day to Trump. I haven't heard the media criticize him for inciting violence and trying to stop free speech.[9]

Instead, the media blames Trump for the violence that Soros and other liberal groups incited and paid for.

What if "White Lives Matter" radicals promised to incite riots if Obama won the election? Well, "Black Lives Matters" leaders have made that promise. Why is no one crying foul?[10]

All of this is happening every day to Donald Trump. And, amazingly, the media is blaming Trump.

If this were happening to Obama, I guarantee you it would be the biggest story in the media around the world, and it would not be Obama being blamed. It would be considered the "shameful, hateful, white conservative extremists and racists, organized by evil right-wing billionaire Donald Trump." That would be the storyline. Guaranteed.

Yes, there are two very different Americas with two very different sets of rules.

In the real world I live in, what the left is doing to Trump is disgusting, unconstitutional, criminal, and, yes, "racist." The left is scared, desperate, and hysterical. They will do anything to stop a Donald Trump presidency—and that includes violence.

Liberals should be very thankful that conservatives don't treat Obama and Hillary the way the vile left treats Trump.

But there is much more liberal hypocrisy.

White Shaming Month

Have you heard about "White Shaming Month" at Portland Community College?[11]

What if the shoe were on the other foot? Would one American college allow "Black Shaming Month"? What if this were a month dedicated to asking blacks to stop killing other black youth . . . to stop allowing drugs to flood black neighborhoods . . . to demand black fathers stay in the home to raise their children? These are all good causes, right? These are all good goals to aim for, right? Yet no college would ever allow "Black Shaming Month." *Ever.*

Straight White Males Not Allowed

Did you hear about the "Equality Conference" being held in Europe that has chosen to ban straight white males? Because, of course, "equality" doesn't include equality for straight white males. Other races, genders, and cultures need "safe zones," which I can only assume are to keep them safe from those terrible straight white males. How can banning straight white males from an equality conference be anything but prejudice, inequality, and closed-mindedness? It makes a mockery of the entire theme of equality.[12]

West Point Hypocrisy

How about the black female cadets at West Point taking a photo, with fists raised, portraying the symbol of the "Black Lives Matter" movement at a legendary American military institution where political displays are specifically banned? The case was dropped. The students involved received no discipline. West Point called their actions inappropriate but not political. Really?[13]

Here's the million-dollar question: What would be the response if twenty white male West Point cadets took a photo on campus with a "White Lives Matter" sign? Or wore T-shirts that read "White Lives Matter"? How about a group photo of white male cadets with a photo of Donald Trump? My educated guess is that white males pulling any of those stunts would have been suspended or expelled from West Point.

That's the hypocrisy of Obama's America. That's the idiocy, corruption, and political correctness of guilt-ridden white liberals in the government and media, and even the military. And that's why we're angry white males.

15

The Media—

The Most Hypocritical of All

Why does the media lie about race? Why do they lie to cover-up for Barack Obama? It started out as embarrassing and pathetic. But it's gotten so bad, it's moved on to pure fraud.

Why does the media allow Obama to give press conferences about the handful of black Americans killed by police officers each year, but there are no press conferences when police officers are murdered by black criminals? It happens frequently, but Obama never says a word about it.

That's his prerogative. But it's the media's job to question him, to point out the inconsistencies, to call him on the hypocrisy and what appears to both police officers and law-abiding citizens as a dangerous double standard that incites violence against police.

Why does the media allow Obama to call Tea Party activists bad people, violent, or radicals when there is not one instance of violence or anyone advocating violence at any Tea Party rally? Yet, the same media, with video proof of protestors at anti-police rallies screaming in unison, "What do we want? DEAD COPS," never question Obama about why he doesn't denounce them.[1]

Given his actions and statements, why is it that when police officers are murdered, the media never assigns blame to the president.

Why does the media allow Obama to give press conferences about the handful of black Americans shot by white people (like George Zimmerman or police officer Darren Wilson), despite these cases being rare, but never question him about the hourly murder of blacks by blacks, including the fact that 93 percent of all black murders are committed by blacks.[2]

And why does the media never mention black-on-black storeowner crime (like looting and burning in Ferguson)?

Or never mention the genocide of the black race perpetrated by black criminals in inner cities like Detroit, Chicago, Baltimore, or Memphis? Where are the nationwide protests for the thousands of innocent black lives taken by black criminals? (I guess a black life taken by a black person isn't one of the black lives that matter.) Are there no money or media headlines or political gain in those kinds of protests?

Why doesn't the media ask the president if black-on-black crime matters to him? If so, why has he never chosen to speak out about it? Why don't they ask Obama to name one victim of black-on-black crime in Chicago this past weekend? Can he name anyone in the past year? Why are their deaths unimportant, insignificant, and anonymous?

Why not ask Obama and Attorney General Loretta Lynch why there aren't teams of Justice Department investigators and prosecutors assigned to black-on-black murders in Chicago (Obama's hometown)? Why isn't the same urgency and number of "boots on the ground" assigned to stop black-on-black crime as that aimed toward a white police officer like Darren Wilson in Ferguson, Missouri?

Shouldn't the media question why the federal government calls it a "hate crime" if a white person kills a black man—even if it was in self-defense and the black man had a criminal record—when a white person murdered by a black man is never called a "hate crime"?

A white Bosnian immigrant while driving through a black neighborhood in St. Louis only days after the Ferguson verdict was murdered by a gang of black criminals who allegedly yelled, "Kill the white people."[3]

Yet there is no "hate crime" designation for that murder, no civil rights investigation, no federal intervention, no national media headlines, no coast-to-coast protests, no press conferences by the president or Al Sharpton. Where is the media? Silent.

What about Al Sharpton? Doesn't the media have the responsibility to see that everyone knows the facts about him and ensure he is brought to justice? After all, it is well documented he is a racist rabble-rouser who was allegedly involved in drug dealing . . .[4]

Who was filmed negotiating cocaine deals . . .[5]

Who was a federal informant doing business with the mob . . .[6]

Who tried to destroy the lives of police and prosecutors back in the 1980s based on false rape allegations by his client Tawana Brawley . . .[7]

Who owes over $4 million in back taxes (as reported by the *New York Times*)[8]

Who is one of Obama's BFFs (best friends forever) and has visited the White House eighty-one times . . .[9] to give the president of the United States advice on racism and race relations.[10]

Are you kidding me? *Saturday Night Live* couldn't make this story up.

Where is the media questioning the role of a "race pimp" and con man like Sharpton hanging out in the White House with the president? What's the difference between Sharpton and a David Duke? Both are racists and haters. Both have made money trying to cause racial division and stir up violence. The only difference is that David Duke was never involved with the mob, has no background in drug dealing, and doesn't owe the IRS over $4 million. Oh, he also isn't a part of the media-protected liberal elites.

Shouldn't the media ask Obama why he isn't embarrassed and ashamed to have a man like Al Sharpton step foot in the people's house eighty-one times (and counting)?

Shouldn't the media be asking what's the difference between white Nevada rancher Cliven Bundy and Al Sharpton? Bundy owed a *disputed* $1 million in back fees to the government,[11] so the government raided his ranch with militarized SWAT teams, airplanes, helicopters, and assault weapons.

But Sharpton owes over $4 million to the same government and there's no raid, no threats or intimidation by government, no police surrounding his New York City headquarters.

Remarkably, Sharpton gets to pal around with the president of the United States. That same guy gets to give advice on race relations to the president. That same guy was awarded a national TV show on MSNBC. That same guy makes a living pressuring (some would call it "extorting") corporations in the name of "racism."[12]

If they pay his organization a "consulting fee," he either says nice things about them or shuts up. But if they don't pay, he organizes national protests against them. Isn't that called a "mob shakedown"? Don't white men with Italian surnames go to prison for decades for the same thing? But a black man involved in the same mob shakedowns gets the red carpet rolled out at the White House? Heck, the president speaks at Sharpton's events, and the media says *nothing.*

What would the same media say if a white Republican president invited an Italian mafia boss to the White House eighty-one times? Clearly, they won't say anything if it is a black Democrat president who is doing the inviting.

What if a white Republican president spoke at a mafia boss's event? Don't mafia bosses shake businesses down? Don't mafia bosses refuse to pay taxes? What's the difference between Sharpton and a mafia boss—other than the color of their skin?

Shouldn't the media also be asking these obvious questions?

Don't police lives matter? Don't white lives matter? Don't black kids slaughtered by black criminals matter? Don't mob shakedowns matter? Doesn't tax fraud on a massive scale matter?

Apparently, none of it matters to the nation's first black president, as long as the people committing all this violence, murder, fraud, shakedowns, racism, and tax evasion on a massive scale are black. And the media says nothing.

Folks, it's official—we are now living in a banana republic.

Before I move on, let me add just one more thing about the hypocrisy of the media. It would be funny if it wasn't such a dereliction of the media's duty to report "the truth, the whole truth."

Imagine if a white Republican president acted just like Obama after the Belgium terror attack.

Imagine the media's reaction if one of the worst terror attacks ever on European soil including dead Americans occurred while a white Republican president was in the White House. A terrible terror attack carried out by our radical Muslim enemies. Not just any radical Muslim group, but ISIS itself.

Imagine some of the Americans who died included the wife of a US military officer, a beautiful young couple, and a young brother and sister. Imagine three Mormon missionaries badly hurt. Imagine other Americans badly hurt, including my own neighbors in my community in Henderson, Nevada (with the husband having part of his leg amputated).[13]

Now imagine this white Republican president was away on a trip visiting a mass-murdering fanatical *right-wing* regime that routinely arrests, tortures, and murders its own citizens who have different political beliefs, just as President Obama was away at the time visiting the radical, fanatical, murdering leftist Castro brothers in Cuba.

Imagine a right-wing regime that imprisons, tortures, and murders liberal dissidents, just as the Castro brothers do to conservative dissidents. A right-wing regime with economic policies that violates civil rights every second of every day and leaves its own people living in misery and poverty, just as the Castro brothers have left Cuba.

Imagine a white Republican president hanging out in that country, having fun, enjoying himself, partying, allowing himself to be photographed and videotaped laughing, smiling, doing the wave at baseball games—all while our citizens and our allies lie dead in the streets of Europe.[14]

You don't have to imagine. Obama did all of that in Cuba in March of this year. Except Cuba happens to be a communist regime run by left-wing murdering despots.[15]

Imagine this white Republican president refusing to cut his trip short and interrupt his vacation to return to Washington, DC, to deal with this terrible terrorist crisis.

Imagine instead this Republican president thinking it's okay to be photographed having fun at a baseball game, smiling, high-fiving, and waving to the crowd while my neighbor's leg is being amputated.[16]

Does this sound like the actions of a leader or even a sane man?

Wait, it gets better. Then instead of going home to deal with this terrible tragedy, which security experts believe signals that America is at risk for an imminent terror attack, too, and while ISIS announces they are sending four hundred specially trained suicide bombers to unleash a new bloodbath across Europe . . .[17]

Imagine in the face of that news, our white Republican president decides it's more important to continue his trip to Argentina, where he dances the tango in front of the world. He might as well put a rose in his teeth and join the cast of *Dancing with the Stars*. It's a surreal scene.[18]

Are these the actions of a world leader? To me, they sound more like the actions and mind-set of a mentally ill psychopath despot of a third-world nation.

Continue using your imagination.

Well, suppose a white Republican president gave a lecture to school kids in Argentina telling them to "stop using labels. Don't worry about Nazism or capitalism. Those are just words. Forget labels; from now on just mix the two. Use whatever works best. Grab some Nazi ideas and mix them with capitalism. No problem."

That's exactly what Obama did in Argentina. He gave a lecture where he tried to convince school kids there's no difference between the greatest economic system in world history (capitalism) and a system that murdered almost one hundred million human beings (communism). Keep in mind he had the time to lecture school kids instead of rushing home to deal with a massive ISIS terror attack.

Don't forget this is the guy who called ISIS "the JV team." This is the guy who swears he has "the best strategy" to defeat ISIS. Yet that JV team carried out two massive attacks in both Paris and Belgium after Obama said that.[19]

And the very day I wrote this, forty-nine Americans were murdered by an ISIS-affiliated radical Muslim in Orlando, Florida.

Is there any doubt how differently the hypocritical liberal media would have responded if it had been a white Republican president rather a black Democrat president?

But it gets worse. Can you imagine the media outrage if that same Republican president then announced he is going to bring more Muslim migrants and refugees to America (whether Congress agrees or not). And he's going to do it knowing that it's almost a certainty some of them will kill Americans once they get here.

Is this not the very definition of insanity?

Imagine if a white Republican president, immediately after a series of Christian right-wing terror attacks, boldly bragged that he intended to bring in more right-wing extremist Christian refugees from that specific region of the terror attack?

What would the media say? What would Democratic leaders say? What would anyone with common sense say?

Why do we need any new immigrants, let alone dangerous or deadly ones, while 94.7 million working-age Americans have no jobs?

There is no money to take care of the health care of 320 million American citizens, let alone millions of desperately poor non-English-speaking newcomers.

What would the media say about a white Republican president of a country in debt and crisis who was this desperate to bring a new wave of poverty, dependence, violence, crime, and death to America?

I know what the mainstream media would say if a white Republican president did all this. They'd say the president is either mentally ill, legally insane, or a traitor out to destroy his own country.

16

Who This Angry White Male Is Really Mad At

So now let me sum up who I'm really mad at—because it's not who you think. As I explained at the start of this book, I'm mostly angry at white, guilt-ridden liberals. I'm not mad at black people, or Hispanics, or any other minority group. Why? For the same reason I don't blame drug addicts. I blame the dealer. For the same reason I don't blame a gun in the hands of a mass murderer or terrorist. It's not the gun's fault. The blame belongs to the murderer. For the same reason I don't blame plaintiffs for suing an honest businessman who did nothing wrong. I blame the lawyers who enticed and enabled them.

I don't sue people. I'm not a fan of lawyers or lawsuits, let alone the biggest scam of the legal world: class action lawsuits. But if my kid were sick, my father had lung disease, I got a disease after taking a medication, or I got fired from a job, even I might be tempted to sue. But only after being hooked by a TV lawyer's advertisement. Those TV ads for ambulance chasers are really appealing. They make you really want to sue. They give everyone an excuse and a chip on their shoulder. They activate the greed in all of us. It's right in front of us. They're screaming at us: "free money . . . free money . . . free money." It's like a blinking neon sign.

So I don't blame all the many Americans taking advantage of the system. I blame the system. And most of all, I blame the white, guilt-ridden liberal politicians (who are almost all lawyers) who make the laws. The reality is that no one would be on welfare or food stamps or disability (without being disabled) unless we offered it to them, and then made it easy for them to qualify. So it's government's fault for offering these handouts, and making the handouts easy to obtain.

Government is like a drug dealer, addicting Americans to welfare. They're offering, sometimes even *begging*, everyone to take it. Is it a surprise that millions of weak-willed people take them up on their offer?

It also isn't the fault of illegal immigrants for crossing the border and then accepting welfare and tons of other "free stuff." First, we practically begged them to cross the border by leaving the borders wide open.

Second, we actually did beg them to take welfare and food stamps. Obama's government runs radio advertisements in Mexico, announcing that illegals can get welfare in America: "Please tell your illegal relatives in the USA to step forward, move out of the shadows, to collect your food stamps and welfare checks." Is it their fault for taking the handouts, when we ran ads begging them to do it—*in Spanish?*

Third, the IRS actually hands out welfare checks disguised as "earned income tax credits" to illegals. If we're that dumb, can you blame them for accepting what we're offering (with a wink)? Remarkably, that same IRS agency refuses to go after illegals who steal the identities of Americans to file fake tax returns.

Can you blame poor people for taking free meals at school for their kids? We're offering "free food."

It's all crazy. And it's mostly white, guilt-ridden liberals offering all this "free stuff." Who wouldn't take free stuff—Obama phones, free contraception, free food, free health care, free meals at school, and free checks (on EBT cards disguised to look like credit cards). The list is LONG. But if it weren't offered, they could not accept it.

So it's all the fault of the system and the stupid, bleeding-heart liberal do-gooders, mixed with a few socialist haters of America. And most of them happen to be white.

Part II

Angry White *Christian* Males

Insanity Reigns

The Transgender Agenda

You wonder why we're angry? The attack has gotten more specific. It's not just a financial attack. It's not just aimed at white males. It's aimed at our beliefs, our faith, our values. It's aimed at Angry White Christian males.

This attack defies common sense. It's so radical and extreme, it boggles the imagination. In my last few books, I predicted the things Obama would do in his last days in office that will shock, offend, and finish the job of "fundamentally changing America." The depth of the attack will be unimaginable. Well, imagine no more.

While writing this book, the attack came fast and furious, from multiple directions. With an economy close to death's door, gross domestic product (GDP) near zero, and the total collapse of good-paying middle-class jobs, Obama decided the number one priority in all America should be transgender bathrooms.

It boggles the mind, but let me assure you, I've played chess with Obama for eight long years, correctly predicting his every move. I know this is nothing but a head fake. The real attack is yet to come. This is only a distraction. Obama is playing with us. He is enraging every Christian and person of moral fiber in America. He is laughing in our faces. He is mocking us. He is purposely endangering our children.

But it's all a distraction for the truly bad stuff to come. In particular, if Donald Trump wins the election in early November, look out for all hell to break loose for the ten "lame-duck" weeks between the election and the swearing in of President Trump. Look for the prisons to be emptied. Look for actions damaging business, redistributing money, and destroying the economy like we've never imagined. Especially, look for a "full Monty" attempt to damage Christianity and religious freedom.

In the meantime, let's look at what Obama and his mentally ill socialist cabal have done to make this a nation dedicated to transgender people. What a strange, radical, bizarre ride we are on.

Transgender America

In May 2016, Obama decided to bombard the nation with laws and directives about transgender peoples. First, Obama's Justice Department sued North Carolina over that state's transgender law requiring citizens to use the bathroom that matches the gender identified on their birth certificate.[1]

To Obama and our federal government, it's "discrimination" to want men to use men's rooms. Obama and his attorney general, Loretta Lynch, compared this battle with the civil rights movement of the 1960s.

Let me ask a few basic commonsense questions.

How do you think Civil War era civil rights hero, Harriet Tubman, would feel about transgender bathrooms and young boys "self-identifying" as girls using girl's bathrooms, showers, and locker rooms?

How do you think civil rights icon Rosa Parks would feel about transgender bathrooms and young boys "self-identifying" as girls to use bathrooms, showers, and locker rooms of girls?

How do you think civil rights icon Martin Luther King would feel about comparing the struggle for equal rights for colored and minority citizens to transgender demands to allow young boys "self-identifying" as girls to use bathrooms, showers, and locker rooms of girls?

Do you think any of them would compare slavery, or blacks sitting at the back of a bus, or "whites only" drinking fountains, or poll taxes, to asking a boy or man with a penis to simply pee in a men's room?

But our president was only getting started. Soon thereafter, Obama sent an edict to every public school in America, demanding they allow children to "sexually self-identify," thereby allowing anyone who claims a different sex to go to the bathroom, shower, or locker room of their choice. Any school district refusing to follow his edict faces the loss of federal funds and federal discrimination lawsuits.[2]

The tyrant is showing his true colors in the last days of his second term. This issue is not black or white. It equally offends every white, black, and Hispanic person of faith. It is an affront to every parent. It is an affront to every man with a penis and every woman with a vagina. It is an affront to anyone who believes in God and a moral code.

It is an attempt by a man who thinks of himself as a dictator or king to micro-manage every classroom, bathroom, and locker room in America. It not only puts our children at risk; there are also all those nasty "unintended circumstances." What about women's sports? Boys simply need to claim they self-identify as a girl to take over spots on the girls' tennis, golf, lacrosse, track, and basketball teams. If they can't make it on the boys' team, steal a spot on the girls' team. There go college scholarships for girls. Colleges will have to give away spots on their women's teams to boys who self-identify as girls. It's also a great way to sleep in the same motel room on overnight school trips or college dorms. Once you "self-identify," no one can stop you. Simply state your self-identify as a girl and you get to sleep and shower with the girls. And let's not forget about the perverts. What's to stop forty-year-old men from "self-identifying" as a woman to hang out in women's rooms everywhere? *Nice move, Obama.*

And you wonder why we're angry white males? In this case we're all just horrified, disgusted, angry American parents!

Offend a Transsexual and Lose Your Business

But the liberals of America weren't satisfied with Obama's edicts—they didn't think he went far enough. New York City Mayor Bill DeBlasio took this madness to a new level. New York City's Commission on Human Rights is clearly in a battle with Obama's Equal Employment Opportunity Commission to see who can pass the most disgusting, outrageous, absurd, anti-business laws. If you thought banning employers from asking black job applicants about criminal backgrounds was shocking, get ready for something so bad it makes that rule look like child's play. New York City's Commission on Human Rights now requires every business in New York to call a transsexual by their preferred title, or be fined $250,000 for "discrimination."[3]

No, this isn't a joke. Men are "Mr." Women are "Mrs.," "Miss," or "Ms." Transsexuals want to be called "zhe" or "hir." Did you know that? You couldn't make this stuff up. And New York is ready to impose a quarter-million-dollar fine for hurting a transsexual's feelings. A simple mistake that anyone could make because no one has a clue who is a woman, man, or transsexual anymore. What if I see a man walk into my store and I say, "Good morning, sir," with a big smile. But he self-identifies as a "she." My life is ruined. I'm a bigot, fined $250,000 and now bankrupt.

I've repeated it enough times that I'm sure you know who owns most of America's small businesses. Yes, it's white straight males. This is an attempt to punish and redistribute the money of white straight males, more specifically white straight Christian males.

This is another example of how to overwhelm the system. The plan Obama and I learned as classmates at Columbia all those years ago always included going after white straight males—and to benefit and tilt the table toward "minorities" and those "born disadvantaged."

Let me mention just a couple of things wrong with the New York law. First, we have free speech and free thought in America. Lawyers who protect free speech and the US

Constitution will have a field day with this one. No government in this country—not local, state, or federal—can use draconian fines as a threat to destroy you if you don't change your thinking or speech to adhere to their rules. That's not America. That's a tin-pot dictatorship. That's a banana republic. In America you simply can't use the force of government to require anyone to address someone the way they want. Not in America.

Second, here's the hypocritical and laughable part that makes DeBlasio and his commie cronies look like Keystone Cops. The law exempts government. You can fine or sue any business, but if government offends you, they are exempt. *Are you hearing this, folks?*

As I was writing this book in May 2016, a new outrage materialized, one so unimaginable it boggles the mind. Transgenders and liberals are demanding that the Veterans Administration pay for sex change operations. Our nation is $19 trillion in debt, and the VA is so short of funding that vets are being put on wait lists to die, yet liberals believe there is money for sex change operations. When will it end? It won't.[4]

Liberals just don't get it. I have nothing against transgenders. Live how you want, do what you want. But do it on your dime. You have no right to my tax dollars for elective surgery. If you feel like a man trapped in a woman's body, or vice versa, pay for your own penis or vagina change. The way they are promoting this issue, there must be no shortage of liberals more than happy to cover your costs.

Does this make you good and angry? I believe we have angry white males, angry white females, angry black Christians, angry Hispanic Christians, and angry patriots of all kinds outraged, shocked, and disgusted at the radical and hypocritical tyrants and bullies running and ruining our country.

This Should Be Trump's Answer When Asked "Is Obama a Muslim?"

The plan to destroy the predominantly white middle class doesn't rely solely on destroying them financially. It also includes executing a plan to destroy the symbols that the middle class of America have always fought to defend: God, faith, religious freedom, and Judeo-Christian values. They are all being targeted. Everything we believe in, everything that gives us hope and comfort, everything that makes us who we are is being desecrated and destroyed. Remember, it was Obama who said we cling to our guns and bibles. That must be why he's so desperate to take them away from us.

My Columbia classmates admitted that they hated America, hated Christians, and despised Judeo-Christian values. We spent our days learning, discussing, and debating a plan to destroy capitalism and radically change America from within. That plan included electing one of their own to the presidency.

Terrorists are laughing at us. We are destroying ourselves from within. The end of America, the world's greatest middle class, and our beloved Judeo-Christian values are being orchestrated from *the White House.*

Just look at the facts.

The news gets stranger every day. And more dangerous. It's time to address the elephant in the room. Whose side are Obama and his socialist cabal on?

Donald Trump will undoubtedly be asked during the 2016 presidential campaign, "Do you think Obama is a Muslim?"

I have a few answers for him.

First, his answer should be a straightforward, "Why does it matter?" Obama is destroying America, American exceptionalism, capitalism, middle-class jobs, Judeo-Christian values, and America's respect and standing all over the world. Whether he's a Muslim or a Christian is meaningless. The real question is "how do we make America great again?"

How do we pay off $19 trillion in debt before it implodes the US economy? How do we create an economy offering something besides low-wage, part-time jobs? How do we save the middle class from Obamacare's doubling and tripling of health insurance costs? How do we save the world from Muslim radicals? Whether Obama is a Muslim or a Christian won't help us solve any of the disasters he has so deftly put into motion.

Second, although Obama claims to be a Christian, it's certainly not dumb or ignorant to wonder if he's telling the truth. After all, he has a history of lying with impunity about so many things.

He looked the American people in the eye and lied when he swore, "If you like your health care plan, you can keep your plan. If you like your doctor, you can keep your doctor."[1]

At the moment Obama made that promise, he was lying and knew he was lying. Internal White House documents reported that ninety-three million Americans would lose their plans.[2]

He promised Obamacare would reduce the cost of health insurance premiums. Another lie, and he knew he was lying.[3]

Then there were his lies about Benghazi—or do you still think it was a spontaneous uprising based on a movie no one ever saw? The facts prove it was known to Obama as a terrorist attack at the moment that he announced it as a protest based on a movie offensive to Islam.[4]

Obama lied about the IRS scandal. It's not small, it wasn't a mistake, it wasn't based in one office in Cincinnati. If you believe that either Obama or one of his political operatives wasn't giving the orders to persecute conservative groups and critics (like me), I have a bridge to sell you in Brooklyn.

Obama called Bush "unpatriotic" for adding $4 trillion to the national debt, and promised to cut the debt in half during his first term.[5]

This was such an audacious lie, and once in office, Obama never mentioned it again. Instead, by the time he leaves office, he will have added at least $10 trillion, almost triple the debt of Bush, and more debt than all the presidents in US history *combined*.

He lied about all of it.

While Obama claims to be a Christian, it may be more appropriate to ask, "What kind of Christian?" Look at the church he chose to attend in Chicago where he followed, befriended, and looked to its minister, Jeremiah Wright, as a spiritual advisor. This is the same Jeremiah Wright who preached hatred for America, white people, Jews, and Israel[6] and screamed "God damn America" to his congregation.[7]

Most Americans would call such a church led by someone like Wright a cult, and his followers (as a best-case scenario) weird, bizarre, radical, America-hating Christians.

So my suggestion that Trump's answer be "What does it matter?" seems right on. My blue-collar butcher father had great common sense. He always said, "Actions speak louder than words."

Let's look at just a few of Obama's actions:

A recent global study reports that the most persecuted, oppressed, and intimidated religious group in the world today is Christians.[8]

Yet our president never says a word about persecution of Christians. He mentions discrimination and prejudice toward Muslims nonstop, but not one word about Christians being killed at the hands of Muslims. In Egypt, seventy churches were burned and Christians killed by the Muslim Brotherhood in 2013, yet Obama said nothing. As a matter of fact, Obama's White House spokesman made a joke about the killing of Christians in Egypt.[9]

Are you aware that during the 2013 Christmas season, VA hospitals banned carolers from singing Christmas songs; censored Christmas cards if they mentioned Christ; banned gifts if they contained the words "Merry Christmas"; and refused to accept delivery of handmade Christmas cards from local school children because the cards included the phrase "Merry Christmas" or "God bless you"?[10]

Why does Obama refuse to use the words *Muslim* and *terrorist* in the same sentence?[11]

He refuses to admit that ISIS is a Muslim group even though their name stands for "Islamic State."[12]

The worst, most telling incident of all was when the French president gave a talk about terrorism at the White House in early 2016. A video was placed on the Obama White House website. But the video was censored. When the French president said the words *Islamist terrorism,* the audio was cut out completely.[13]

Obama has quietly supported a nonmilitary Muslim invasion of America by importing about one million Muslims into America during his presidency. *One million.*[14]

If we were admitting, say, five million Europeans at the same time as one million Muslims, perhaps that would make sense. But the government's own numbers indicate Obama has awarded twice the number of green cards to Muslims than to Europeans. Why? What do they offer us in risk-reward?[15]

How many are terrorists? How many want to live under Sharia law?

Well, we don't have to guess. A new poll came out literally on the day I finished writing this book. Fifty-one percent of American Muslims support Sharia law over the US Constitution, and 25 percent support violence against Americans as part of global jihad. Note that these are Muslims already living in America.[16]

How many are on welfare, overwhelming the system, with middle-class taxpayers picking up the tab? Earlier in the book, I reported on Labor Department statistics that show over 90 percent of recent Muslim refugees are on food stamps, and almost 70 percent are on welfare.[17]

Obama claims we're winning the war against ISIS when the facts show we are losing.[18] He appears to be purposely doing nothing and buying ISIS valuable time to grow stronger. Soon they will be impossible to stop. The day after he made the claim that we are winning, 130 people were killed in an ISIS attack in Paris.

Within days, there was another terrible radical Islamic terrorist attack in Mali.

But Obama refused to back down. He demanded that even more Syrian refugees be welcomed into the United States—into *your* middle-class neighborhoods and schools, of course. Not his wealthy DC or Hawaii neighborhoods, or his daughters' exclusive DC private school.

At the same time that Obama is demanding we import dangerous Muslim refugees, he is sending Iraqi Christians back. He talks about compassion for Muslim refugees but deports Christians.[19]

Russia reported Obama's policies actually helped ISIS.[20]

Our own pilots report that Obama's policies block 75 percent of air strikes. So Obama's tough talk about bombing

ISIS is just like his famous quote, "If you like your insurance, you can keep your insurance." It's just another lie.[21]

He's left our borders wide open. Many illegals from the Middle East have been caught trying to sneak across the border. How many were never caught?[22]

An unusual number of Middle Eastern military males have been caught at the San Diego border in the past year. My friends in the Border Patrol fear this is a sign that terrorist cells are already in the United States—a ticking time bomb waiting to go off.[23]

Ironically, Muslims don't even need to sneak in. *Obama is inviting them in.* I've already told you about the one million Muslim immigrants he's imported.

But he also wants tens of thousands of Syrian refugees resettled here.[24]

Just within a week of the Orlando terror attack, when a Muslim terrorist killed forty-nine gay Americans in a nightclub, 441 Syrian refugees were brought to America—441 in a matter of days. Is one of them a ticking terrorist time bomb?[25]

The media reports that Obama is actually in such a rush to import Syrian refugees, he has decided to "surge" them into the country. What's the rush? Are we flush with cash? Are there too many jobs with no applicants in America? Why is Obama so desperate to bring in Syrian refugees? Nothing adds up, except that he's a Muslim sympathizer, the likes of which America has never seen in high office of any kind.[26]

Syrian. Say that word slowly. Understand its meaning. Terrorists from ISIS lurk among these strangers being forced down our throats. Keep in mind it was an Islamic terrorist leader who recently bragged that over four thousand terrorists have been smuggled into Europe disguised as refugees.[27]

Obama's own Department of Homeland Security and FBI have publicly admitted we cannot vet the incoming Muslim refugees. The FBI director says we have no records, therefore no way to distinguish between moderates and extremists.[28]

But Obama doesn't care what his citizens think. He doesn't care what governors think. Obama's State Department says governors have no say on who he dumps in their state.[29]

Obama announced that he will veto Congress if they dare to require closer screening of Syrian immigrants.[30]

Obama is so extreme in his thinking about Syrian refugees that even the normal wimps in the House of Representatives ignored his threat and voted with a veto-proof majority. An unheard of forty-seven Democrats voted against Obama.[31]

Even a few brave Democrats now understand that on the topic of fighting radical Islam, our president has gone off the rails. Something is wrong, very wrong.

Obama leaped at the chance to bring a Muslim boy to the White House who was accused of building a bomb, yet he has never once brought the young child of a Marine, or Navy Seal, or police officer killed in action to the White House.[32]

Obama ordered his Equal Employment Opportunity Commission to take the side of Muslim delivery truck drivers who refused to deliver beer. Our own government forced companies to pay a $240,000 fine to Muslims in our country, refusing to do a job for which they were hired, based on *their* laws, not ours.[33]

Obama took their side. Think about that for a minute.

Obama even recently proposed banning pork at federal prisons. I'm not joking.[34]

What president would get involved in a decision about pork? Obama is paralyzed with indecision about how to stop ISIS; he refuses to ban refugees from Middle Eastern war zones; but he's more than happy to ban pork!

And look at how this president, who claims to be a Christian, treats Christians:

Are you aware Christian prayers have been banned at some military funerals?[35]

Are you aware Christian military chaplains have been harassed and banned from praying in Jesus's name or reciting passages from the Bible?[36]

Are you aware the Obama administration has prohibited Christian ministers from taking part in prayer services on federal property?[37]

Are you aware Christian minister Franklin Graham believes the military's effort to ban him and other Christian leaders from the National Day of Prayer observance at the Pentagon is nothing short of an effort to stamp out Christianity in the military?[38]

Are you aware that at a routine meeting held at a Mississippi military base with various leaders of the 158th Infantry Brigade, an "equal opportunity officer" objected to the usage of the word *Christmas*? That officer claimed it was the

US Army's rules that the word *Christmas* might offend non-Christian soldiers.[39]

Yet all of this pales in comparison to the damage Obama has done to world peace and safety with his Iranian deal. It is not a stretch to say that Obama and his supporters, including Hillary Clinton, will be directly responsible for the deaths of millions of Jews and Christians.

Since the mainstream media has largely ignored it, and Republicans in Congress seem unable or unwilling to fight, it is extremely important that every American understands just how dangerous Obama's Iranian deal truly is. The simple fact is Obama has ensured that the world's most radical Muslim terrorists (who have openly vowed they can't wait to use them) will have nuclear weapons. Worse, Obama even gave them the money to pay for it! Not just white American males, but freedom lovers worldwide have every right to be angry and to be afraid, very afraid.

With Iran, Obama agreed to the single most pathetic and dangerous treaty in American history—a treaty that lets a terrorist state monitor itself. A treaty filled with secret agreements Obama won't even allow US senators to see.[40]

Obama's Iranian deal makes it a certainty that extreme radical Iranian Mullahs will have a nuclear bomb. As a bonus, Obama gave this terrorist regime $150 billion to build their nuclear weapons and fund terrorism around the world.[41]

And get this: Obama promised that the United States would *protect* Iran's nuclear facilities from Israeli attacks.[42]

Obama's own former advisor admits he purposely alienated and distanced the United States from Israel to win the trust of Iran. Is there any other world leader who would denounce an ally to win the trust and support of a terrorist regime?[43]

To implement this obscenely dangerous deal, Obama then acted like a banana republic dictator, ignoring the Constitution that requires the support of two-thirds of Congress to ratify a treaty.[44]

Fox News's Bill O'Reilly suggested that Obama might be suffering from mental illness. He asked if Obama is "delusional."[45]

Since everyone else seems unwilling and too intimidated to say it, let me: I believe Obama's a true believer. He loves the Islam of his childhood in Indonesia and is too compromised to see the truth.

In his autobiography, Obama said the sweetest sound he knows is the Muslim call to prayer; and in a speech at the UN he said, "The future must not belong to those who slander the prophet of Islam."

Are there "peace-loving, moderate Muslims" out there? Obama seems to see something the rest of us don't. I believe recent events prove Obama is seeing a mirage. Even so-called "moderate Muslims" aren't so moderate. Muslim crowds in "moderate" Turkey recently booed and chanted "Allahu Akbar" during a moment of silence for the victims of the Paris attack by ISIS. *Lovely.*[46]

And then, there's that 51 percent of American Muslims who support Sharia law. Lovely.

I don't know if you're a Muslim, Mr. President, but I know you're not on our side. I know you are compromised. I know you are a biased Muslim sympathizer.

Even those Americans who are unwilling to admit they were wrong with their votes in 2008 and 2012 and want to keep their heads buried in the sand must admit that this is bizarre behavior for an American president, even one who is a member of a bizarre, radical Christian cult.

So Donald Trump's answer should be . . .

"With friends like Obama, Christians don't need enemies."

Still wonder why we're angry white males? What's happening to America right in front of our eyes is right out of a fictional movie. Real-life is stranger than fiction.

19

Mr. President, You Disgust Me

This is a P.S. to the section about what Obama is doing to a specialized group of angry white males—the Christian ones.

I wrote this commentary the day of the worst mass shooting in America's history: June 12, 2016. This was my response to Obama's address to the nation after a Muslim terrorist murdered forty-nine gay men and women in a nightclub in Orlando, Florida.

I've known for eight long years what a poor excuse for a man we have as a president. I've known for eight long years what a deep, dark hole he is leading this country down. I've known for eight long years that he is either mentally unstable, incredibly ignorant, or an extreme Muslim sympathizer like we've never seen in the White House.

I hope other Americans are waking up after today's pathetic presidential address to the nation about the Orlando Islamic terror attack.

It's time to talk frankly. Obama's speech was the most insulting, revolting, and embarrassing speech *ever* by an American president. It made me sick to my stomach.

Obama is the commander-in-chief. He certainly knows far more than an average citizen like me—certainly far more than the journalists on Fox News or CNN.

Obama knows what the FBI chief knows, what the Orlando police chief knows, what the CIA knows, what military intelligence knows. His press conference was even pushed back by thirty minutes. Obviously, he wanted the absolute latest intelligence.

Yet at the moment he walked to the podium, I already knew:

1. The mass murderer was Muslim.
2. He pledged allegiance to ISIS.
3. ISIS itself warned publicly three days earlier about a pending terrorist attack in Florida.
4. The murderer called 911 to give credit to ISIS before walking into the gay nightclub.
5. He yelled "Allahu Akbar" before opening fire.

Only minutes after Obama was done with his pathetic address to the nation, it was reported that ISIS actually took credit for the attack. That was also undoubtedly known to him when he walked to that podium.

Yet with all of those facts at hand . . .

Obama *still* did not mention the words *Islamic* or *Muslim* or even *radical Islam* in the entire address to the nation. No mention was ever made of the religion or background of the worst mass murderer in US history.

Obama *still* would not say the words *Islamic* and *terror attack* in the same sentence.

Obama *still* would not assign blame to Islam, or radical Islam, or jihad.

He knew exactly at that moment in time what this attack was. But he could not bring himself to mention those words.

But he was certainly angry. Steam was clearly coming out of his ears because he had to admit the attack was in fact "terrorism." We've been through this so many times before; he's always quick to blame guns or Republicans, but the word *terrorism* rarely ever comes out of his mouth.

But this time was different. All the facts were in. This was 100 percent ISIS verified *before* Obama walked to that podium. So he had to admit it was a "terror attack." Even Obama knew he couldn't avoid that.

That had to burn him. He looked so angry and shocked that I half expected a Muslim prayer to end his speech. I could almost hear "Salaam Alaikum" rattling around in his brain.

I know my old Columbia college classmate like the back of my hand. I waited for the old tried-and-true liberal attack on guns. Obama didn't disappoint. He had his usual hissy fit about guns being to blame. It was the gun's fault. It had to be. The man who picked it up was a Muslim.

We are under attack by radical Islam, most of the time by lone wolf attackers like this one, where one American citizen with a gun could end the attack and save many lives. But, amazingly, Obama's only impulse is to disarm the innocent victims, leaving us helpless to defend ourselves.

Just absorb a few of these facts about Obama and his Muslim connection:

Obama is a man who wants to rush the process of importing more Muslims refugees into the United States (even military-age males from war zones), even though his own Homeland Security chief warns we cannot vet them.[1]

Obama's not just purposely importing Muslims, he's bringing them in at a record pace.[2]

Obama refuses to secure the border, even though Muslim terror cells are surely entering the United States hidden among the hordes of illegals from Mexico and Central America.

Obama is the man who brings in twice the number of immigrants from Muslim nations versus European nations.[3]

Obama is the man who cut $2.6 billion in funding for US veterans, while at the same time adding $4.5 billion to the budget to relocate Syrian refugees to America.[4]

Obama is the man who is *obsessed* with disarming Americans, at the exact same time he arms Muslim terrorists—remember, he recently handed back to the terrorist state Iran $150 billion *plus* interest to buy weapons that will be used to murder Americans, Israelis, and other Westerners.

Obama is the man who has claimed that terrorists have "legitimate grievances."[5]

Obama is the man who refused to use the word *Muslim* at a terrorism summit.[6]

But remarkably he opened that summit with a Muslim prayer. [7]

Obama is the man who claimed "Islam" has been woven into our country's fabric from the first days of America.[8]

Obama is the man who refused to meet with Israel's prime minister during a US visit, but found time to meet with head of a Muslim country (Qatar) that supports terrorism during that same week.[9]

Let's never forget this is the man who refused to place the US flag at the White House at half-mast for almost a week after a terror attack at a US military base. But on Sunday after a mass murder of gays, Obama ordered the White House flag to be lowered almost *instantly.*

You couldn't make this stuff up in a fiction movie. You'd be laughed out of Hollywood.

Obama's actions are revolting. His address to the nation on Sunday was both embarrassing and insulting. But more importantly, it was *telling.* No true American could or would *ever* give a speech like that.

Can you imagine Democrat President FDR refusing to mention the word *Japanese* in an address to the nation after the attack on Pearl Harbor? Can you imagine FDR refusing to mention the word *Nazi* when discussing our war with Germany? Would he say, "We are at war with certain European and Asian individuals"? How absurd. How insulting.

Mr. President, you disgust me.

It's time for Obama to resign from office, or be removed forcefully by a United States Congress with balls.

Oh, and one other thing . . .

Pray for President Donald J. Trump.

Yes folks, angry white males have plenty to be angry about.

Part III

Donald Trump to the Rescue

20

Braveheart—
Trump Is Sir William Wallace

History repeats. And, those who fail to study history are destined to fail.

Braveheart is my favorite movie of all time. I've watched it a half-dozen times. Recently, when I watched it again with my two young sons, a light bulb went off. I suddenly realized we're watching history repeat. *Braveheart* is the story of America today, with the predominantly white middle class fighting for its very survival. *Braveheart* could have been called *Angry White Male.*

Braveheart is the story of Scotland's battle for freedom and self-determination against the powerful British empire. It's the same battle America's predominantly white middle class is fighting today against Washington, DC. It's not just Obama. It's Obama, Hillary, Bernie, John Kerry, Nancy Pelosi, and Harry Reid. They're all in it together. They're all to blame. The whole socialist cabal known as the Democratic Party, their media and big business coconspirators, and entrenched Republican political elites. Their goal is Big Brother government and full control over every aspect of our lives. Their goal is 90 percent tax rates, making us all dependent on government for survival. And, of course, they believe we should thank them for "allowing" us to keep 10 percent of our money. How generous of them.

The hero of *Braveheart* is Sir William Wallace, a passionate, enthusiastic, heroic, and principled leader and warrior. Wallace didn't fight for personal gain. He fought only to achieve freedom for his people and he was willing to die for that cause. He was perhaps the first "angry white male."

Who represents Sir William Wallace today? First it was the Tea Party. That's why big government, politicians of all stripes, power brokers, corporate crony CEOs, and the mainstream media were so desperate to stop the Tea Party. It threatened their very existence. It threatened to upset their apple cart. It threatened to end their gravy train. The Tea Party had its moments of initial success, but overall, little changed.

Why? There were two problems. First, the Tea Party movement didn't have the money to compete with the establishment lawyers, lobbyists, unions, the elite wealthy class, and, of course, big business donations.

Second, big business and these establishment power brokers managed to use the mainstream media to brand the Tea Party as "racists," "radicals," "extremists," and "violent." I spoke at hundreds of Tea Party rallies and never once heard or witnessed a single act of racism. Even though millions attended thousands of Tea Party events across the country, there was never any violence. As far as the "radical" charge, the Tea Party represented the exact same views as our Founding Fathers. America was founded to give power to the people, not the government. There's nothing "radical" about that.

The establishment never imagined the Tea Party movement was just the start, an appetizer for the main event to come. The Tea Party was the spark.

Donald Trump is the fuel and the fire.

Trump is the Tea Party on steroids. Trump really is a modern-day embodiment of Sir William Wallace. Trump doesn't just threaten the interests of big government. He promises to do something about it. He doesn't just threaten to end the gravy train. He is a bull in a china shop. He threatens to turn Washington, DC, upside down. He will break it into a million pieces. He will put people who lied and stole from the citizens and taxpayers in prison. He will upset the apple cart. He will end the gravy train. He threatens "business as usual." He is a threat to "the good old boys network." Trump owes nothing to anyone. He is so rich, he can't be bought or blackmailed.

Trump understands how to use the media to sell his brand and spread his message. Sir William Wallace became a folk hero because, like Trump, he understood how important it was to tell a great story, then spread it far and wide.

Why is Trump succeeding? Trump is strong in all the areas where the Tea Party was weak. He has the money, celebrity, and the media firepower to compete with the big boys. Liberals can't stop or even slow Donald Trump. He is the Tea Party on steroids!

That is why Trump is denigrated, slandered, and maligned by Obama, Hillary, Bernie, the Democratic Party, the GOP establishment, lobbyists, lawyers, CEOs of multinational corporations, the entire mainstream media, and entire countries (like Mexico and China). Trump threatens to end their scam. They are desperate.

Donald Trump does not fight for corporate interests. He only fights for what he believes is best for the American people. He believes in the little guy. Donald Trump believes people should keep more of their own earned money. He believes people shouldn't have to work their entire lives just to pay off the government's debt. And he believes in giving more power to the people. So yes, Trump is a modern-day Sir William Wallace.

The evil, bad guy of *Braveheart* is the King of England, Edward Longshanks. Today, the embodiment of King Edward Longshanks is Barack Obama, Hillary Clinton, and the other big government politicians (including many establishment Republicans).

Just like the multitudes of big government politicians today, the king was out to control the people lock, stock, and barrel. Just like Obama and Hillary, he believed your money is his money. Just like Obama and Hillary, he believed every decision should be made by government, every conversation should be listened to, and your rights and guns must be confiscated as a threat to his rule.

And just like Obama and Hillary, the old king of England was arrogant and vicious. King Edward stopped at nothing to hide his true intentions. He repeatedly broke his word to set up his enemies for defeat. Obama and Hillary lie just like King Edward. But their biggest lie is their nonstop claims that they are on the side of the middle class. This entire book proves otherwise.

King Obama must have taken notes from King Edward. He tells the people anything and everything to distract them while he takes control of our lives and livelihood. He uses the power of government to get his way, to silence dissent, to steal your property, to control your lives. Obama uses the government as a weapon to intimidate and persecute his own people—IRS, NSA, EPA, SEC, FDA, ATF, DOJ, DHS (Homeland Security)—you name the government agency and they are at war with the people they are supposed to serve and protect.

Like King Edward, Obama's goal and his every policy has been aimed at creating a two-class society leaving only the super-rich (wealthy royalty) and the masses (serfs). Tyrants can only survive in a two-class society where the super-rich are easily bribed and the poor are beholden to government for survival.

Hillary is a carbon copy of Obama. All you need to do is look at the Clinton Foundation to understand her goals, priorities, and personality. Hillary is all about one thing: Hillary. Only someone as corrupt as the Clintons could dream up creating a family foundation, then with Hillary in office accepting billions in "donations" (aka bribes) from foreign governments and handing those same powerful donors government contracts and awards, paid for with taxpayer money. Hillary is more King Edward than even Obama. She has taken arrogance and corruption to a new level.

I call that level "treason." She accepted those bribes (she calls them donations) while secretary of state. She handed out coveted government contracts based on those bribes. That's treason. I'd also bet allowing classified emails to fall into the hands of hackers and foreign governments is also called "espionage." In US political history, no candidate for president has ever been so compromised as Hillary.

Obama, Hillary, and the entire political class love the super-rich. To get their money to stay in power, politicians must dance to the puppet strings of the super-rich, which includes willingly selling out the middle class. Of course, tyrants need the support of the helpless, hopeless, clueless poor folks. They ensure that by keeping them dependent on government—hooking them on welfare checks the way a drug dealer hooks addicts on heroin. Ironically, the government is the very group that destroyed their middle-class lives in the first place. The poor huddled masses and serfs now have little choice but to vote for the tyrant who keeps the government checks coming.

What is even more ironic is that the money to fund these government checks these tyrants hand out comes from the hides of the hard-working middle class. You couldn't make this stuff up. Keeping the people helpless, hopeless, desperate, and dependent, and having the middle class pay for it, is the perfect mix for how corrupt tyrants and arrogant kings stay in power.

The one group a tyrant can't abide is the middle and working class. That's why it has to go. Just like in *Braveheart*, the middle and working classes don't fit into the plans of a tyrant like Obama or Hillary. The middle class is not easily bribed. They believe in personal responsibility and don't want government dependency. They will stand and fight for things like God, country, American exceptionalism, and Judeo-Christian values. They are willing to die for those principles.

Obama knows that. Remember his own words during the 2008 presidential primaries. Obama said that "working class people get frustrated and bitter, and cling to their guns and religion. . . ."[1]

So, just like in *Braveheart*, Obama, Hillary, and their socialist cabal must eliminate the middle class. The middle class must be driven into poverty. Suddenly, they lose their faith in God, country, and capitalism. Then they'll get down on their knees begging for government to save them and their children. That's how you get middle-class people to cling to government, instead of guns or religion.

That's why Trump is so hated and feared by all the politicians and people in power. His entire agenda is designed to help the middle- and working-class Americans. He riles them up by telling them the raw truth they've never heard in their lives from a politician. He scares the hell out of anyone currently in power—both Democrat and Republican.

Braveheart is like today's America in one other important way. For hundreds of years, the noblemen of Scotland sold out their own people through "negotiating" and "compromise." The excuse of these frightened cowards, traitors, and sellouts was that the Scottish people could never defeat the powerful British army. "So why try? We're better off compromising."

That was the excuse. But in reality these noblemen sold out the people for their own personal gain: titles of royalty, land, and fancy estates. The noblemen of *Braveheart* are embodied today by establishment GOP leaders in Washington, DC.

Just like today's GOP leadership, the Scottish rulers cut deals and "compromised" with the king of England to turn the people (the middle class) into serfs. The people got nothing, while the noblemen got rich and fat, while acting like they were the friends of the people. History repeats. Remind you of anyone? Like maybe John Boehner, Mitch McConnell, Paul Ryan, Jeb Bush, Mitt Romney, John McCain, Lindsey Graham, and so many others who despise Trump? Or how about Supreme Court Justice Roberts? They all talk a good game. But they aided and abetted Obama every step of the way. I believe they have either been bribed or blackmailed.

The good news is that *Braveheart* had a happy ending. After centuries of slavery, cowardice, and traitorous behavior by their leaders, the Scottish people rose up and defeated the British. Starving, outmanned, and outnumbered, the peasants defeated the "unbeatable" British army and won their freedom—inspired by Sir William Wallace.

With Donald Trump leading the charge, the same outcome is possible today, but only if Trump leads with the same passion, intensity, enthusiasm, and principles of Sir William Wallace.

Only if we defeat the negotiating, compromising, country club establishment Republicans (i.e., noblemen) who sell us out every day in DC and shutter, shake, and genuflect whenever King Obama or Queen Hillary walks into the room.

These are the same country club Republicans who show up at a gunfight with knives. They are the same people who sell out the middle class for a committee chairmanship or millions of dollars in corporate campaign contributions. Or if they lose reelection after doing the bidding of the DC elite and crony capitalists, they get a lobbying job, law firm partnership, or millions deposited into a Swiss bank account. That's how the game is played today. Paul Ryan, the latest speaker of the House, is perhaps the most disappointing example ever. I thought he was a great guy. I thought he wanted to cut spending and the size of government. But instead, it's clear he's another fake. As soon as he got the top job, he sold the taxpayers out. He went along with everything Obama wanted, including the most obscene, corrupt spending bill in history.

We will win only if we understand that our opposition is playing for keeps, with a purposeful plan to destroy our country, capitalism, our economy, our freedoms, and, most importantly, the middle class. The American Dream is being extinguished, and the predominantly white middle class is being murdered. It's all about greed, bribery, and blackmail.

Our GOP "defenders" are not playing for keeps. They are either too docile, fearful, or naïve to fight back; too "country club elite" to even understand what is happening to the middle class; or too concerned with amassing a fortune to secure their own families' future (just like the noblemen of Scotland). In other words, they've sold us out.

We have only Trump to fight for us. We either fight for keeps, or our children and grandchildren will be enslaved to big government, big spending, big taxes, and the loss of all privacy and civil rights.

It's time to fight fire with fire. It's time to support Trump—our Sir William Wallace. A leader with passion, fire, and fighting spirit. A war leader.

It's time to bring a rocket launcher to a gunfight, before we wake up and find it's all gone. It's time to call the people who are trying to take the American Dream away by their proper names: elitists, traitors, thieves, tyrants, Marxists, Fascists, and assorted socialists and communists.

And let's not forget RINOs (Republicans in name only) because there is only one thing almost as bad as a communist trying to "murder the middle class" and snuff out the American Dream. That is a DC establishment Republican who goes along with the plan out of naiveté, fear, or to enrich his own family's future.

It's time to fight with passion and enthusiasm and to throw caution to the wind. It's time to fight like a cornered wolverine. It's time to fight with a daredevil attitude that comes from knowing your freedom, your life, and your family's future depends on it.

Because it does.

It's time for all angry white males, as well as other assorted peasants and serfs of all colors and sexes, to support our generation's Braveheart. It's either Trump or the light goes out, the fight is officially lost, and America is gone forever. It's time to fight back. It's time to fight for every inch.

It's Trump time.

21

Why Is the Establishment So Desperate to Stop Trump?

Many powerful people are very nervous. They are getting desperate: Obama, Valerie Jarrett, Eric Holder, Hillary Clinton, and Jon Corzine, to name just a few. Let me tell you why.

There is an unholy conspiracy between big government, big business, and big media. They all benefit by the billions from this partnership, and it's in all of their interests to protect one another. It's one for all and all for one.

It's a heck of a filthy relationship that makes everyone filthy rich. Everyone except the American people. We get ripped off. We're the patsies.

But for once, the powerful socialist cabal and the corrupt crony capitalists are scared. I've never seen them this outraged, this vicious, this motivated, this coordinated. *Never* in all my years in politics have I seen anything like the way the mad dogs of hell have been unleashed on Donald Trump.

When white extremist David Dukes ran for governor of Louisiana, even he wasn't treated with this kind of outrage, vitriol, and disrespect.

When a known fraud, scam artist, and tax cheat like Al Sharpton ran for president, I never saw anything remotely close to this.

When Libertarian Ron Paul ran for president promising to reign in big government and restore power to the people, nothing like this ever happened.

The over-the-top reaction to Trump by politicians of both parties, the media, and the biggest corporations of America has been so swift and insanely angry that it suggests they are all threatened and frightened like never before.

Why? Because David Duke was never going to win. Al Sharpton was never going to win. Ron Paul was never going to win. Ross Perot was never going to win as a third-party candidate. None of those candidates had the perfect combination of celebrity, brand name, money, or chutzpah it takes to beat the political establishment and the powerful entrenched special interests. But Donald Trump has that rare combination that gets that rare someone through the gauntlet and into the White House.

No matter how much they say to the contrary, the media, business and political elite understand that Donald Trump is no joke and can actually win and upset their nice cozy apple cart. Trump is a real threat. A serious threat. The gifted one.

Saying this in the fall of 2016 (as you read this book) is no big deal. But I wrote these exact words in July 2015. This chapter was published back then as a commentary at many top conservative websites. Back then, I was the only national political commentator saying these things—predicting Trump's success, predicting Trump would win the GOP nomination, predicting Trump would win the presidency, and warning of the over-the-top backlash from the desperate establishment of both parties. I made some remarkable predictions way back then.

It was no coincidence that everyone got together to destroy Donald. I guarantee you this was a coordinated conspiracy led by President Barack Obama himself. Obama himself made the phone calls and gave the orders to his buddy and billionaire donor George Soros; to communist-backed protest groups; to illegal immigrant groups; to major corporations who depend on government contracts, loans, and investments; to the country of Mexico; and to the mainstream media. Obama is the ultimate intimidator who plays by the rules of Chicago thug politics.

Why was this so important to Obama? Why did he personally get involved? Because all of the other Republican presidential candidates are part of the "old boys' club." They talk big, but in the end they wouldn't change a thing. Why? Because they are all beholden to big money donors. They are all owned by lobbyists, unions, lawyers, gigantic environmental organizations, and multinational corporations like Big Pharma and Big Oil. Or they are owned lock, stock, and barrel by foreigners like George Soros, who owns Obama and most Democrats, or foreign governments, who own Hillary with their Clinton Foundation donations.

These run-of-the-mill, establishment politicians are all puppets owned by big money. But one man—and only one man—isn't beholden to anyone. One man doesn't need foreigners, or foreign governments, or George Soros, or the United Autoworkers, or the Teachers Union, or the Service

Employees International Union, or the Bar Association to fund his campaign. Donald Trump doesn't need anyone's money. He'll take it, with no strings attached. But he alone doesn't need it.

Billionaire tycoon and maverick Donald Trump doesn't care what the media says. He doesn't care what the corporate elites think. He isn't intimidated by Obama's IRS or Securities and Exchange Commission. That makes him very dangerous to the entrenched interests. That makes Trump a huge threat. Trump can ruin everything for the bribed politicians and their spoiled slave masters.

Haven't you wondered why the GOP never tried to impeach Obama? Haven't you wondered why John Boehner, his successor Paul Ryan, and Mitch McConnell all talk a big game but never actually try to stop Obama? Haven't you wondered why Congress holds the purse strings, yet they've never tried to defund Obamacare or Obama's clearly illegal executive action on amnesty for illegal immigrants? Bizarre, right? It defies logic, right? Until you start putting two and two together.

First, I'd guess many key Republicans are being bribed.

Second, I believe many key Republicans are being blackmailed. Whether they are secretly gay, having affairs, or stealing taxpayer money, the National Security Agency (NSA) knows *everything*. They're listening in on phone calls, they're reading emails and texts. They know everyone's dirty little secrets. Obama has shown no hesitancy to use all this snooping for blackmail.

Ask former Republican House Speaker Dennis Hastert. The government even knew he was withdrawing large sums of his own money, from his own bank account, in a bribery scandal. But why him? Of course, because he's a Republican. Putting a former GOP speaker of the House in prison sends a powerful message to all politicians.

Trust me—the NSA, SEC, IRS, and all the other three-letter government agencies are watching every Republican political leader. They know everything.

I'm no fan of Dennis Hastert. He is a low-life pervert who took advantage of teenagers who looked up to their wrestling coach. But how did the government know? How did they catch "a needle in a haystack"? The point of paying blackmail is so no one ever finds out. How did the Obama administration know? My educated guess is they are watching every Republican politician, big donor, activist, and high-profile critic of the president. We are all under surveillance. And if they find or hear something, that's when they have control over us. They either control our votes, ruin our reputations, or maybe even send us to jail.

As I was in the midst of writing this book, famous Las Vegas businessman and philanthropist Billy Walters was arrested for "insider trading" on Wall Street. Billy also happens to be a big-time Republican donor. Is he guilty? I have no idea. Maybe he is, maybe he's not. I'll let a court decide. But I know Hillary Clinton has done far worse: espionage in her email scandal and treason and bribery with the Clinton Foundation. As of the writing of my book, she is still walking around "scot-free."

I know Jon Corzine was chairman of MF Global when a billion dollars went missing. But he happens to be a top Obama donor and bundler. He was never indicted.

I know Al Sharpton owes millions to the IRS. Yet he's never been indicted. Heck, he visited Obama's White House eighty-one times. He's a counselor and confidant to the president of the United States. It pays to be a big-government Democrat.

Not a single big shot official at the IRS has been indicted or even fired for one of the worst scandals in the history of US politics. And while what happened is so bad the GOP Committee with oversight over the IRS is threatening IRS Commissioner John Koskinen with firing and loss of his pension for refusing to cooperate, it is a safe bet it will never happen.[1]

Do you understand how bad this scandal is? I was a target and victim of this IRS persecution. I've always believed Obama stole the 2012 election by using the IRS to target, intimidate, persecute, distract, and bankrupt conservative groups, critics, and Tea Party groups. Conservatives had momentum until it was destroyed through IRS attacks. I believe Obama ordered the IRS attacks with the specific goal of changing the outcome of a presidential election. The blatant disregard for laws of the United States by the IRS commissioner indicates I'm right.

As described elsewhere in more detail, the Obamacare scandal is even worse. This is the world's first trillion-dollar scam, all passed through using lies, misrepresentation, and fraud. The architect of Obamacare, MIT

Professor Jonathan Gruber, was caught on tape admitting to lying, withholding facts, and committing fraud to fool "stupid voters."[2]

No one was ever charged.

Fast and Furious was another massive Obama scandal. Attorney General Eric Holder tried to block Congress. Obama himself used "executive privilege" to keep the facts from getting out to the American people. The facts are they sold guns to Mexican drug lords, and lost track of the guns that wound up killing many victims, including a US border agent. This was all a planned, anti-Second Amendment attempt to force the American public to accept more gun control. It failed miserably and Obama and his staff covered it up. No one has ever been charged.[3]

US Senator Harry Reid entered the Senate with very few assets and is leaving in January as one of the richest members of the Senate. Now he's worth $10 million.[4]

He now lives in a suite at the Ritz Carlton in DC. How did that happen? Did it have anything to do with his push for federal funding for a bridge connecting Laughlin, Nevada, with Bullhead City, Arizona? Neither state cared about that bridge. There was no fierce lobbying. But "Dirty Harry" happened to own one hundred sixty acres near the new bridge. Before the bridge was approved by Congress, that land was valued at $250,000. Post building of that bridge (with taxpayer money), it's now worth as much as $5 million. It's listed as Reid's single biggest asset.[5]

Is anyone investigating?

Yet the Obama government is going after Billy Walters, a GOP donor, for insider trading. I don't know if he's guilty, but I sure don't see any top Democrat politicians or donors being investigated, indicted, or prosecuted. Funny how that works.

Finally, why criticize Obama or call him out for his crimes, let alone demand his impeachment and risk being called a "racist."

So . . . why rock the boat? After defeat or retirement, if you're a "good ole boy," you've got a $5 million per year lobbying job waiting.

The big money interests have the system gamed. Win or lose, *they win.*

Enter Donald Trump. Do you still wonder why voters are angry, pissed off, in a foul mood . . . sick and tired of "business as usual?" Donald Trump doesn't play by these rules. Trump breaks up this nice cozy relationship between big government, big media, and big business. All the rules are out the window if Donald wins the presidency. Career politicians of both parties will protect Obama, Hillary, and their friends from prosecution. But Donald won't.

Remember, Trump is the guy who publicly questioned Obama's birth certificate. He questioned Obama's college records and how a mediocre student got into an Ivy League university.[6]

Now he's doing something no Republican has ever had the chutzpah to do: question our relationship with Mexico[7]; question why the border is wide open; question why no wall has been built across the border; question if allowing millions of illegal aliens into America is in our best interests; question why so many illegal aliens commit violent crimes, yet are not deported; question why our trade deals with Mexico, Russia, and China are so bad.[8]

Donald Trump has the audacity to ask out loud why American workers always get the short end of the stick?

Good question.

I'm hopeful Trump will question what happened to the almost $1 billion given in a rigged no-bid contract to college friends of Michelle Obama at foreign companies to build the defective Obamacare websites.[9]

By the way, that tab is now up to $5 billion. In the private sector, secretaries go to prison for embezzling a thousand dollars. What about $5 billion? Why isn't anyone ever sent to prison for embezzling $5 billion of taxpayer monies?[10]

Trump will ask if Obamacare's architects can be charged with fraud for selling Obamacare by lying. He will ask if Obama himself committed fraud when he said, "If you like your healthcare plan, you can keep it."[11]

Trump will investigate Obama's widespread IRS conspiracy, not to mention Obama's college records. Liberal reporters might ask why are those important? Well, I'd ask why they were sealed for Obama's entire eight years as president. It sure seemed important to Obama to make sure no one ever saw them. I think the citizens and taxpayers have a right to know.

Trump will prosecute Hillary Clinton and Obama for fraud committed to cover up Benghazi before the election.

How about the fraud committed by employees of the Labor Department when they made up bogus job numbers in the final jobs report released before the 2012 election.[12]

Obama, Hillary, the multinational corporations, and the media desperately need to stop this. They recognize this can get out of their control. If left unchecked, telling the raw truth and asking questions everyone else is afraid to ask, Donald could wake a sleeping giant and mess up their gravy train.

Trump's election could be a nightmare for big government proponents. It could be an even bigger nightmare for Obama and Hillary who I believe have committed many crimes. Only Trump will dare to prosecute. Once Donald gets in and gets a look at "the cooked books" he won't hesitate. The game is over. The jig is up. The goose is cooked.

Obamacare will be defunded and dismantled.

What I call "The Obama Crime Family" could be prosecuted for crimes against the American people. Hillary, Bill, and maybe even Chelsea Clinton could wind up in prison for what they did at the Clinton Foundation. Eric Holder could wind up in prison. Valerie Jarrett could wind up in prison. Obama bundler Jon Corzine could wind up in prison. The entire upper level management of the IRS could wind up in prison. Even Obama himself, if not in prison could wind up ruined, his legacy in tatters. Don't be surprised to see a long, long list of midnight pardons the night before Obama leaves office.

Trump will investigate. Trump will prosecute. Trump will go after everyone involved—just for fun. That will all happen on Trump's *first day* in the White House.

Who knows what Donald will do on day two?

That's why the dogs of hell have been unleashed on Donald Trump. That's why we must all support Donald. This may be our only shot at saving America, uncovering the crimes committed against our nation, and prosecuting those involved. It is our last chance to save the great American middle class.

I wrote these words in July 2015, when 99 percent of experts believed Trump had no chance to win the nomination, let alone the presidency. Today, those words ring more true than ever. Today, Donald Trump is inches away from the White House—making the establishment's worst fears come true.

22

Proof of the Conspiracy

Donald Trump, Paul Ryan, and the Biased Judge

As I was writing this book, a controversy erupted about Trump University. The New York judge overseeing the class action lawsuit was criticized by Trump for being biased due to his membership in a radical Hispanic organization. Once again, in a repeat of what happened when Trump announced his run for president, the GOP establishment turned on Trump. Republican Speaker of the House Paul Ryan accused him of racism.

I have a message for Donald Trump: *don't change a thing.*

Donald, don't listen to these people. The GOP establishment is a bunch of sellouts and sore losers. From the moment you started running for president, the biased liberal mainstream media, government bureaucrats, career politicians, lawyers, lobbyists, establishment Republicans, and various corporate CEOs, who are all in bed together, have tried to damage you, destroy you, or change you.

But you stuck to your guns. You charged ahead and did it your way. Don't change a thing. Continue to speak directly to the people. Speak over the heads of these elitists, globalists, and "one world-ers." You understand they don't have the best interests of America, American workers, or the great American middle class in mind.

And it worked.

The Republicans who criticized you are all wrong. You've marginalized them one by one. Mitt Romney. Jeb Bush. John McCain. Lindsey Graham. Mitch McConnell. Let's not forget commentators like Charles Krauthammer, Bill Kristol, Erick Erickson, Ben Shapiro, and the editors of *National Review*. They are all now meaningless.

When Karl Rove and George Will go on air, we all now change the channel! We know exactly what they think and are about to say—they are anti-Trump because Trump truly means real change, not Barack Obama's B.S. change, but real change! And they don't want it. Trump has rendered them meaningless.

Now it's Paul Ryan's turn.

Donald, you've beaten them all. Their thinking and language doesn't appeal to the working and middle class, and it certainly doesn't win elections. These establishment types no longer matter. The GOP is *your* party now.

You tell the truth. You speak with raw emotion. You are politically incorrect. You tell it like it is, even if it shocks some who've never heard straight talk before. It worked. You vanquished the sixteen best candidates in GOP history. You destroyed them. You made them disappear.

Even more remarkably, they raised and spent hundreds of millions. You spent almost nothing. And you won! Your raw truth beat their big money.

Heck, these politicians all became rich men on our money. Not just Harry Reid, but thousands of others who feed from the public trough and manipulate the system, often illegally. Donald is the only one who can put a stop to it. The "test run" that proved his remarkable success was beating all the big money interests and their candidates in the GOP primary.

Donald, if you stick to your guns, you will do the same to Hillary Clinton. This election is yours if you just be Donald. Don't change a thing. That's what got you to this amazing place in time.

Now it's Paul Ryan's turn to become irrelevant in his own party, to become meaningless, to disappear.

On a national basis, Republicans have won nothing with Paul Ryan's image and ideas. He's boring, traditional, moderate, vanilla, and establishment. He won't take a gamble. He's scared of his own shadow, just like our last two presidential candidates, McCain and Romney, and the other feckless GOP leaders intimidated by Obama for eight long years.

Donald, on the other hand, you're a riverboat gambler. You've been up and down. You've been close to disaster. Yet you've come out of it with billions of dollars and one of the great business empires and brands in history.

What's Paul Ryan built? He's been in GOP leadership for eight long years while Obama damaged the economy and the country. He was there while Obama stuffed taxes, regulations, spending, Obamacare, and outrageous illegal executive orders down our throats while Ryan and his GOP establishment buddies did nothing. They were powerless, feckless, impotent cowards. They allowed it all to happen.

They didn't fight like Americans. They waved a white flag like the French.

So when Paul Ryan disavows your comments about the Mexican American judge in your Trump University case and calls your words "racist," consider it a badge of honor. He's the coward and appeaser who waves the white flag every time the left cries foul.

You know why they cry foul? Because *you're winning!* Right when victory is upon us, inches away, at the very moment our tactics are working—that's when liberals cry foul and scream "racist" and GOP establishment weaklings and cowards cry "Uncle." *That's Paul Ryan.*

Ryan is the typical Republican leader who brings a knife to a gun fight. He plays by gentleman's rules, while liberals bring machine guns and cut us to shreds. They're banging our brains in, and Ryan keeps playing by gentleman's rules. He thinks it's badminton with Muffy at the country club. But it's war. And we need a wartime leader. That's you, Donald.

Quite simply, Ryan and his fellow establishment cronies are either idiots or sleeping with the enemy.

Trump didn't say anything racist. He just told the truth. It isn't his Mexican heritage that makes Judge Gonzalo Curiel unfit to oversee the Trump U case. It's his membership in a La Raza lawyers group. La Raza by the way means "The Race." It's his past statements about his Mexican heritage. It's his being on the selection committee for a La Raza event to hand out college scholarships to illegal aliens. It's his membership in a group that called for a boycott of Trump businesses because of his promise to build the wall.[1]

This judge can't be trusted to oversee a Donald Trump case any more than the Democrat mayor of "sanctuary city" San Jose and his allegedly La Raza–sympathizer police chief can be trusted to be impartial.

That San Jose police chief appears to have ordered his 250 riot police to stand down and do nothing, while Trump supporters were beaten and bloodied right in front of them. How is a judge with the same beliefs any different than a police chief who may have allowed innocent people to be beaten because of his dislike for Donald Trump? It's time to speak truth. It's time to admit the fix is in. The deck is stacked. These people in power have an agenda. They're not on our side. They're not on Trump's side. They are on the side of illegal aliens and big corporations looking for cheap labor, subsidized by government welfare checks. Everyone wins except taxpayers and the predominantly white middle class.

By the way, talk about liberal hypocrisy. Anytime a black criminal is shot dead by a white policeman, don't black leaders immediately cry "racism"? So if that's the case, that a white policeman can't be trusted because he's white and he has a bias, then isn't it fair to question the bias of a judge who is on record as supporting illegal immigration, awarding scholarships to illegals, and joining La Raza?

The reality is none of the people in power can be trusted anymore, whether they be white, black, Mexican, or any other race or creed. They are all part of "the system." They are all out to protect the way things are, to protect their power, their crony capitalism, their obscene pensions, and the open borders that enrich them but kill middle-class jobs and lower our wages. They are all a part of the scam to destroy America's working and middle class to make us dependent on government, to give the power to the elite, to leave the rest of us powerless and at their mercy.

Donald hit the nail on the head again. This case is about so much more than a judge's race or heritage. It's about a corrupt and biased judiciary and legal system, in bed with the DC establishment ruling class.

Here are the questions that need to be asked about Trump's case:

1. Who put lawyers in charge? Lawyers and law firms contribute more to political races than any other group, the vast majority to Democrats. Who says they have our best interests in mind? Or is their only goal to protect the government and the "ruling class" and hurt people like Donald Trump who stand up against the power elite?

2. A judge is supposedly 100 percent impartial. Really? How is that possible when he belongs to advocacy groups opposed to what Donald Trump and conservatives stand for?

His Mexican heritage does not matter. But his belonging to organizations giving scholarships to illegal aliens and advocating boycotts of Trump's businesses matters very much. Paul Ryan is either stupid, paid off, or simply too scared to be called a "racist" to tell the truth.

Could an innocent black kid get a fair trial from a judge who belongs to a white supremacist group?

Could a white cop get a fair trial from a judge who marches in "Black Lives Matter" protests and denounces cops as "racist"?

Any judge who belongs to groups that oppose the defendant's views must be removed from the case due to conflicts of interest.

3. Why doesn't the system require that both parties to any legal action agree on the judge? Why should any defendant's case hinge on the luck of the draw? Why should a defendant have to pray for a judge who is fair—versus one with an agenda?

Donald Trump should turn this into a teachable moment about the unfairness of the legal system. It is time to shine light on the fact the deck is stacked against anyone fighting the system and the elite DC establishment.

Add a corrupt legal system and biased judges to big government, big business, big media, politicians, lawyers, and deep pocketed lobbyists, stacking the deck against anyone fighting corruption, fighting big government, fighting the system. The conspiracy to hurt the middle class and stop

Trump at all costs goes from big government to judges to police chiefs to CEOs to Republican leaders like Paul Ryan.

Don't run from it, Donald. Don't back down. Instead, DOUBLE DOWN. You'll become a folk hero—and the next President of the United States.

As far as Paul Ryan—ignore him. He's the old guard, and the people will soon throw him out. His weak message and nonstop apologies are a losing image for the GOP. He's another Mitch McConnell. He's the new John Boehner. Paul Ryan is the reason the GOP is losing. If the GOP wants to win over angry white males and middle-class Americans, the answer is simple . . .

Donald J. Trump.

23

A Message for Christians Who Don't Support Trump

I wrote this commentary on June 20, 2016, on the day I finished writing this book. I believe it is the most powerful and important message I've ever communicated in my life. I wrote it after saying my morning prayers and reading my daily Bible verses. It came to me at that moment. I believe it was inspired by God. I wanted to include it in this book.

I have a message for Christians who don't like Donald Trump: **"YOU'RE MISSING THE BOAT."**

Christians have Trump all wrong. God sends messages in many forms. You're just not listening. God is talking, but your eyes and ears are closed.

Here's a famous joke about God and how he talks to us.

"A deeply faithful Christian man is stuck on the roof of his home because of massive flooding up to the second floor. A rowboat comes. He says, "No, I'm waiting for God. I've prayed and I know he's coming." Second rowboat: "No, I'm waiting for God." Third rowboat: "No, I'm waiting for God."

The water rises. The religious man drowns. Now he's meeting God in heaven. Dead guy says, "Where were you? I prayed. I was faithful. I asked you to save me. Why would you abandon me?"

God says, "Hey stupid, I sent you three rowboats. What are you, blind?"

Trump is our rowboat. Trump is our life preserver. Did you ever consider that Trump is the messenger, sent by God?

Maybe God is trying to tell us something important—that now is not the time for a "nice Christian guy" or a "gentleman" or a typical Republican powder puff. Maybe now is the time for a natural born killer, a ruthless fighter, a warrior.

Because right about now we need a miracle, or America is finished.

Maybe the rules of gentlemen don't apply here. Maybe a gentleman and "all-around nice Christian" would lead us to slaughter. Or do you want another Mitt Romney, Bob Dole, John McCain, Gerald Ford, or Paul Ryan? Did any of them win? Did they lead the GOP to "the promised land?" Did they change the direction of America? No, because winning is what matters. If you don't win, you have no say. You have no seat at the table of power.

Paul Ryan couldn't even deliver his own state, Wisconsin!

And as leader of the House, Paul Ryan rolls over to Obama like my dog rolls over for a scrap of food or a steak bone. He's a useful idiot. Nice, but obedient. I mean Paul Ryan, not my dog. My dog is actually a pretty good defender and loyal. Paul Ryan is none of those things.

Maybe God is knocking on your door loudly, but you're not listening. Maybe God understands we need a war leader at this moment in time. Maybe God understands if we don't win this election, America is dead. It's over. The greatest nation in world history will be gone. Dead and buried. Finished. Kaput. Adios.

And with one last breath, one last inch of open window, our very last chance, what we need to save us at the last second is someone *different*. Someone you haven't ever experienced before because you weren't raised in rough-and-tumble New York. Someone you've never had in your home because your dad was a "nice guy." Someone you've never watched on stage at your church. Maybe, just maybe, all of those things would not beat Hillary and her billion dollars and her best friends in the media who will unleash the dogs of hell upon the GOP nominee.

I guess you think God is only nice and gentlemanly. *Really?* Then you've missed the whole point of the Bible. When necessary, God strikes with pain, death, and destruction. When necessary, God inflicts vengeance.

Maybe you think God is too nice for Trump. Trump is too vicious, rude, and crude. Not true. When we won WWII, was God nice? Were we "gentlemanly" when defeating Hitler? Were we gentlemanly when firebombing Germany? Were we gentlemanly when dropping atomic bombs on Japan? Is God ever nice on the battlefield? Or does he send us vicious leaders like General George S. Patton so the good guys can defeat evil?

It's pretty clear to me God sends the perfect choice to be war leaders. That's a different role than a pastor or church leader. God understands that.

Maybe God purposely sent Trump instead of the nice Republican powder puffs like Paul Ryan, or Mitt Romney, or John Kasich because he wants us to win.

And maybe it's time to redefine "nice." Maybe Mitt Romney and Paul Ryan aren't nice at all—because they led us to defeat. And losing again would mean the end of America. And God can't allow that.

Maybe Romney and Ryan mean well, but the road to hell is paved with good intentions.

Or maybe they're just jealous that they had their chance and blew it. Maybe they'd rather help elect Hillary than allow Trump to expose them as weak, feckless, and incompetent.

I was reading the Bible this morning and I found the perfect verse that explains the success of Donald Trump:

Isaiah 40:30–31

Even the youths shall faint and be weary, and the young men shall utterly fall: but they that wait upon the Lord shall renew their strength; they shall mount up with wings as eagles; they shall run, and not be weary; and they shall walk, and not faint.

It's almost like God created this verse for Donald Trump and this moment in history.

Trump is our energy. More energy than any candidate *ever*. He took on the sixteen best candidates in GOP history—all younger than him, all with better political credentials—and destroyed them with his energy. You mean that kind of energy in a 70-year-old isn't inspired by God?

Trump renews our strength. Or does the all-time record turnout and all-time record votes for a GOP presidential primary candidate not define "strength"?

With Trump we mount up with wings like eagles. With Trump as our leader there is nothing we can't do. Any man who can build skyscrapers in Manhattan and wind up victorious against billion-dollar bankers, and vanquish sixteen GOP opponents, while spending almost nothing, can lead us to the heights of eagles.

With Trump we run, we are not weary. Just when we get tired of the fight against Obama, Hillary, big government, big business, big media, big unions—just when it all seems impossible to overcome the powerful forces of evil—along comes Trump to reenergize us, and to help us dream big and win big.

Trump inspires us. Trump gives us hope. Trump gives us confidence in victory. Trump gives us just a touch of arrogance. Maybe God understands that's exactly what we need right at this final moment to save America.

So let me repeat my message to Christians: **"YOU'RE MISSING THE BOAT."**

God is about miracles. We don't need a "nice guy" or a "gentleman" right now. It's the fourth quarter and we're losing 21–0. We need a miracle. A Hail Mary.

Trump is our miracle.

Trump is our rowboat. Except he's more like a *battleship!*

On the wings of our soaring eagle Trump this November we shall taste victory . . . we shall overcome . . . and we shall take back our country.

It's time to see the light. Because God can't knock any harder. It's Trump or it's the end of the America we love. The choice is easy. #TRUMP.

God bless America.

24

Trans Pacific Ponzi

Proof of the Murder of the Middle Class

This chapter could have been in the first section of the book, where I explained why angry white males are angry and what kinds of agenda and policies are being used to damage or destroy the predominantly white middle class. But this bill called TPP is so associated with the establishment, with big business, with Obama, with dark global forces who believe in "one world," that I decided it belongs here at the end of the Trump section. It represents everything Donald Trump rails against. Bills like TPP created the need for Trump. TPP represents everything we should all be not just angry about but outraged about. Only Donald Trump can save us from TPP now. Let's hope he gets the chance.

Want to hear about a bill so terrible for the American middle class that both parties support it? Our wonderful government calls their favorite new bill "TPP" for Trans Pacific Partnership. But it's really a bipartisan Ponzi scheme. It should be called "Trans Pacific Ponzi." It's a trillion-dollar rip-off of the American people and American workers. Obama wanted "fast-track authority" because he wants to put the end of America as we know it on a fast track. He got that fast-track authority, but as of the writing of this book, he has not yet passed TPP itself.

My hope is he won't be able to pass it during election season, when so many eyeballs are watching what each senator and congressperson does. If Trump wins the presidency, he can then kill TPP. But I'm betting Obama teams with Paul Ryan over the summer to try to bring it up for a vote. If that fails, there's always the "lame duck session" between the election and the day in January when the new President Trump is sworn in.

Trust me, don't ever assume TPP is dead. Like Freddy Krueger of *Nightmare on Elm Street*, it will keep coming back from the dead. Because the billionaires and billion-dollar multinational corporations want TPP. The powers that be won't give up. They will not rest until it passes, by hook or by crook. And since they are *all* crooks, they'll use any means necessary to get it passed. Electing President Trump is our only chance to kill it for good.

My book, *The Murder of the Middle Class,* describes the unholy alliance of the socialists like Obama and the crony capitalist corporations who own both political parties. The TPP is the perfect example of "the murder of the middle class" in one devastating treaty. Passing it requires secrecy and fraud carried out by both Obama and his partners in the Republican Party. Fraud and treachery makes for strange bedfellows.

The worst part isn't even what's in it—and it certainly contains a toxic brew that will destroy millions of middle-class jobs. More on that later. But the worst part is how it's been hidden from the people by Obama and the Republican leadership, working as a tag team like this is a World Wrestling Federation match.

Remember when Nancy Pelosi said, "We have to pass Obamacare to find out what's in it."[1]

We all know how *that* turned out. Obamacare is killing jobs, dramatically increasing the national debt, and bankrupting the middle class with gigantic increases in health insurance premiums. That's precisely why no one wanted you to read it, study it, or take the time to analyze it.

These disastrous billion-dollar bills need to be hidden and then passed quickly before anyone has a chance to understand their implications. They are written by lobbyists and lawyers, and never closely read by the very politicians voting for them. It's all about dollars. Corporations and fat-cat donors make billions, and the politicians collect millions in legal bribes (i.e., campaign contributions) and million-dollar lobbying jobs after they retire. That was the storyline of Obamacare.

The exact same scenario is playing out with the TPP. Do you know what's in the details? I don't. Neither do any of the Republicans voting for it. They openly admit it. Members of Congress need "security clearance" to be "allowed" to read it.[2] Leading GOP TPP supporter Senator Orrin Hatch admits he doesn't fully know what's in it.[3] GOP Majority Whip Steve Scalise and GOP Rules Committee Chairman Pete Sessions both admit they haven't read it.[4]

Paul Ryan channeled Nancy Pelosi when he said, "It's classified. You'll find out what's in it after we pass it and it's declassified."[5]

Are you kidding me? The GOP now thinks its own voters are as dumb and ignorant as Democrats? Paul Ryan thinks he should be allowed to pass bills the citizens aren't "allowed" to read? Really? Then it's time for the citizens to remove Paul Ryan from office.

Folks, Obamacare was 2,000 pages of legal-ese that no average citizen could understand. That was the tip-off that it was a rip-off (excuse the rhyme). But TPP makes Obamacare look open, honest, and transparent.

TPP is kept under lock and key. No citizen has access. No citizen has a clue what's in it. Only senators and congressmen with security clearance can walk into a room in the Capitol building to read it—alone. Then they are required to leave without making copies or taking notes.[6]

Does this sound strange to you? Does it sound surreal? Does it sound like it's good for the people? Because to me it sounds like a scam. A Ponzi scheme. Only criminals want their victims to sign contracts without reading them. It's quite clear: the ruling class and the corporate elite think we are serfs, and they are our masters.

At this point I don't care what's in it. If they don't want us to read it—if Congress thinks they should pass it without knowing what's in it—then our job is to burn it down. Stick a knife in its heart. Stab it until it can never again rear its ugly head.

But what is actually in it? Well, Wikileaks has leaked small parts of it. It appears it is a killer of American sovereignty. The TPP appoints a commission of soulless corporate lawyers with sweeping authority to override US laws and our Constitution.[7]

That commission will have sweeping power over US trade, labor, immigration, environmental, and commerce regulations. In other words, foreign and corporate powers will be running the United States of America. You think they care about American workers or middle-class jobs?

Unelected foreign lawyers representing multinational corporations will have more power than American citizens and even our politicians. And America only gets one vote on this commission. We'll have no more power or importance over rules regulating our lives than Brunei or South Korea.[8] How does that sound to you?

But I don't need to know all that. All I need to know is it's supported by Barack Obama. Heck, it has been nicknamed "Obamatrade." If Obama created it, it must be a toxic brew of onerous job-killing government regulation, insane job-killing climate change rules, illegal immigration amnesty that opens our borders to the poor and dependent of the world (i.e., future Democrat voters), and higher minimum wages that will drive small businesses out of business and guarantee millions more jobs are shipped overseas (where they can pay employees pennies on the dollar).

Obama doesn't support free trade. He supports Big Brother government and "the murder of the middle class." He loves to fool and defraud you by using cute cuddly names. The bill that made your health care unaffordable was named "The Affordable Care Act." Now the bill that destroys America's free trade economy is disguised as "free trade."

Unions are bitterly opposed to the TPP. They're siding against Obama—it must be *that* bad. For once I'm on the same side as the unions. This is a treaty that will destroy good-paying American jobs. It will destroy middle-class quality of life in America. The goal of TPP is "equality." Putting working people on equal footing around the world. Does that sound appealing to you? That sounds like a law designed by bureaucrats and lawyers to lift other people around the world up, by pulling our middle class down.

Equality always produces "shared misery." People who live well are always pulled down to the level of people who live a lousy quality of life. The rest of the world has always been jealous of our high standard of living. I guarantee you this is their attempt to reduce us to their level. It will make the American Dream unaffordable. It's time to rise up and kill TPP. And if the GOP won't listen to its own voters and supporters, then it's time to kill the GOP.

As usual, Donald Trump is our only hope. And that's why Paul Ryan, Mitt Romney, and so many others in the GOP establishment who clearly want to make us all government-dependent serfs hate Trump so much. He is the fly in their ointment. They were winning the battle to put billionaires and billion-dollar multinational companies in charge of our lives, until Donald came along to ruin their plan.

Pray for President Trump.

Now it's on to the section you've been waiting for: SOLUTIONS!

Part IV

Solutions

God, Guns, Gold, Tax Cuts, and Term Limits

We must all hang together or we shall surely hang separately.
—Ben Franklin

Every Angry White Male needs a battle plan. Here is yours!

25

Relentless God, Faith, and Prayer

Even the youths shall faint and be weary, and the young men shall utterly fall; but they that wait upon the Lord shall renew their strength; They shall mount up with wings like eagles; they shall run and not be weary; and they shall walk, and not faint.

—Isaiah 40:30–31 King James Version (KJV)

The key to my success is *The Power of Relentless.* That was my most recent book. I hope you'll have a chance to read it. To win this battle for the soul of America, and to save the great American middle class, every Angry White Male and every other patriot (regardless of race, creed, gender, or religion), we will need to be *relentless.*

The verse above is my favorite Bible passage. It gives me great comfort. It gives me faith. But most importantly, it gives me *energy!* Whenever I'm feeling down, I read that passage. Even youths are weary, but with God's strength, anyone can run like the wind! Then I stand up to my challenges, mount up with wings like eagles, and run through any obstacle or roadblock standing in my way. This verse is *The Power of Relentless* personified.

Even though that has been my favorite Bible verse for over a decade, you read in the last chapter how it fits Donald Trump perfectly. It was tailor-made for this man and this moment in history. Trump is our "wings like eagles." Trump gives us our energy, confidence, strength, and momentum.

But no man is Superman—not even Donald Trump. No *human* is superhuman. We all need help. We all need a boost of energy and faith now and then.

We all need a team to support us. I am a firm believer that God leads that team. God gives us the horsepower of a Ferrari or Maserati. When we need strong shoulders to hold our problems and stress, God gives us the shoulders of ten thousand bodybuilders. Faith is the foundation of success.

Let me tell you about the importance of faith, prayer, and gratitude and how I use them to improve my well-being. But if you are an atheist or nonbeliever, don't fear, and don't skip this section.

I was born Jewish and became a born-again Christian. That's my personal faith and testimony. But I'm not here to preach any one faith, although I can testify about the strength, energy, and passion I've enjoyed since taking Jesus Christ as my savior.

Know that I find inspiration in the writings of many different religious leaders throughout time. I want every reader of this book to enjoy the power of faith, no matter your religion. If faith and prayer are not your thing, think about it as being an extension of positive thinking. Prayer is meditation. It is affirmation and visualization. It is exercise of your mind and, for believers, your faith. It is a perfect, holistic, organic diet of positive thought. It is perfection. It is team building. It is a synergistic combination of everything I believe in.

Prayer to God is about faith in something greater than yourself. Gratitude, or thanksgiving, if you like, is about thanks and acknowledgment to God for the blessings in your life.

As we are told in 1 Thessalonians 5:16–18, few things can change our lives more than turning our complaining into thanksgiving.

"Rejoice evermore; pray without ceasing; in everything give thanks: for this is the will of God. . . ."

The key words here are "in everything give thanks." Prayer is my anchor. It is the ROOT (excuse the pun) of my passion, energy, enthusiasm, positive attitude, confidence, tenacity, and, of course, it is the foundation of my *Power of Relentless.*

My personal faith in God inspires me and motivates me. It gives me confidence in knowing I'm not alone. My shoulders simply could *not* carry the weight all by themselves.

How do I know this? Because all the truly great things in my life happened only after I developed a deep faith in God. A whole new world was opened to me. My faith inspires me to believe in miracles; to make the impossible, *possible*; to move mountains; and to ignore critics and the limitations set by naysayers.

I firmly believe no man is an island. We all need support and help. If two heads are better than one, having God on your team is . . . *INFINITY.*

A faith in God reduces stress and fear, and with that out of the way, creativity comes alive.

This may sound simplistic, but perhaps most of all, prayer makes me happy. It is the ultimate extension of positive thinking (aka relentless optimism). No matter how low my mood, prayer lifts it. That's why for me, spiritual wealth has led to material wealth. I recommend prayer to start each and every day. I wouldn't start my day without it!

AUTHOR'S NOTE: To read about my entire prayer program in detail, you'll need to read a copy of *The Power of Relentless*. I lay out a detailed plan involving prayer, gratitude, forgiveness, thoughtfulness, bible reading, and tithing in the chapter on faith.

But prayer is only the start of my amazing, aggressive, life-changing daily routine. It took me twenty-five years to perfect it. I call it "Positive Addictions." The program combines prayer, meditation, morning walk, yoga, affirmation, visualization, daily aerobic and strength training, holistic and healthy diet and lifestyle, and—here's the biggest part other than prayer—mega vitamin supplementation. I lay it all out in detail, including the exact vitamins I take each day that give me the energy of a thousand men (or one Donald Trump).

I've never been sick one day in my life. I haven't had even a common cold in five years. I haven't had the flu in ten years (and I don't need a flu shot). I work sixteen-hour days, without ever getting tired. I am excited to get up early each morning, and I go at a hundred miles an hour until midnight most nights. This program works. It's all gift-wrapped in detail in *The Power of Relentless,* available at Amazon.com or your favorite bookstore.

As I end this section, I want to share one more of my favorite prayers. I read it aloud every morning and it has given me great peace, strength, faith, energy and of course, "The Power of RELENTLESS."

And I am convinced that nothing can ever separate us from God's love. Neither death nor life, neither angels nor demons, neither our fears for today nor our worries about tomorrow— not even the powers of hell can separate us from God's love. No power in the sky above or in the earth below—indeed, nothing in all creation will ever be able to separate us from the love of God that is revealed in Christ Jesus our Lord.

—Romans 8:38–39 New Living Translation (NLT)

A Bold GOP Message That Wins the 2016 Presidency and Beyond

The GOP has one root (excuse the pun) to victory. We need a positive message. Here is the three-part plan that guarantees a presidential win in 2016.

We need to guarantee a job for every American, *not* a welfare check. Americans want two things:

1. They want a job, and
2. They want a system that is fair.

Why would anyone go to work, if others get to stay home, sleep late, watch *Dr. Phil*, play with their kids, and collect welfare and food stamps? This system is unfair, and it's leading to the decline and eventual collapse of the US economy.

President Trump needs to promise "a job in every pot." He must declare, "I am the jobs president. I'm going to get America working again come hell or high water. I will guarantee every American a job over the next four years. PERIOD. And if I don't deliver, fire me."

But for those on welfare or other government checks, you get a job whether you want one or not. Everyone must work. If you want to work, we'll find you a job. Your government checks will keep coming, but you'll earn the check.

If you refuse to work, you're on your own. All government checks will stop coming.

The state of Maine recently tried this model and it worked like *magic*. As soon as welfare recipients learned they had to work in order to keep their check, the welfare rolls dropped dramatically. Great! Mission accomplished. Less burden for taxpayers.[1]

Finding everyone a job is much cheaper (in the long run) than a welfare check. It's cheaper than food stamps for forty-six million Americans (for forty months in a row).[2]

To accomplish all this, President Trump and the GOP Congress will have to agree to spend more on jobs, not welfare. We'll have to invest billions in training workers; we'll have to spend money to hire job counselors and job placement experts; we'll have to give businesses incentives to hire the unemployed; and if we still can't find you a job in the private sector, we'll give you a job in the public sector. I don't care if you hold up STOP signs at construction sites, or pick up garbage along the highway, or help little children cross streets. But you will have a job, so that you earn your welfare check.

Everyone will have to work during a Trump presidency. PERIOD.

No one can ever again see their neighbor collecting a government check for staying home and not working. No longer should anyone's goal in life be welfare, food stamps, disability, or free health care. Obama is turning America into Cuba under Castro (his new BFF). Well, America is not Cuba. And we cannot ever allow it to become Cuba.

But we won't let anyone starve either. If you need a job, we'll give you one. If you need a check, you'll get it—but only if you work.

Now to Part II

Democrats *claim* they don't want people on welfare or dependency. They *claim* they want Americans to work. They *claim* they want a higher minimum wage. Our GOP candidate should call their bluff. We'll support new spending for jobs, training, and placement; and we'll spend money to create jobs for those who appear unemployable; and we'll even raise the minimum wage (a little bit).

Democrats and the media claim they want compromise. They claim compromise is good. Here's the deal President Trump and the GOP should offer in early 2017: In return for more spending on jobs training and a higher minimum wage, we want to lower personal and business income taxes to a flat tax of 15 percent. That's the tax rate and flat tax system of Hong Kong, the most prosperous, booming economy in the world.

Everyone wins. Millions of new jobs will be created because of dramatically lower business and personal income taxes. And with a higher minimum wage, employees will feel more prosperous, too. Will Democrats cut taxes for small businessman, in return for a higher minimum wage and more investment in jobs? They'd be crazy to say "no." I dare them. I *double* dare them.

Now to Part III

The border must be sealed and secured. Our jobs are being given away to the cheap labor of illegals. Government has allowed our working class to be decimated. That's not fair to American citizens. An American president should guarantee a job for every American citizen, *not* foreigners. The border must be sealed. We must build the wall. No more free rides for illegal aliens. No more cheap labor that takes away middle-class jobs. No more entitlement checks to illegal aliens. No more "earned income tax credits" for illegal aliens. No more incentives by our own government for companies to hire illegal aliens over you—an honest, law-abiding American citizen.[3]

We are killing the spirit of legal American citizens. This is outrageous. It must end with President Trump. It's time a president puts America first, America second, America forever. And announces "America fair," too. Every American will be guaranteed a job. No one sits at home. You either work or you lose your welfare check. The system must be fair and reward work, not welfare.

Game over. Announce this plan and Trump and the GOP win in a landslide.

The Tax Plan That Saves Middle-Class America

We need a bold, contrarian new vision to save the great American middle class. We need a bold, game-changing, conversation-changing tax plan. Donald Trump's tax plan is darn close to what I'm proposing here. I sent Donald my plan and lots of notes. I hope my recommendations had something to do with inspiring his tax plan. But I have more details and many new ideas here. And Trump will need a GOP Congress to go along with him. There are some creative ideas in this section. This is my plan:

First . . .

A National Income Tax Vacation (NITV)

That's right—I want to start with the boldest idea in modern American political history. With my plan, the middle class and small business get a holiday from paying taxes. For one year middle-class Americans get to keep 100 percent of what they earn. *Your money belongs to YOU.* And here's a really cool wrinkle: I've found a way for it to cost 0. As in zero. More on that in a minute.

To Obama and his socialist cabal, the idea of a "tax cut" is to cut the taxes of only those with little or no income (i.e.,

Democrats). The group that is left "out in the cold" just happens to be the economic engine of the US economy—middle-class private-sector taxpayers and small business owners (i.e., Republicans).

Like it or not, you cannot turn around an economy by giving "tax cuts" to people who don't pay taxes, who have no idea how to create jobs, who are not "rainmakers." That achieves nothing. If you don't believe me, see Exhibit A, Obama's "stimulus" that gave away $2 trillion to poor people, unions, and a few select Democrat donors (like green energy companies), but produced nothing and created only crappy, part-time, low-wage jobs.

This plan aims the tax cut directly at the only people who can ignite the economy and dig us out of this hole: the innovators, rainmakers, and entrepreneurial risk-takers.

Or as I call them **"FINANCIAL FIRST RESPONDERS."**

My plan incentivizes the people who start the businesses and create the jobs. This plan doesn't just refill their fuel tanks; it puts racing fuel into a turbo-charger. It's Ronald Reagan—*on steroids.* I can't help the fact that the vast majority of these people who start businesses, create jobs, and pay into the system happen to vote Republican. As Dillinger once said, "That's where the money is." Those are the people you have to incentivize to create an economic boom. I can't help it that they're not your voters! They're the ones who pay into the system; they are the only ones who can start a recovery and save the US economy.

Stand back and watch the economic explosion when middle-class taxpayers and small business owners capitalize on this once-in-a-lifetime opportunity. They will do what all smart and ambitious entrepreneurs do with money: spend it, invest it, and risk it to start new businesses or expand old ones. And they will do it quickly because for the next year (or two, if this works) they get to keep all of it. That's all you have to tell an entrepreneur and they are off and running, with a smile, and a gleam in their eyes! Democrats claim rich people are "greedy." Well, guess what? This plan capitalizes on that greed. It forces the people with the money—taxpayers, business owners—to spend their money like never before, in order to take advantage of the greatest opportunity of their lifetimes.

Obama and his Marxist cabal will scream, "But how can we run government without taxes?" That question never bothered Obama when he spent almost $1 trillion on his failed stimulus plan. But the true cost has ballooned to the range of $2 trillion.[1] Not one member of the media ever asked where the money would come from.

Here's the beauty of my plan: My income tax vacation is aimed at the first $147,000 made by any and all taxpayers. All of them get one year off from paying taxes on that amount of income. This gives relief to millions of working- and middle-class Americans who have yet to recover from the disastrous Great Recession we've been in for the past eight years. Instead of giving the money to people who don't work (that's Hillary's plan), this plan gives it to those who work and pay into the system. How do I know? Because you only get the tax holiday on taxable "earned income." Someone who earns nothing, or collects welfare, gets nothing. Why should they? They don't pay any taxes, so why would they get a "tax cut"? This is only a reward for WORKING!

The working class and middle class need this to heal from this terrible economy. They can use the extra money to pay off their mortgage, or credit card debts, or student loans, or medical expenses, or buy a new car, or buy a new home, or remodel their home, or start a new business. It's a once-in-a-lifetime break for the working man and woman. It's about time someone rewarded them for what they do, what they sacrifice. These are the people who will make America great again.

And who benefits? Job creators. Banks. Construction firms. Real estate firms. Stock firms. Retirement planners. Retail sales will soar. Home sales will soar. Car sales will soar. Small business start-ups will explode. Job creation will dramatically increase. And even the government will benefit from higher tax collections resulting from a booming economy. Like Reagan's tax cut, this middle-class tax holiday will create the greatest recovery and then economic expansion in world history.

But don't forget all the wealthier business owners who will also get a tax vacation on the first $147,000 of their income. They may not need it for credit card bills or student loans. But they will use it to start or expand businesses, buy stocks, buy homes, buy investment real estate. As a result, middle-class jobs will be created by the millions.

But the truly amazing part is the cost: ZERO.

It doesn't cost a thing. It's 100 percent paid for by allowing corporations to bring back home to America about $3 trillion (or more) held offshore and paying only a one-time 10 percent tax. That will produce about $300 billion in one-time tax revenues, to pay for the approximately $300 billion bill for this middle-class income tax holiday.

Here is the math directly from the Laura Saunders in *Wall Street Journal*. Saunders reported on a Pew Institute study of taxes. The total income tax take for 2014 (the latest figures) was $1.4 trillion. Twenty percent of that take came from income between $47,000 and $147,000. That adds up to a total cost of $280 billion.

Please note this is only a holiday from income earned by *labor*, such as from your job or owning a small business. Investment, interest, and capital gains income would still be taxed.

One more benefit comes from the offshore money brought back to the United States—after paying $300 billion in taxes, there is $2.7 trillion left to use for investment. That $2.7 trillion will be used by companies to create millions of additional middle-class jobs.

What synergy! Everyone who works or wants to work wins. This is just common sense and a truly amazing plan!

Other candidates have talked incessantly about helping the middle class, but no one has ever actually done it, except Reagan. Donald Trump and the GOP can forever lock in the loyal votes of middle- and working-class Americans with this plan. If you work and pay taxes, we celebrate your contributions and reward you.

Obama's trillion-dollar stimulus plan created nothing, inspired no one, did not create one job, and as a "bonus" added $2 trillion in debt for our children to pay. Oh, and Obama lied. Long after the money was spent, he made a joke out of the fact that there were never any shovel-ready jobs.[2]

Why did this stimulus never work, never improve the economy, or never create any large number of jobs? It never worked because the money was handed to the wrong people: FOBs (Friends of Obama), big government donors, welfare addicts, and unions. All the groups that have the political class bought and paid for. None of those groups could find a job if it hit them in the face.

But my NITV (National Income Tax Vacation) empowers the right people to keep 100 percent of their income for one year. Who are the right people? Small business owners and small investors. This is exactly what Reagan did when he cut tax rates from 70 percent to 28 percent—he helped only those who paid taxes in the first place.

Reagan's idea worked because, like my plan, it empowered the right group: the people who pay all the taxes. To get the economy going, no one else matters.

Simply put, taxpayers will be so excited, they will begin an investing spree that will create millions of jobs, which will quickly increase tax revenues. If critics are worried about the cost, let them find corresponding spending cuts. *That makes my plan even better!*

Oh, my NITV plan also includes a "Small Business Payroll Tax Vacation."

Note to the GOP

A plan like the one I've proposed is how you change the conversation. This is how you use boldness and courage to turn a historic bust into a boom. This is how you inspire voters. Reagan gave us the greatest tax cut in history to save us from Jimmy Carter. Today, we need to cut taxes to *zero* for a year (or two) to save America from what Obama just did to us. The Obama economy is even worse than the Carter economy. So the jolt must be that much more dramatic. An income tax vacation will start a revolution to save capitalism and take back our country.

Now comes part two, the permanent tax plan that saves the great American middle class.

It's All About the Taxes, Stupid!

Remember James Carville's famous words, "It's all about the economy, stupid." Well, Ronald Reagan proved that saving the economy from assorted America haters, socialists, Marxists, and ignorant fools (like Jimmy Carter and Barack Obama) deserves a new jingle.

It's all about the taxes, stupid.

Or are you forgetting that Reagan completely reversed the worst economy since the Great Depression in only two years and created the greatest economic expansion in world history with just one simple magic bullet: he cut taxes from 70 percent to 28 percent. It really was that simple.[1]

Liberals and the mainstream media (I know, I repeat myself) have spent the past thirty years trying to make you forget that simple magic formula. And even conservative Reagan fans have a foggy memory of the facts. Conservatives remember Reagan's smile, his jokes, his positive attitude. They think that was the key to Reagan's success. But the actual facts of the amazing Reagan economic revolution have become blurred.

It's time to revisit the facts of what Reagan produced. Lower taxes reward the work ethic. Lower taxes encourage the people that matter (business owners and job creators) to want to risk and invest our money, achieve, produce, and contribute. That's what made America great and will "Make America Great Again."

By keeping taxes low, Reagan fought for capitalism, for small business, for taxpayers, for working Americans. The result was SPECTACULAR SUCCESS. Reagan turned the misery, malaise, decline, depression, and disaster of the Carter years into the greatest and longest economic expansion ever. Reagan's low taxes produced an era of prosperity unlike anything in history.[2]

Reagan exploded the economy: $30 trillion in goods and services was created. Net assets like stocks and real estate went up by $5 trillion—an increase of 50 percent.

Reagan's low tax policies created nearly twenty million jobs in a short span, increasing US employment by a remarkable 20 percent. In one year alone, the GDP increased by 6.8 percent—the largest increase in fifty years. In only seven years, the economy grew by a staggering one-third. The economic boom lasted ninety-two consecutive months—the longest peacetime boom in world history. It shattered the previous record of fifty-eight months by almost 60 percent.[3]

These aren't good stats. These aren't even great stats. These are *remarkable* stats. These are miracles. And all Reagan did to achieve them is cut taxes dramatically and therefore leave more money in the hands of the taxpayers, instead of the people who take, take, take, and give nothing back in return.

Reagan was a believer in the famous "80/20 Rule of Business." You make all your money in business from your best customers, the 20 percent at the top. You waste your time if you're worrying about the others, the bottom 80 percent. It works with employees, too: Jack Welch of GE, perhaps the greatest CEO ever, achieved his success by giving raises to his best managers and firing the bottom 10 percent each year. Success is always about paying attention, rewarding, and celebrating the best.

But today, our nation is the hands of the worst: Barack Obama. Obama has destroyed the economy by lavishing attention, rewards, and celebrating the worst—the people who want welfare checks but give nothing back. Obama has proven (just like Jimmy Carter before him) that redistribution of wealth from the rich and middle class to the poor produces economic disaster. Giving money to the poor not only bankrupts a country and creates mountains of debt, but no one wants to work anymore. That could be why there are now over ninety-four million working-age Americans no longer working. Good luck with that.

Now the media hates Donald Trump. But Trump has put forth a tax plan that replicates Ronald Reagan. Since our economy is now performing exactly as it did under Jimmy Carter, Trump's plan is exactly what the doctor ordered.

Trump's new tax plan is Reagan-esque. It's a blast from the past. Like Reagan, Trump is relentlessly on the side of the makers, not the takers. Trump's plan is great for the people who want to work and pay taxes. Trump will produce a new era of Reagan prosperity by rewarding the financial risk creators and job creators.

Finally, someone is relentless on *our* side.

Reagan's tax plan was simple, lower, fairer, flatter, with rates of 15 percent and 28 percent. That did the trick. That unleashed an economic tsunami. That's all Reagan did.

Trump's plan is just like Reagan's: simple, lower, fairer, and flatter. The four rates are 0 percent, 15 percent, 20 percent, and 25 percent—almost identical to Reagan's, except the top rate is even LOWER! *Brilliant.*[4]

But Trump goes even further. Trump eliminates the marriage penalty, rewarding marriage and family. *Bravo.* His plan also eliminates the dreaded AMT (alternative minimum tax) that has ripped off middle-class American taxpayers.

And Trump's tax plan eliminates the estate tax, so anyone who has worked their whole life to build something and already paid their fair share of taxes on it can leave it to their children and grandchildren without the greedy government stealing it.

Trump also listens. In all my previous books, commentaries, and personal correspondence with Donald Trump, I've stressed the importance of a flat tax *combined* with keeping tax deductions for mortgage and charity. Nothing is more important to America, your family, or your neighborhood stability than your home and your church. Trump kept those deductions 100 percent intact. Bravo.

But here's where Trump "trumps" Reagan. Trump cuts corporate tax rates to a flat 15 percent and incentivizes US companies to bring their $3 trillion parked offshore back to America with a 10 percent rate. Suddenly, America will go from the worst corporate tax rate in the world to the best. Trump's plan will create REVERSE INVERSIONS. Every company in the world will want to relocate here in America! This is how you create millions of jobs.

Is Trump's plan perfect? No. But it's damn good. It's close to perfect. If I could have my way, I'd replicate the exact tax system of Hong Kong, the most prosperous place on earth, where individual taxpayers get the same 15 percent tax rate as corporations.

And instead of eliminating the estate tax, I'd have chosen to dramatically cut capital gains taxes. Hong Kong's capital gains tax is zero. Guess what the capital gains tax rate is in China (our number one economic competitor)? Zero.

Why is this important? Because the average American doesn't pay estate taxes, so they don't care. But everyone will sell a home, sell a stock, or sell a small business in their life-time. Cutting those taxes is the greatest thing you can do for anyone who ever risks a dime on any business or investment. So that's how I'd tweak Trump's plan.

But never let the "perfect" get in the way of the good. Trump's plan is damn good. It is damn Reagan-esque. Trump's plan is RELENTLESS—but this time it's relentless for the people who work, achieve, produce, and contribute. Trump's plan will truly make America great again! Bravo, Donald.

Because "it's all about the taxes, stupid!"

29

The Middle-Class Contract with America

Remember when the Newt Gingrich–led GOP created a "Contract with America." It was the greatest success in the history of modern politics. Well, it's time to create a new version. But I'm not worried about rich people. I'm only concerned with the great American middle class. I want to create a plan that puts America first. I want to create a plan that creates middle-class jobs. I want to create a plan that convinces working- and middle-class Americans that America is now open for business and work will be rewarded and celebrated.

I created just such a plan when I was asked to give the 2016 Tea Party Response to the President's State of the Union. That response has always been given by sitting US senators or congresspersons. The one exception was former GOP presidential candidate Herman Cain. I was honored to be the first nonpolitician to ever be asked to respond to the president of the United States. I cannot say it any better, so I'll reprint my entire speech and plan right here.

2016 Tea Party Response to the President's State of the Union

Hello, I'm Wayne Allyn Root. It is a great honor to be here tonight representing the Tea Party and the American people in responding to "the State of the Union" address by President Barack Obama. I want to start by thanking the Tea Party Express and millions of Tea Party members for giving me your trust and this sacred responsibility.

As a DC outsider, patriot, and anti-politician who believes in the American Dream and American exceptionalism, I am proud to follow previous Tea Party leaders who have delivered this response to President Obama in previous years—US Senator Rand Paul, US Senator Mike Lee, Congresswoman Michelle Bachman, Congressman Curt Clawson, and former presidential candidate and business leader Herman Cain.

Tonight the American people are being given three visions for how to move this country forward. You've just heard the president's vision and the traditional response from the opposition Republican Party. Now, in this remarkable nation "of the people, by the people, and for the people," you are about to hear a third vision delivered by someone just like you. I'm an S.O.B. (son of a butcher), a taxpayer, a successful small businessman, and a homeschool dad.

The remarkable irony is that I am the college classmate of President Barack Obama, Columbia University, Class of '83. We graduated on the same day, from the same college thirty-three years ago. And we've never had anything in common, ever again.

I'm not a part of the political class. I'm the proud founder of AARP—"Americans Against Rotten Politicians." The NFL's Seattle Seahawks honor their twelfth man before every football game. They acknowledge the fans as the beating heart of their team. It is the fans who give their team the supernatural energy to win the battle. I believe the American people, the taxpayers, the small business owners, the middle class are the true heroes, the beating heart, the twelfth man of America, and the US economy.

We are the important ones—not the politicians, not the government bureaucrats, not the media elite, not the lawyers, lobbyists, or arrogant Ivy League intellectuals. It is the people—the taxpayers—who made America the greatest nation in world history, and I am proud tonight to be here representing the American people.

The vision I will lay out tonight is "of the people, by the people, for the people."

President Obama left an empty seat tonight next to the first lady to symbolize victims of gun violence. I think that empty seat is appropriate. But it should represent the dying middle class. The good people of America who have lost their jobs because of Obama's high taxes, nonstop new laws and regulations, and the massive expense of Obamacare. Obama is destroying the twelfth man; the great American middle class is being wiped off the earth. That empty seat should be a memorial to the vanishing middle class.

When it comes to the economy, Obama summed up the attitude of the arrogant political class when he said to the American people, to the taxpayers, to the business owners of this country, "You didn't build it." The president believes government built it. But he has it all backwards because government earns and produces nothing. Without taxpayers, there is no government.

The government only exists due to the fruits of our labor. Our hard work, creativity, ingenuity, and courage to risk our own money to build businesses and create jobs, creates all the money that funds government. All those wonderful things Obama and Hillary and Bernie and all the other career politicians take credit for are in reality made possible by the taxpayers. We built the schools, not government. We built the highways. We built the airports. We funded the military. We pay government employee salaries and pensions. The American people who paid the taxes BUILT IT. Not the other way around. The politicians and the government built nothing.

My hero, Ronald Reagan, once said, "The nine worst words in the English language are, "I'm from the government and I'm here to help." Barack Obama has spent seven long, destructive, ruinous years proving those words true.

So I'm not here tonight representing "business as usual." This is a very different "State of the Union" speech and a very different vision. I'm here to take the shackles off the American people. I'm here representing "We the People." I'm here representing economic and personal freedom. I'm here to shine a light on another way forward that takes power away from government and returns it where the Founding Fathers believed it belonged—with the American people.

So, start dreaming with me about a country returned to its roots. . . .

A country where you are in charge. . . .

A country where the government doesn't lie to the people. . . .

A country where the President doesn't dump thousands of pages of new regulations on the people on the Friday before every holiday so the people won't notice their rights are being taken away. . . .

A country where new laws aren't 2,000 pages long and voted on by Congress without ever being read. . . .

A country where the president, Congress, and government bureaucrats must live under the exact same laws as the rest of us—and if they break them, they lose their jobs and go to prison just like the rest of us.

A country where the president doesn't run sweatshops filled with lawyers, whose job is to create new ways of killing small business, stealing your hard-earned money, and taking more control over your life. . . .

A country where the government doesn't call you "greedy" for wanting to keep more of your own money, the money you worked for, you sweated for, you risked your life savings for. A place where the government understands it's not their money—it's *your* money. You earned it; it belongs to you. And when they take some of your money, they always say "please" and "thank you." Folks, that's the true American Dream.

The true definition of "greed" is government stealing the money of the people who earned it to redistribute it to those who didn't, in order to buy their votes so they can stay in power. That's greed. That's the root of what's wrong with America. That's why we're failing. That's why the American Dream is dying.

And that's why polls show a majority of Americans no longer believe the American Dream is alive.

Polls show a majority of Americans fear their own government. Polls show a majority of Americans feel like foreigners in their own country. People are angry and enraged because they know the deck is stacked against them. Their government is not just failing them—*it is actively working AGAINST them.*

America has endured seven years of a failed presidency. Almost every problem cited by President Obama in his campaigns has gotten worse under his disastrous leadership. But you didn't hear about those disasters in his State of the Union speech tonight. President Obama, his socialist cabal, the greedy entrenched political class, and the media elite are involved in a cover-up of epic proportions.

Well, it's time to tell the truth. It's time to face the facts of what President Obama and the political class has done to this once great country that is now drowning in almost $19 trillion in debt, whose economy is stuck in quicksand, and whose new job market is reduced to minimum wage jobs, cleaning toilets, mowing lawns, washing dishes, or tending bar—an entire economy built to make the richest among us far richer and the rest of us serfs begging for crumbs.

Whether it is domestic policy, economic policy, foreign policy, or national security policy, the result has been the same—a singularly failed presidency. Whether these failures were created by incompetency, ignorance, or a purposeful attack upon capitalism and American exceptionalism from within the White House, the result has been the devastation of America, especially its once great middle class.

On the other side of Obama, Hillary, Bernie, and their socialist Big Brother cabal stands the Tea Party. The Tea Party has been the most profound political movement in modern political history, making dramatic changes in Congress and state legislatures across our great country. In 2010, the Tea Party provided the energy for Republicans to win the House of Representatives with historic margins. By the time the 2014 elections were over, Republicans had won the most House seats since 1928, taken control of the US Senate, won more state legislatures than at any time since 1928, and elected a near record thirty-one governors.

The reality is that President Obama isn't winning any more than Charlie Sheen is winning. Under Obama's leadership the country has turned to a sea of Republican red at the state and local level. In seven years under Obama, Democrats have lost an unheard of 900+ state legislature seats, twelve governors, sixty-nine House seats, and thirteen Senate seats. Obama is the greatest Republican salesman in history!

Yet the media hides this success. They are scared you might realize big government is failing and those who support it will lose their power.

That's why it's time for the Tea Party to match its Congressional and local level success, and take back the presidency. But just electing any Republican is not the answer. If it was, I'd be giving the Republican response to the State of the Union. I'm representing the Tea Party and the people of America who keep voting Republican and feel like they are getting the shaft. We've got to elect the *right* Republican who will actually cut spending, taxes, and debt; kill Obamacare once and for all; and cut the size and scope of government.

To end this long national nightmare, our next Republican president must pledge to erase everything Obama has done—his agenda, policies, and executive actions. He must also pledge to investigate, prosecute, and convict those found guilty of lying, defrauding, and stealing from the American people.

We can take back the White House and turn around America. It's really not difficult. Just follow the Founding Fathers and put your faith in the people. Just reverse Ronald Reagan's famous saying and repeat after me, "The ten best words in the English language: I'm from the private sector and I'm here to help." The plan I'm about to unveil gives the people more freedom and less government.

Ronald Reagan turned the Jimmy Carter disaster into the greatest economic turnaround—and the longest economic expansion in world history. And Reagan produced this miracle in record time. All he did was dramatically reduce taxes and regulations. He let the people do the rest. The American people have never failed and will never fail. Just get government's boot off our necks and watch us make America great again. Here are the thirteen points. Why thirteen? One for each of the original thirteen colonies. It's time to get back to what made America great. It's time to remember why our Founding Fathers risked everything to fight and die in an American Revolution—to limit the size and scope of government, to protect our God-given rights, and to restore power to the people.

1) Simple. STAND DOWN. We can only turn around this economy if the next president understands government doesn't create jobs. And government doesn't improve the economy. But it can create the environment conducive for economic growth and high-wage, middle-class job creation. You do that by getting government the hell out of the way. STAND DOWN. Streamline it, make it smaller, limit its power, fire incompetent and redundant government employees (we have twenty-two million of them), reduce government employee pensions, reduce taxes so the people have the money, not the government, and rip regulations to shreds. Ronald Reagan proved it works—with twenty million new jobs created almost overnight, by simply cutting taxes on individuals from 70 percent to 28 percent, and dramatically cutting regulations. He did it in the middle of the same kind of economic malaise and misery as we suffer from today. It really is *that* simple.

2) Throw out the entire IRS Code and empower American taxpayers and small business with a flat tax. This tax reform emulates the most successful and prosperous economy in the world—Hong Kong—with a 15 percent flat tax, including deductions for mortgage and charity, and it includes a capital gains tax rate of zero. It's a proven winner. This one Reagan-esque action will empower small businesses across the United States and unleash the greatest economic expansion and job creation in history.

3) Empower American business with the same 15 percent flat tax rate as individuals, plus a one-time "tax holiday" to bring $3 trillion kept offshore back to the United States—an instant windfall to create millions of new jobs. In combination with the new flat tax, pass major tort reform that prevents frivolous lawsuits. That will create jobs instead of lawyer fees.

4) Repeal and replace Obamacare. Obamacare is destroying the US economy—killing jobs, raising taxes, imposing onerous regulations, and raising insurance premium prices and prescription drug prices through the roof for middle-class Americans. This is why GDP growth is zero. This is why manufacturing, shipping, and retail sales are all a disaster. The people are out of money. The US economy cannot recover unless we kill Obamacare. We can't play around the edges. Stick a cross through its heart like a vampire.

The answer is so simple: freedom. Health freedom, health savings accounts, make all health costs tax deductible, and pass tort reform—bankrupt the lawyers, not the American people.

5) Repeal every regulation imposed by both Obama and George W. Bush. The biggest regulation years in history were all under Obama and the last year of the Bush administration. Regulations are strangling the economy.

This is how we create record job growth. It's time for a reset. Let's go back to the year 2000, the last year of Bill Clinton. Our economy was prosperous and growing. Even Democrats should agree on that. Bill Clinton was your President! We lived just fine with the laws in place at that moment in time. I didn't hear any Democrats complaining back then. So why do we need the thousands of costly new regulations on the books since then? Let's erase every regulation passed by both Obama and Bush and reset to the year 2000.

6) Reign in the EPA and reduce job-killing green energy regulations. Do you want to know why we are losing our middle class? In Texas, the *average* energy job pays well over $100,000 per year. Obama's regulations are wiping those high-wage jobs off the map and replacing them with low-wage and part-time jobs. Not only do global warming and green energy regulations kill jobs, but they are also dramatically raising electric bills that the poor and middle class simply can't afford.

The answer is to repeal regulations, pass the Keystone Pipeline, open offshore and on-land drilling of oil and natural gas to make the United States less energy dependent on hostile regimes across the world. In one commonsense move we create high-wage jobs, lower the cost of living, save the middle class, and starve the funding of terrorism.

7) Build the wall and secure our borders with both Mexico and Canada. We must secure the border to protect our country, economy, and the safety and health of our citizens. The only job of the American government is to protect the jobs and wages of AMERICANS. Illegal immigration is overwhelming the system with debt, spending, and entitlements.

Building the wall, securing the border, defunding sanctuary cities until they decide to obey the law, and stopping anyone in our country illegally from collecting welfare, food stamps, or entitlement checks of any kind must be a top priority of the next president.

The wall and a strict e-verify system will also ensure all of our citizens—including *legal* immigrants—will have their jobs and wages protected from illegal immigrants flooding into America competing for the same jobs. The bonus is a secure border that prevents radical Muslim terrorists from entering our nation.

8) Declare a national debt emergency. Our national debt is a disgrace and national security emergency. Debt is a job killer. Just look at the so-called PIGS of Europe: Greece, Spain, Portugal, Italy. Debt has destroyed their economies while creating unemployment rates of 20 percent and above for adults and 50 percent or higher for youth. The president must declare a national emergency to make paying down the debt the top priority of this nation.

We can start by cutting incompetent and redundant government employees (we now have twenty-two million of them) and reducing the salaries and pensions of government employees to the level of the same jobs in the private sector. Why are they a privileged class?

We must audit every government agency from top to bottom and expect government to operate like a successful business. If they aren't performing, close them down.

Finally, the president must fight for a balanced budget amendment. It's time to force Congress—by law—to spend within our means.

9) Term-limit the politicians and hold them accountable. We cannot make America great again unless we fire career politicians. No one has a right to stay in office for life.

And from this day forward, Congress has to live by same rules as the American people. Anything Congress passes applies to them and all government employees as well.

10) We must reform and limit entitlements. Every able-bodied American collecting welfare or any other government entitlement check must be required to work. No more free rides. If you need welfare, you'll get it. No one will starve in America. But you've got to work for that government check. Middle-class Americans get up and go to work each day. Why shouldn't every person on welfare have to do the same thing?

Like the laws in place in the United Kingdom, each family will be limited to a maximum income from all entitlement checks combined. No person or family on welfare should ever again receive more money than a hardworking middle-class family. Otherwise, why would anyone go to work each day?

11) One of the most important issues in America is choice—school choice. The next president needs to repeal Common Core, eliminate the Department of Education, distribute all the federal money back to each state to use as they decide is best, and bring education closer to the only people that matter—the children and their parents, not the teachers' unions. Education should be run from the bottom up, not top down.

The federal dollars we're spending on education now are failing miserably. My daughter was homeschooled and graduated Magna cum Laude from Harvard. Today, she is on full scholarship getting her master's in economics and political science. It doesn't take a teachers' union to raise a child; it takes two great parents who give a damn. No amount of federal money or intervention can change that.

12) We must rein in government agencies like the IRS and NSA. The next president must pledge to investigate, fire, and prosecute anyone who was involved in the persecution of President Obama's political opponents and critics. The IRS works for the taxpayers, not the other way around. Those that deliberately targeted conservatives because of their political beliefs and those that covered up this travesty must be prosecuted and sent to prison. There can never again be harassment by the IRS (or any other government organization) of taxpayers for their political beliefs.

The next president should also pledge to pass privacy laws to limit the NSA's domestic surveillance on American citizens.

13) Maintain a strong national defense. We must restore the greatness of our US military, improve pay, increase morale, and make taking care of our most valuable resource—our veterans—a number one priority. No vet will ever again die on a waiting list at a VA hospital. Everyone involved in that VA scandal must be fired and prosecuted.

And to keep our citizens safe, we must stop the importation of Syrian refugees and immediately cancel the dangerous, reckless, outrageous Iran treaty. We must all agree to make it a national priority to protect and support our great ally, Israel.

And it's time to end that curse called political correctness before it gets us killed. Obama is endangering our children's lives by being unwilling or unable to name our number one enemy and national security threat—Islamic extremism—and we should be determined to destroy this threat with no option off the table.

Finally, we must put military leaders, not lawyers, in charge of war and all rules of engagement.

That's my vision for saving America, saving capitalism, saving American exceptionalism, saving the great American middle class and small business, and turning this Obama

Great Depression into the greatest economic turnaround in history.

But we must recognize this isn't just politics; it's a battle for our survival, for your children's future. Winston Churchill is one of my heroes. He was perhaps the greatest war leader in world history. He should be our role model. His words inspired his nation and the entire world to keep fighting Hitler and the Nazi empire at our darkest moments, when all seemed lost. I want to quote Winston Churchill's words from a speech that rallied the UK people from brink of destruction.

". . . We shall not flag or fail. We shall go on to the end, we shall fight in France, we shall fight on the seas and oceans, we shall fight with growing confidence and growing strength in the air, we shall defend our Island, whatever the cost may be, we shall fight on the beaches, we shall fight on the landing grounds, we shall fight in the fields and in the streets, we shall fight in the hills; we shall never surrender, and even if, which I do not for a moment believe, this Island or a large part of it were subjugated and starving, then our Empire beyond the seas, armed and guarded by the British Fleet, would carry on the struggle."

That, ladies and gentlemen, is how you fight to win. And that's how we win the fight. With every fiber in your body. With every ounce of courage. With heart and will and spirit. We must fight with the power of RELENTLESS. We must never ever, ever give up or give in. We must fight to the end to save this country—the greatest nation in world history.

It's time to relentlessly defend America and American exceptionalism before it's gone *forever.*

I am confident the American people will reject the Barack Obama–Hillary Clinton–Bernie Sanders socialist Big Brother blueprint in the election this November. Then, America can be proud to stand again as that shining city on a hill.

Thank you for listening. Good night. God bless you, and God bless America.

30

The Middle-Class Dream

Once and for All,
Deal with Illegal Immigration

Solving our illegal immigration problem has more to do with saving the predominantly white middle class than any other issue. But as a bonus, it's also a godsend for every black working-class American who can't find a job. All it takes is a simple two-step commonsense plan. The GOP needs to have the brains and the courage to lay out this plan to the American people.

Step 1: This one is simple. Demand we secure the border before anything else gets done. Period. Without securing our porous, crime-ridden, drug-smuggling border first, I'd agree to nothing. Zero. Zip. There is no negotiation. I think Donald Trump has already made this one crystal clear.

It won't be easy without a substantial GOP majority and GOP President Trump. Obama, Hillary, and their amnesty crowd don't want a secure border. It's bad business for Democrats, who rely on poor, uneducated, helpless, dependent voters who support big government. Obama and his socialist cabal want millions of additional illegal immigrants to keep crossing the border, simply because they see them as millions of future Democratic voters.

Obama and Hillary's mentor, Saul Alinsky, famously taught, "The ends justify the means."[1]

That's why Democrats distract us from the truth. They claim the wall is too expensive to build. I'm sure Donald Trump would find spending cuts, bring the wall in *under budget,* and as a "bonus" find a way for Mexico to pay for some or all of it.

But we can create a combination real wall and VIRTUAL WALL with high-tech surveillance. All we need is drones and cameras. Not one person could cross a border protected by drones—with border patrol, or National Guard, or US military positioned to swoop in the moment a drone notifies them that anyone has crossed the border.

Obama has created a Soviet-style surveillance state that snoops on his own law-abiding citizens. The NSA can listen in to all our communications without a warrant, and the IRS intimidates the president's political opponents. Soon our skies will be filled with drones. Funny, and telling, how when it comes to protecting our border, the president suddenly forgets how to put the same high-tech tools to use. Drones can create an impenetrable virtual wall, at a fraction of the cost of a brick-and-mortar wall.

Step 2: Here's the big one. Here's where the GOP is disconnected from its own voters. Conservatives welcome immigrants, *legal ones.* We have no problem letting legal immigrants who want to work and contribute into our country. A major problem with our immigration policy, or at least the way it is implemented, is that there is too little differentiation between those applicants who are willing and able to work and contribute versus those who aren't.

Real immigration reform must deal with this head on. Here is the simple solution: New immigrants must give up the right to welfare and government subsidies. *Forever.* That's the agreement. You can become a legal resident, and if you came into the country legally, you can become a citizen, but only if you give up any right to welfare, food stamps, housing allowances, aid to dependent children, free meals at school, and hundreds of other entitlement programs. Did you come here to work or to collect handouts? That's the key question we should be asking before we let *anyone* into America.

America is generous, but let's not be stupid. We'll let you in, but only if you're here to work. We won't let you in if you're here to mooch off us. I didn't say you have to be rich to get in. But you need to have skills, contacts already here, and a job lined up so you are not a burden from day one.

Why would taxpayers invite strangers into our country to collect handouts that raise our taxes and debt? Why would we invite you in so you can lower our quality of life and that of our children? *We're not THAT dumb, are we?*

Well, actually, under President Obama, **we are.**

The Republican Party should be leading the charge for immigration reform that bans welfare, in return for working and living in this great country. That has to include the "earned income tax credits" that have allowed billions in tax refunds for illegal immigrants who never paid taxes in the first place.[2]

Immigrants who are here to work and contribute will welcome this gift of a lifetime and thank those who propose and support it. So would Democrats if they actually cared about the well-being of immigrants. But they don't. The Obamas and Hillarys of the world only want illegal immigrants who are scared, desperate, poor, and have no skills. That makes them perfect targets for the Democratic Party. That kind of immigrant desperately needs cradle to grave welfare. They will vote loyally for any politician who promises to keep the checks coming.

That's it. That's the plan. As Steve Jobs always said, K.I.S.S.—Keep It Simple Stupid. This is the plan that will fix our immigration problems, expose the Democrats as the hypocrites they are, and win elections for the Republican Party. Because anyone can understand it.

31

Term Limits

I've always thought a crucial solution for saving America is term limits. Every politician should serve exactly two terms—one term in office and one term in prison!

What we all saw on display at the 2016 GOP presidential debates is symbolic of a major problem with America: a bunch of career politicians on the stage and an audience stacked against the only non–career politician, Donald Trump, filled with fat-cat donors, lobbyists, consultants, and DC lawyers. They hate Trump because they can't bribe him. They clearly own all the other candidates lock, stock, and barrel.

The massive chorus of BOOS you heard directed at Trump are proof positive he's the right man to clean up the swamp in Washington, DC. This stranglehold by special interests rooting for crony capitalism and bigger government is clearly what has infested and corrupted our government and ruined our country.

Donald Trump is an outsider. He is the anti-politician. Politically incorrect, willing to tell the raw truth, even if it offends. Willing to say, "YOU'RE FIRED."

That's why the perfect theme for Trump is to brand himself as "THE TERM LIMITS PRESIDENT."

There is a speech I would love to hear him give. It will so excite the American people that Trump will become more

than the next president of the United States. He'll become a
folk hero!

Here is Trump's speech:

> As an outsider running for president, I will spend the next
> eight years in the White House "throwing the bums out." And
> as part of that fight, I will lead the fight for a Constitutional
> amendment to term-limit Washington, DC, politicians.
>
> I am campaigning for president because, like you, I know
> Washington is broken. It's become a place where politicians
> go to line their pockets. Electing a non-politician like me as
> president is a great start, but even with the commitment and
> energy a Trump presidency will bring to the White House,
> it is only a start and will remain an uphill battle against the
> power brokers and political elites.
>
> What is needed is a long-term fix, and that means for-
> ever getting rid of the entrenched political class, who look out
> only for their own best interests, not yours.
>
> **The answer is TERM LIMITS.** Strict term limits, so
> those elected can spend their time looking out for the people
> who elected them, rather than selling their vote to the corrupt
> lobbyists financing their next campaign. Under my proposal
> there will never be a "NEXT CAMPAIGN" for any national
> politician ever again.
>
> Here's the plan: Congresspersons serve only one four-
> year term. Senators serve one six-year term. And you only get
> the one term in *either* house. We'll structure it so every two

years, half of the congresspersons and one-third of the senators will be brand new.

This will ensure we'll see a constant infusion of new citizen politicians who truly are in touch with the people they represent. They will bring new ideas and new energy to fight the government bureaucrats and battle waste, fraud, and outright corruption.

Did you know that right now the average representative has been elected and reelected almost five times and been in office nine years? It's even worse in the Senate, where the average senator has been in office ten years,[1] which is more than a little misleading since more than half of them served several years in the House of Representatives before being elected to the Senate. The 114th Congress convened with more ex-US representatives than at any time since 1899.[2] Quite frankly, it's shameful but shows crystal clear what a good job the entrenched politically elite have done looking out for themselves at your and this great country's expense.

On the campaign trail, I have found that Americans are practical, commonsense people. The argument you are sure to hear against term limits is "the value of experience." That's a con job meant to fool the people into reelecting the same frauds and crooks year after year. Experience at what? Stealing your money and making sure crime and time in DC pays? We don't need that kind of experience.

All you need do is look at the latest obscene federal spending bill where the politicians on both sides of the aisle handed out all the goodies they could to those who will pay to get them reelected, while stealing our children's future by plunging them ever deeper in debt. What a disgrace.

This latest budget will destroy the future of America. And it's bipartisan. Because the crooks are on both sides of the aisle. I'm going to Washington DC to change all that. No wonder the audience of donors, lobbyists, and special interest lawyers booed me so loudly at the presidential debates.

So much for "the value of experience!" That spending bill that bankrupts your children's future was created by "experienced" politicians.

Well, I say, "THROW THE BUMS OUT" and term limits is the way to do it.

The next question I'm sure to be asked is "How can we do it?" It will take a Constitutional amendment, and Congress will never allow that. The answer is a Convention of the States as proposed a few years ago by popular conservative national talk radio host Mark Levin. While hotly fought by career politicians, thirty-six states (particularly those that allow citizen initiatives) have passed term limits for Governor. Twenty-one states voted for term limits for their state legislators (although courts overturned them in six of those states).

While we're at it, term limits for the Supreme Court is undoubtedly also a good thing. How about eight years? Why should anyone serve in any office for life, ruling over our lives?

The fact is folks, it won't be easy and it won't be fast, but as the ancient wisdom says, "A journey of a thousand miles begins with one step." It's time get the ball rolling.

Term limits will be a major focus of my campaign, along with repealing and replacing Obamacare and building a wall to secure our border. A vote for Donald Trump shows your support for killing "business as usual" in Washington, DC.

To "Make America Great Again," we need to kick out the career politicians who think and act as rulers and tyrants and bring back sanity and common sense. I'm Donald Trump, and I want to be your president.

That's a speech that will go a long way to electing President Donald Trump.

32

Send a Message

Send Architects of Obamacare to Prison

Fraud:

Act or course of deception, an intentional concealment, omission, or perversion of truth. . . . Willful fraud is a criminal offense which calls for severe penalties, and its prosecution and punishment (like that of a murder) is not bound by the statute of limitations.[1]

Term limits are a crucial part of this plan to save America and the middle class, too. But there's a part two to term limits. Remember my joke: one term in office and one term in prison. Well, it's no joke! We need to send a message. The dirty politicians who ripped off middle-class Americans need to be punished, or the fraud and theft will continue. There must be consequences. We need to start with Obamacare, because that is the foundation of their plan to bankrupt the middle class and make us dependent on government.

Almost three years ago, I asked at Fox News, "Is President Obama too big to jail?" I was referring primarily to the crime of fraud and misrepresentation used to sell Obamacare.[2]

Later, I publicly compared the fraud and deception used by Obama to sell Obamacare to the fraud committed by TV infomercial scam-artist Kevin Trudeau.[3]

He was convicted in 2014 for using lies and misrepresentation to sell his products on television.[4]

The US government rightfully claimed Trudeau couldn't have sold his product (a book about weight loss) without lying to consumers. The government claimed without Trudeau's lies, deception, and misrepresentation, no one would have bought his book. He was sentenced to ten years in prison.

Lo and behold, we now have proof that Obamacare was sold by Obama and his socialist cabal with the same kind of lies, fraud, and misrepresentation used by Kevin Trudeau. The words of none other than Jonathan Gruber, the MIT professor and architect of Obamacare have come back to haunt the Obama administration (clear as a bell on video).[5]

I'm no lawyer, but it's clear the selling of Obamacare was built on lies, deception, and misrepresentation. Gruber admits (actually brags) that Obamacare could never have passed if the American people knew what was in it.

Gruber brags that the bill was saved by a "lack of transparency." That's a nice way of saying we lied to sell this fraud.

Gruber calls American voters "stupid." Isn't that what con men like Kevin Trudeau and Bernie Madoff think of their victims?

Gruber then admits the bill was written in a "tortured way" to hide the truth: that Obamacare was always designed as a big fat tax to redistribute money. He says if the Congressional Budget Office "scored it" as a tax, it could never have passed into law. So the facts had to be hidden.

Gruber doesn't mention the biggest whopper of all: "If you like your insurance, you can keep it." Obama told this lie while his own internal White House reports showed that up to ninety-three million Americans would lose their insurance because of Obamacare.[6]

Yet Obama kept repeating that famous line to the media and at speeches and rallies across the country. Isn't that the very definition of fraud? Can you imagine if a private-sector CEO told the same lie over and over again in front of TV cameras and large audiences? A jury would take fewer than fifteen minutes to send him to jail for thirty years (or longer).

Obama lied to sell Obamacare to "stupid American voters." How does that differ from Bernie Madoff taking money from gullible investors by telling them he could produce massive returns year after year?

How does that differ from Kevin Trudeau telling TV infomercial viewers that he had a system that made weight loss easy?

All these crooks and scam artists have one thing in common—they needed to lie and misrepresent to get victims to buy into their Ponzi schemes.

Gruber just spilled the beans—on video.[7]

If Obama had truthfully admitted, "This is a massive wealth redistribution scheme," who would have supported it? If Obama had truthfully admitted, "If you like your insurance, there's a darn good chance you'll lose it," who would have supported it?

Or "if you like your doctor, too bad. You'll probably need to find another." Or "if you like your price for health insurance, get ready for the price to double or triple." If Obama had truthfully admitted any of that, he never could have sold Obamacare to the American public. So he had to lie, deceive, and misrepresent. That's the definition of fraud.

Then there's the really sad part of all of this. Madoff is away in prison for life. Trudeau is away in prison for ten years. But neither put a gun to the head of their victims. They simply advertised or promoted. Victims willingly came to them, or bought from them of their own free will. Yet that's still (of course) fraud because victims willingly handed over their money based on lies and deception.

But Obama's crime is far worse. He didn't just lie and misrepresent. Obama sold his scam at gunpoint. No one had free will. Obama forced every American with the force of government and IRS fines to buy his fraudulent product. Obama is a criminal of the highest degree.

And for the purposes of this book, guess who the victims were? They just happen to be the predominantly white middle class and millions of small business owners (who also happen to be 85 percent white according to CNBC). I rest my case on behalf of all the "angry white males" of America. We have every right to be angry. We were defrauded.

It's time to put the architects and salesmen of Obamacare in prison. Kevin Trudeau's act cost about one million consumers a paltry $30 each. No one's life was ruined. Madoff cost a few thousand wealthy investors a few billion dollars. Many lives were ruined.

But Obama is in a league all his own. Obamacare is the biggest fraud in world history. Over time it could cost middle-class consumers trillions of dollars in new taxes, higher premiums, deductibles, copays, and higher prescription drug costs. Or in the case of victims who are terminally ill and lose their insurance altogether, million-dollar bills, or worse— their lives. And how about the job losses and downgrades from full-time to part-time work for millions of American employees.

Now remember the second half of the definition of fraud . . .

Willful fraud is a criminal offense that calls for severe penalties, and its prosecution and punishment (like that of a murder) is not bound by the statute of limitations.[8]

It's time to make the people that committed fraud to sell Obamacare pay. I think life in prison is getting off easy for the pain and loss they've caused to millions of middle-class consumers and patients. We cannot change DC, or change the dysfunctional system, or save the middle class without setting an example by putting the frauds, cheats, crooks, and bad guys away in prison. It'll never change if we don't set an example, right here, right now.

Sadly, Obamacare is only the most obvious and grievous fraud the Obama/Hillary administration has perpetrated on the American people. If Trump is elected as president, you can bet there will be panic among the politicians and bureaucrats who committed fraud to advance the agenda to make us all dependent on government—in particular the architects of the Obamacare and IRS scandals. I'm betting you'll see a long list of midnight pardons issued as Obama leaves office.

Author's Note: For more details about all of my many ideas for turning the GOP into the party of the middle class, please read my book *The Murder of the Middle Class.* You'll see 390 pages of details.

33

Invest in Lead

Remember what I said to start this book? This book is not an attack on any group. Rather it is self-defense because we are under attack. I can think of no greater weapon of self-defense than owning a gun.

My father was a blue-collar butcher who taught me to watch what a man does, not what he says. My father died in 1992, but he must have been looking into a crystal ball.

Obama is the poster boy for saying one thing—and then doing exactly the opposite. Hillary, Bernie, or any liberal do-gooder politician would be no different. It all sounds so good, until, as you've learned in this book they lie—*about everything*. They were taught "The ends justify the means."

So what does this have to do with guns? It's the same story. Every time there's a crisis, big government politicians learn the wrong lesson, come up with the wrong solution, and always use the crisis as a reason to take away our freedoms and grow government bigger.

Now liberals like Obama and Hillary want our guns. Their reasoning is they want to "save" us and protect us. Better grab your gun and your wallet. Bad things happen when government comes to "save" us, and it always costs us.

Obama says he "supports the Second Amendment and doesn't want to take our guns away." He only wants to protect "the children." What a guy! He wants to protect your children with "gun-free zones," even though virtually every mass killing in recent American history has occurred in a "gun-free zone."

Obama wants schools to be "gun-free zones." Meanwhile, Obama's children attend an exclusive private school protected by a security force of armed guards, plus an army of heavily armed Secret Service agents.

Obama also wants your place of business to be disarmed, while he's protected by armed agents and a tall fence around the White House (with steel spikes at the top).[1]

Obama wants to ban assault rifles, while Homeland Security stocks up on assault rifles, armored vehicles, and 1.6 *billion* rounds of hollow point bullets—the kind that explode in your body upon impact.[2]

That's enough for a twenty-year war. The question is: *with whom?*

Is Obama perhaps worried that the inevitable economic collapse produced by his radical spending and debt policies will result in unrest, anarchy and revolution in the streets? Are those 1.6 billion bullets aimed squarely at the middle class of America? Is that why Democrats want Americans disarmed?

Obama says he's being "reasonable" and "moderate," only looking to stop mentally ill people from getting guns. Think about that. We know that just as my father warned, Obama says one thing and does another, so what is his real goal?

Obama is smart and devious. He knows banning guns is a losing argument. So he claims to support guns, while plotting to take our guns away. How? First, by appointing justices to the Supreme Court who are dedicated to overturning the Second Amendment. He's done that with Justices Sotomayor and Kagan. Hillary plans to finish the job, if Donald Trump can be defeated. Then, our gun rights are gone forever.

But Obama and Hillary have more devious plans straight from the Saul Alinsky communist playbook. You don't need to ban guns to disarm the citizens, just tax bullets to the point they're unaffordable. Or order Homeland Security to buy so many billions of rounds that drastic bullet shortages are created. *Voila*—there are no bullets for the citizens' guns.

I've saved the best for last. "Mental illness" is the issue Obama and Hillary will use to fool and disarm American citizens. New York is leading the way. Citizens in New York who have been prescribed antidepressants are now having their guns confiscated. Think about that. We are not talking about people who have criminal records or who have been committed. Yet their guns are being confiscated.

But here's a very important question: How do the police know you've been prescribed these drugs? Aren't our rights to medical privacy being violated?

With Obama and his socialist Nanny State collective, there is always a secret clause or technicality buried inside one thousand or two thousand pages, written in "lawyer-ese." Inside the federal HIPAA policy (Privacy Rule) is a clause, "provide and promote high quality health care to protect the public's health and well-being." Obama and his cronies apparently believe they can use that clause "to protect the public's well-being" to require doctors notify authorities of prescriptions issued for antidepressants and then order immediate confiscation of guns.

Then there's the military. Many vets coming home from Iraq and Afghanistan have suffered some level of stress, fear, depression and PTSD (posttraumatic stress disorder). Aren't they encouraged by their superiors to report their problems and seek help? Now it's being used against them.

I've been contacted by the mother of a soldier who saw his best friend's legs blown off. He suffered a brain injury himself in that same IED explosion. He took meds for a year while recovering from his brain trauma. Now, healed, healthy, and ready to reenter civilian life with a job offer as an armed bodyguard, the army has informed him he is banned from ever owning a gun because of his PTSD. Is this Obama's new scam? Obama and his team of gun grabbers have figured out a way to legally disarm the bravest group of gun owners in the country—returning veterans. These people are the most trained and most likely to own guns. They are also the most likely to lead a battle to protect the citizens from overreach by our own government. Yet if they are ever treated for PTSD, Obama is stripping them of their Second Amendment rights. Nice way to treat our heroes.

Obama, Hillary, and their socialist cabal cannot be trusted. Watch what they do, not what they say. Don't agree? Perhaps you should check with Austin, Texas, Democratic City Councilman Mike Martinez who stated matter-of-factly during a speech that the Obama long-term agenda is a total firearms ban.[3]

Or listen to the words of Hillary Clinton, who admits her goal is to emulate Australia's gun confiscation.[4]

My answer? Join the NRA, get armed, trained, and stock up on ammo. Because the only way to protect our civil rights and save the middle class from being destroyed by an arrogant, out-of-control, overreaching federal government is if the people are armed and the government fears its citizens.

I'm not your typical NRA member. I'm Jewish, New York born and bred, Ivy League-educated, and have been a member of the mainstream media (I started my career as an anchorman and host for CNBC, then called Financial News Network).

Here are the reasons why I am a proud NRA member.

First, I believe it's clear that our politicians have come to all the wrong conclusions. Why would we rush to ban guns, when almost all of our mass murders and most of our violent crimes occur in places with the strictest gun control? Why rush to create more "gun-free zones" when almost all mass shootings occur in "gun-free zones"? This response is idiotic. It's almost as if our own government wants to get us all killed. *Almost.*

The worst violent crime and murder rates in America occur in places like Detroit, Chicago, Cleveland, New Orleans, Baltimore, and Washington, DC. Strict gun control clearly does not work. It only disarms the honest, law-abiding citizens, who are left helpless and defenseless. Criminals never have a problem acquiring guns. Therefore, gun laws are not only useless, they are dangerous.

But don't just look at big cities in America. Let's look across the Atlantic Ocean for the best example. Our friend and ally England has a complete ban on guns. No UK citizen can carry a gun. Period. Not a one. Result? The UK violent crime rate is three and one-third times higher than America. The FBI reports 386 violent crimes per one hundred thousand in the United States. The UK Home Office reports 1,361 violent crimes per one hundred thousand in England. Gun control may be a failure, but the UK experience proves that outright gun bans are an unmitigated disaster.

But this is nothing new. Leftist, big government, Nanny State politicians always come to the wrong conclusion about most issues.

Groucho Marx said it best: "Politics is the art of looking for trouble, finding it everywhere, diagnosing it incorrectly, and applying all the wrong remedies."

Rahm Emanuel put it differently: "Never let a crisis go to waste." Our leftist big government politicians are trying to turn a terrible tragedy into a gun crisis. Their solution is to try to demonize and ban guns. They not only seem hell-bent on bankrupting the middle class, they want us defenseless, too.

Thank goodness the American public has more common sense than the politicians and media big shots. A recent Rasmussen poll shows that while 27 percent think stricter gun control laws are the solution, a dominant 48 percent believe the answer is more action to treat mental health issues.[5]

It is obvious that many Americans agree that guns do much more than kill (in the wrong hands). More often than not, they save lives and prevent violence.

Here are a few proven facts that are too often missing from the gun debate (thanks to Gun Owners of America and ZeroHedge.com for these statistics): Based on a 2000 study, Americans use guns to *defend* themselves from crime and violence 989,883 times annually. Banning guns would leave about one million Americans defenseless from criminals who have no problem acquiring guns illegally.[6]

A nationwide survey reported over a five-year period 3.5 percent of households had a member who used a gun to protect themselves, their family, or their property. This also adds up to about the same one million incidents annually.

Each year, about two hundred thousand women use a gun to defend themselves from a sexual crime or abuse.[7]

The Carter Justice Department found that of more than thirty-two thousand attempted rapes, 32 percent were actually committed. But when a woman was armed with a gun or knife, only 3 percent of the attempted rapes were actually successful.

Newer studies all point toward a figure of 2.5 million: that's the new expert guesstimate of how many times Americans defend themselves from violent criminals each year.

Guns save lives.

Now that we've polled the citizens, how about we see what the felons have to say:

A survey of male felons in 11 state prisons across the United States found that 34 percent had been scared off, wounded, or captured by an armed victim of their crime.

Sixty-nine percent of felons knew other fellow criminals who had been scared off or captured by an armed victim.

Fifty-seven percent of felons polled agreed that "criminals are more worried about meeting an armed victim than they are about running into the police."

Statistical comparisons with other countries show that burglars in the United States are far less apt to enter an occupied home than their foreign counterparts who live in countries where fewer civilians own firearms.

These facts (and many more too voluminous to show here) prove that guns—in the right hands—defend citizens, families, and children. In short, guns save lives.

But for me, it's always been a personal and emotional argument, even more than a factual one. I'm a proud Jewish American. Over six million of my fellow Jews were enslaved, starved, tortured, and then slaughtered by Adolph Hitler. Before it could happen, in 1938, Hitler banned gun ownership for Jews.[8]

That act on November 11, 1938 (one day after the infamous Kristallnacht) was the beginning of the end for German Jews. Millions of Jews were left defenseless from that day forward. Just like the criminals in the studies above, who were far less likely to break into a home or attack a victim, if they feared the victim was armed, Hitler only started his murderous genocide after first ensuring his victims were disarmed, defenseless, and helpless.

The reality is that throughout history, the first thing all tyrants do, is disarm the citizens. Then the mass killings begin.

In the end, we all have to remember our second amendment was not put in place to protect us from criminals and random crime. It was put in place to protect us from our own government.

Or didn't you realize ninety-four million human beings were murdered in the twentieth century by communist governments around the world. Communism was the leading ideological cause of death in the world between 1900 and 2000.[9]

Could it happen here? Well, Obama addressed a class of high school students in Argentina and told them there is no big difference between capitalism and communism. "Just choose from whatever works," he said. I guess he missed the news that ninety-four million souls are dead because of communism.[10]

In every case, communist governments seized all the guns from the citizens before the mass murders began.[11]

Thomas Jefferson put it best:

"When governments fear the people, there is liberty. When the people fear the government, there is tyranny."

Or as Ronald Reagan said, "Trust but verify." Owning a gun and being prepared to use it is the best way to "verify."

I'll be glad to give up my guns when the elites in DC, Manhattan, and Hollywood agree to disarm their bodyguards. . .

. And when President Obama takes the tall fence with spikes and armed bodyguards away from the White House, when Obama starts traveling without armed Secret Service, and when elitists like Obama stop sending their children to safe, exclusive private schools with an armed security force.

I'm a proud card-carrying member of both the NRA (National Rifle Association) and JPFO (Jews for the Preservation of Firearms Ownership).

If we want to keep the American middle class intact, it is in all of our best interests to proudly carry on the American tradition of gun ownership for self-defense. Just always remember, it's not the criminals you should fear most, it's your own government. If you don't believe me, ask the ninety-four million human beings murdered in the past century by their own governments.

If they had a second chance and a voice today, do you think they'd arm themselves? I'll bet the farm on that one.

34

Your Family's Survival

Here is a closing warning to all my readers and fans—straight from my heart (and gut instincts). I believe the storm of a lifetime is coming to our shores. How bad could it get over the coming months or years? No one can answer that. But it's time to prepare for the worst-case scenario. As one of my favorite sayings goes, "Always expect the best but prepare for the worst."

It's time to start preparing, or you'll wind up in line waiting for food, water, and protection from the government, with the rest of the masses of helpless, unprepared citizens. You and I know in our hearts that protection will come late, be insufficient when it comes, or never come at all. Ask the people of New Orleans how quickly help came after Hurricane Katrina. Ask the people of the Philippines how quickly help came after Typhoon Haiyan. Ask the people of Thailand how quickly help came after the massive tsunami.

When the "Big One" hits Los Angeles or San Francisco (or both), how quick do you think government will be there to help you?

What if there's a cyber attack on the banking system, or the Internet? How quickly will the streets become filled with desperate, dangerous, and deadly criminals looking for food and money?

We got very lucky with Ebola, but we may not get lucky with the next pandemic.

In 1929 when the stock market crashed, America was not deeply in debt. A crash today would be far more devastating than the one in 1929. The Fed is out of bullets—there is only so much money you can print, and interest rates can't go much lower than zero.

So it's time to prepare for worst-case scenarios. This mind-set could save your family's life.

In my national bestseller The Ultimate Obama Survival Guide, *I included a very painstakingly detailed chapter about survival preparation, as defined by a Special Forces expert. That chapter and those details for surviving a worst-case scenario could save your life. I encourage you to read that book.*

But here in this book, I wanted to at least include information on where to buy the supplies you'll need. Don't wait, hesitate, or procrastinate. Order the survival supplies you need and store them in a safe place, so they are ready to use when you need them. I personally recommend you buy a minimum of two years' supply of freeze-dried food that lasts up to thirty years for every family member, a minimum of 1,500 calories per person per day. It is important to buy several survival stoves to boil water and cook food. It is also a good idea to buy GMO-free seeds in long-term storage containers.

My favorite company is DrVita.com. They offer vitamins that are nitrogen flushed like freeze-dried foods, to extend shelf life for many years. Most survival food lacks adequate vitamins or minerals. DrVita changes all that. I recommend a two-year supply of DrVita multivitamins and triple strength fish oil.

I've arranged a special deal for the readers of this book. Use the **promo code "WAYNE"** at DrVita.com for special discounts, free shipping, and free gifts for the readers of this book.

I also recommend you purchase several water filters that can remove harmful organisms from thousands of gallons of water. It is also important to stock up on solar recharging panels and devices for batteries along with rechargeable batteries. Emergency LED lighting, communication devices, and radios are very important.

You cannot survive without clean water, food, protection, light, and communication. Further, these are items you can use for barter, as your credit cards, checks, and cash could become worthless in a serious or prolonged crisis. This commonsense strategy could be the difference between life and death.

WAR
Wayne Allyn Root

Sourcing Data:
Vitamins, Food, Survival Supplies, Water Filters, Solar & Stove Sources:
http://drvita.com/911
*Use Promo Code "WAYNE" to get your special discounts, free shipping, and free gifts.

Survival Websites:
http://www.tacticalintelligence.net/blog/top-10-most-influential-survival-and-preparedness-blogs.htm

Weapons:
http://us.glock.com/
http://www.mossberg.com/
http://xcr.robarm.com/

35

Homeschool to Harvard

This "Angry White Male" is a firm believer in school choice and alternative education. My personal choice is home-schooling. And do I have a story that proves it works! But first a word about the government-run public school system.

If you want to know why America is failing, public schools are ground zero. The public school system is no longer about education. The primary purpose of public schools is simple: they are daycare warehouses and brainwashing/indoctrination centers. They exist to keep teachers' unions in business. The more taxpayers spend, the worse the results. Then they point to the horrible results and demand even more. But the one thing that might improve the results is never factored in: competition. It seems competition has worked out pretty well for IBM and Microsoft, for Mercedes and BMW, for Coke and Pepsi. So why not public schools? Because the government and teachers' unions prefer a monopoly on horrible performance. Who cares? After all, it's only the future of our children's lives at stake.

The decline of America can be traced to the dumbing-down of generations of our children. Public schools teach them how to be order takers, not freethinkers. No one is taught how to actually earn a living, start a business, create jobs, fund a business idea, or balance a checkbook. This is why generations of kids are no longer becoming entrepreneurs, and no longer becoming contributing, tax-paying members of society. Public schools are just warehousing kids, preparing them for nothing but a miserable life, menial jobs, and minimal pay.

Am I wrong? Is this just the opinion of a conservative "Angry White Male?" Well, actually no. Every single wealthy Ivy League–educated liberal I know chooses to send their kids to expensive, elite private and prep schools where the bill is $25,000 to $50,000 per year—including President Obama's two precious daughters Sasha and Malia. If public schools are providing a quality education and the cost is zero, why do so many educated liberals choose to waste $25,000 to $50,000 per child on a private school education. *Why indeed?*

Their expensive choice is all you need to know. If someone chooses to spend $25,000 to $50,000 per child versus free, you know exactly what free is worth. Common sense tells us it's got to be worthless. Or smart people would choose a free education every time. Instead, they keep telling you how great public schools are, while the kids fail and graduate unprepared to do anything beyond take orders at McDonald's. Those public schools are plenty good for *your* kids, but not certainly not theirs. As my wise butcher father used to say, "Always watch what a man does, not what he says." Liberals are pathetic hypocrites, but at least they provide a solid road map for you to follow. At all costs, get your kids out of public schools.

The problem is very few middle-class parents can afford private or religious school alternatives for their kids, especially if they have multiple kids. But the good news is I have discovered, tested and PROVEN an alternative that works and costs far less.

My daughter, Dakota Root, was homeschooled here in Las Vegas. Dakota scored perfect SAT scores of 800 in reading and writing. She was a National Merit Scholar and Presidential Scholar nominee. She was accepted by many of this nation's finest universities including Harvard, Stanford, Duke, Columbia, Penn, Brown, Chicago, Virginia, and Cal-Berkeley. She actually had the confidence to turn down an early acceptance offer from the Yale fencing coach before she had gotten any of her other acceptances. *My kid turned down Yale!*

At Harvard, she earned straight A's, not to mention the John Harvard award for being in the top 5 percent of her class. She attended Oxford University in England during her junior year, where she was again at the top of her class. She graduated magna cum laude from Harvard University.

Harvard and Oxford are rated as the two best colleges in the world. Dakota is both a scholar and an athlete. Fencing for the elite Harvard team, she earned Second Team All-Ivy League honors. I am proud to say Dakota is among the best and brightest ever produced by the great state of Nevada. She represents what all of us hope and pray for our children.

But she isn't done. Today, Dakota is on full scholarship for her master's degree in economics and political science.

What makes Dakota's story so remarkable is that she was educated in the same city (Las Vegas) that produces some of the worst public education results in America. So how did it happen? Can others learn from Dakota's story? Can others replicate her remarkable "Homeschool to Harvard" story? *YES, they can!*

Here's the message that politicians need to hear loud and clear: it doesn't take a village, or a government, or a teachers' union to raise a child. It takes a mother and father who give a damn.

Even more impressive, our personal homeschooling success story continues. My two boys have followed almost exactly in Dakota's footsteps. Both tested as "Post High School" (meaning college level) on national exams in sixth grade. I have a gut instinct that my youngest daughter Contessa is the smartest of them all.

So now you have a remarkable pattern. One child achieving those results is fantastic, two is remarkable, but three performing the same way (a decade apart) is proof positive that we are on to something remarkable.

The key is the same as achieving success in all other areas of life: taking action, taking charge, taking personal responsibility and being RELENTLESS. It requires taking back power from government. Dakota Root's story is a testament to the power of the individual and understanding that when it comes to educating our children, "government is too big to succeed."

My advice as the homeschool dad of a Harvard and Oxford superstar scholar and athlete: Take control. Take charge. Take action. Be proactive. Become the CEO of your child's future. "If it's to be, it's up to me."

Dakota's story proves that middle-class parents can save their children's future—but only by taking action and taking control. Only by understanding that parents know what is best for their children, more than government. Dakota's story proves the American Dream is still alive and future generations of the middle class can be saved, if only we'd stop depending on government to save us.

What exactly did we teach Dakota that isn't being taught in the public schools of America? I've got that story laid out in detail in my book *The Ultimate Obama Survival Guide*. If you're a parent and want to learn more about our exact educational program and philosophy, I suggest you read a copy of that book.

Angry White Males Need
Financial Self-Defense

I've saved the best for my very last "Middle-Class Solution" because I want you to do more than survive. I want you and your family to financially THRIVE!

In all my years in school and college, no one ever taught me this lesson. I wish I could go back in time and learn, at the start of my career, about the two most relentless investments in the world. These two unique investments relentlessly protect "what's yours" against all forms of economic crisis. And they relentlessly appreciate in good times and bad like no other investment or asset. These two amazing relentless investments are precious metals (gold and silver) and Rare Color Diamonds.

This country (and most of the world) is in serious economic trouble. Debt is exploding and getting worse every day. Governments are desperate to spend more money, print more money, as well as add to the debt, in order to try to keep the economy afloat. Yes, stock markets are dramatically higher, but that too is based on debt (printing fake money), which you and your children owe back.

But this is not a uniquely American problem. Global debt is almost three times larger than the entire world economy.[1]

We are heading for a cataclysmic event-debt crisis, dollar crisis, currency war, world war, stock market implosion, cyber attack, or widespread economic collapse. Throw in a long overdue massive earthquake in California that could cost hundreds of billions to recover from, and our country is in a world of trouble.

The worst news of all: Interest rates are being kept artificially low, the lowest in history. Any increase in interest rates in the future would result in just interest on the debt exploding to levels that would eat up the entire budget and send the US economy into a death spiral.

- In January 2001, when President George W. Bush took office, the Treasury was paying an average interest rate of 6.620 percent on its marketable debt.

- In January 2009, when Obama took office, the Treasury was paying an average interest rate of 3.116 percent on its marketable debt.

- In January 2016, according to the Treasury, the United States paid an average interest rate of only 2.063 percent on its marketable debt.[2]

Do a little basic math. That means that the average interest rate on the US government's marketable debt is now less than a third of the interest rate we were paying in 2001, when our marketable debt was only about 25 percent of what we owe now. If interest rates were to rise up from the historically low rates they are at now, our economy would be destroyed, the assets that you've worked for your entire life would become worthless, and our children's future would be doomed.

So what's the solution?

Part I: Precious Metals

We start with precious metals (gold and silver). Precious metals are the perfect financial instrument for a book called *Angry White Male*. We should all be angry at what has happened to our country and economy. Both are dysfunctional and in decline. But there is hope, at least for you—because gold and silver are quite simply the most relentless forms of currency in world history.

There are many reasons to lose sleep at night. Our country is headed in the wrong direction. The things that have destroyed every country in world history are big government, big spending, big taxes, big entitlements, and big debt. That last one (debt) is the poison of all poisons. I've already laid out the debt tsunami that America is facing.

Over the past hundred-plus years (since 1913 when the Fed was founded), if you kept your money in dollars, $1 million in cash is now worth about **$41,000** (in today's buying power). The dollar has declined in value by about 96 percent during that period.

But if you had kept your assets in gold, $1 million today would be worth about **$67,000,000** (over a 6,000 percent rise, as of the writing of this book).

I don't know about you, but my math says $67 million beats $41,000 every time.

From January 1, 2000, to December 31, 2013 (fourteen years), gold outperformed every other asset class by a mile. Gold beat stocks, bonds, real estate, and even inflation. By how much? The NASDAQ was up over those fourteen years by 16.40 percent. The S&P 500 was up by 56.50 percent. Gold bullion was up by 446 percent.[3]

Since 2014, gold has been down. But as my investing hero Benjamin Graham said, "Buy low, sell high." Buying gold or silver each time they dip is my definition of a bargain.

Gold has started 2016 on an upward rampage, up over 20 percent as I finished writing this book in June. Understanding the historical role of gold versus debt, many experts believe we are at the start of a thirty-year bull market in gold—what some might call a "Golden Age."

What accounts for gold's over-the-top success for such a long period of time? It's actually pretty simple. Gold is more than an investment, or a form of currency. It's "wealth insurance."

You don't expect to die today, yet you pay for life insurance. You don't expect to be sick today, yet you pay for health insurance. You don't expect to wreck your car, yet you wouldn't even think of getting into your car without auto insurance. Insurance protects you from disaster (an unexpected event that could wipe you out).

In that same way, buying gold is "wealth insurance"— it protects you from overall economic disaster. Gold is your hedge. While paper money issued by reckless governments declines in value, gold holds its value. Gold has served as wealth insurance for thousands of years. It has successfully held its value during major wars, economic collapses, debt crises, hyperinflation, and unrest in the streets.

While the typical investor has slowed their purchase of gold since 2014, the smartest, most sophisticated investors in the world have gone on a gold-buying binge: *central banks.*

In the year 2012, central banks bought more gold than in all the years since 1964 *combined.*[4]

In the year 2013, central banks around the world bought more than $3 trillion of physical gold.[5]

In the year 2014, central banks did it again. They bought 477 tonnes of gold, 17 percent more than in 2013, and the second most gold bought in a year in the past half-century (topped only by 2012).[6]

In 2015, the buying spree continued unabated.[7]

So why isn't any of this in the news? Why isn't it a headline in the media? Why does no one teach you about gold in high school . . . or college . . . or even business school?

If the smartest bankers in the world reach for gold to protect their country's assets, why shouldn't middle-class Americans do the same thing? Why does no one mention that the antidote to a debt crisis is gold?

Here's the most important question of all: If gold rose over 400 percent from 2000 to 2013 due to the massive debt being accumulated by the US government (because of out-of-control spending), why wouldn't gold be an even better investment now that debt is *dramatically* higher both in America and around the world in 2016?

If you understand math, and you know history repeats itself, then you know we have a big problem. This will not end well.

But I come bearing gifts! I have the solution. Knowing how many bad things could happen, the ownership of precious metals should be a crucial part of any portfolio. Keep in mind US tax law now allows you to own precious metals inside your IRA accounts.

Gold and silver are my insurance policy. Gold and silver give me "staying power" in case of disaster or tragedy. Gold and silver protect my family, income, and assets. Gold and silver help me sleep at night. Gold and silver often appreciate, while other forms of investment decline or collapse. Gold and silver are my middle-class weapons of self-defense.

Again for a more detailed look at why gold and silver are so valuable, please read a copy of *The Power of Relentless*. I go into much more detail there.

For more information on how to purchase gold and silver, contact THE authority that I trust:
Swiss America
Website: www.RelentlessGOLD.com
PH: 800 519-6270
Dean Heskin is the President of Swiss America
Dean's personal email: Heskin@SwissAmerica.com

Part II: Rare Color Diamonds
But I'm not done yet. There's a part deux to wealth protection and appreciation. Precious metals have a "kissing cousin."

But if you thought the knowledge about precious metals was obscure in our educational system, try Rare Color Diamonds on for size. The knowledge about this product is literally nonexistent among the masses. But the super-wealthy have a keen understanding of the power of Rare Color Diamonds. Rare Color Diamonds are one of the crucial financial weapons of self-defense that allow the super-wealthy to *stay* super-wealthy! Why shouldn't you take advantage, too?

Rare Color Diamonds are a unique asset class all their own—some have called them "indestructible wealth." This specific and exclusive kind of rare diamond is nothing like the ordinary and common diamonds you buy at a mall jewelry store. The difference is night and day. It's like saying we both own cars, but yours is a Honda and mine is a Rolls Royce. They are in fact both cars, but they are not even in the same universe, right? One is ordinary, common, and inexpensive. The other is exclusive, special, valued, desired, beloved, and very expensive.

Because of their rarity, much like rare collectible coins, or rare works of art, Rare Color Diamonds have proven to hold their value or dramatically appreciate during times of great economic crisis, instability, and uncertainty.

History shows Rare Color Diamonds have been one of the best performing assets during periods of inflation and currency devaluation. Since formal records began in the 1970s, prices for the highest grades of color diamonds have increased in value by an average of between 10 and 15 percent per year (with rarer colors and higher grades enjoying the greatest appreciation).[8]

Perhaps more importantly, the appreciation of Rare Color Diamonds has no direct correlation to stock market or bond prices—thereby giving investors true diversification.

"Rare" is the key. Regular coins that your child keeps in his piggy bank—pennies, nickels, dimes, quarters—never go up in value. A nickel is worth exactly five cents. But rare collectible coins are a very different breed. Just one rare coin from the late 1787 sold at auction in 2014 for $4.58 million. The coin contained 26.66 grams of gold, worth about $400. That's the importance and value of "rarity."[9]

In 2013, a 1794 silver dollar sold for $10 million at auction. An ordinary dollar (the kind you keep in your wallet) may not go very far anymore, but a rare collectible dollar has *ten million times* the value![10]

Don't you wish in all your years of schooling, someone, anyone had taught you about the value of rare collectible assets?

In late 2014, the "Fancy Color Diamond Index" showed a 167 percent appreciation of Rare Color Diamonds since January 2005. This compared to a 58 percent increase in the Dow Jones Industrial Average, 63 percent in the S&P 500, and 82.1 percent increase in London real estate prices. Pink diamonds showed the greatest appreciation—up 360 percent over the past nine years. Clearly a hard asset that you can appreciate, while it is appreciating![11]

Rare Color Diamonds have been a hot commodity, with record prices being achieved. For example, twenty years ago, a fancy intense pink color diamond sold for approximately

$70,000 per carat. Today that same diamond is worth $500,000 per carat. The highest price ever paid for a color diamond was achieved at Sotheby's in 2013 when a pink color diamond sold for $83.2 million.[12]

But there's another aspect to fancy Rare Color Diamonds. Just like gold, they are a "wealth insurance" policy. But Rare Color Diamonds offer a different kind of insurance policy. What if your city, state, or country descends into crisis or chaos? What if you need to leave your home to keep your family safe? Diamonds are the easiest, lightest, and most *portable* asset class on earth.

One tiny Rare Color Diamond, about the size of a button, fits in your shirt pocket. It has a weight that is virtually undetectable. You can fit literally millions of dollars of fancy Rare Color Diamonds in an envelope that weighs about two ounces. It can fit in your briefcase, your pocket, a woman's purse, or even your sock. Try that with 250 pounds of gold, or your twenty-five-unit apartment building! And Rare Color Diamonds are invisible and undetectable by the security machines at the airport. Think about the value of that.

Rare Color Diamonds are a one-of-a-kind *portable* "wealth insurance" policy. Combined with precious metals (gold and silver), they are the most *relentless* middle-class weapons of self-defense in the financial world.

Please note that when anyone acquires Rare Color Diamonds, they should come graded and certified with GIA grading papers and accompanied by a GIA graduate Gemologist appraisal.[13]

Again for a more detailed look at why Rare Color Diamonds are so valuable, please read a copy of *The Power of Relentless*. I go into much more detail there.

For more information on how to purchase Rare Color Diamonds now, contact THE only authority that I trust:
The Diamond Market
PH: 1-877-432-6291
Website: www.thediamondmarket.com
Adam J. Lowe is the president of The Diamond Market; his direct email is: CEO@TheDiamondMarket.com

In Conclusion, Just Be Relentless

I want to close with my philosophy in life. I call it "The Power of Relentless" (the name of my bestselling business book). In the end, success is all about being relentless. Who wants it the most. Who is the most committed, tenacious, and combative. Who has the most spirit, enthusiasm, and will. Who is hungry. My whole life I've been STARVING!

I may not agree with any of the beliefs, policies, or agenda of Obama, but I sure do respect his relentless mind-set. He is relentless in destroying America, American exceptionalism, capitalism, economic freedom, personal responsibility, and Judeo-Christian values. What Obama has accomplished to damage this great country and the great American middle class is remarkable. *Amazing.* A real-life testament to how one man can make a difference, either for good or evil. The key is to set a goal, refuse to accept defeat, and then just be relentless until you achieve your goal. Just keep moving forward. Never look back. Always be pitching (selling your vision), never be bitching. That's Obama. He is the most relentless leftist warrior in modern history.

I saw the same attributes and mind-set in Donald Trump early in the game. I saw the light, the energy, the enthusiasm, the nonstop action, the relentless mind-set, the competitive spirit, the aggressive always-on-the-attack personality, the vision of a winner. That's why I attached my wagon to his star early before anyone else in America besides Donald himself and his family. I was there from day one. I knew I'd found a lion and leader for capitalism, conservatism, and "Always America First."

Relentless will take anyone a long way. As far as they can go. Donald Trump won the GOP nomination against all odds. He beat out the strongest, deepest field of presidential candidates in GOP history, spending almost nothing. He did it with sheer willpower, with pure "Power of Relentless." That's my kind of guy. I'll always fight for that kind of candidate. I'll always stand in his corner.

I'm a pretty relentless guy, too. I've pulled off miracle after miracle in my business careers. Everything every "expert" told me could not be done, I did. I proved them wrong again and again. Nothing is impossible in this world if you have a strong vision, belief in yourself, faith in God, a great plan, and "the Power of Relentless." As one of my heroes Winston Churchill once said, "When you find yourself in hell, keep going." America is in hell right now. We need to keep going, keep fighting, keep attacking relentlessly, keep praying, stay positive, stay on the offensive, and never accept defeat. *Never*.

But in the end, Obama isn't the perfect "model" for relentless. Donald Trump isn't the perfect model for relentless. I'm not the perfect model either. It's my mother's story that is the perfect model, the perfect inspiration for angry white males, conservatives, and capitalists everywhere.

I want to leave you with one final, extremely personal example of RELENTLESS. It is the remarkable, magical, extraordinary story of the last twelve hours of life of my mother, Stella Root.

My mother and father died of cancer twenty-eight days apart in 1992, the toughest year of my life. I spoke at my father's funeral in New York and flew back to my home in California only to get a call a few days later from my sister telling me that our mom had gone into a tailspin after the funeral. Only days later, she was gone. But it was the remarkable last hours of Stella Root's life that I will remember and cherish forever. They drive me to new levels of RELENTLESS in every aspect of my life.

I'll never forget the call I got from my mother's oncologist. "Wayne, I'm sorry to tell you this, but your mom is gone. We've done all the tests. Her brain is dead. We just disconnected life support. Her battle is over. So please don't rush home. We don't want any more tragedies in your family. Take your time, spend time with your family, and come home in a few days. Doctor's orders. Got it?"

My sister Lori grabbed the phone and said, "Don't listen to a word the doctor said. You and I both know Mom and she's not going to die until you get here to say goodbye. So please rush home!"

Lori held my mom's hand the whole night and said over and over again, "Don't die, Wayne is on the way. You can't die until Wayne gets here." It took me about twelve hours to catch the redeye flight from Los Angeles and arrive at my mom's hospital room in Westchester County, New York. Yet when I ran through the door to her room, I heard the most beautiful sound in the world:

Beep . . . beep . . . beep . . . beep

Her heart was still beating twelve hours after doctors disconnected life support. Brilliant doctors and medical science may have already declared her dead, but my mom had other plans. You're not dead because your brain is dead. You're only dead when your heart stops beating. My mother had lived through the night on sheer willpower.

Some might call it a miracle. I simply call it The Power of RELENTLESS.

I hugged my mom, kissed her cheeks, and thanked her for staying alive for those twelve long hours. I told her I loved her, then gave her permission to leave. "It's time to rest now," I told her. "You've fought a great fight. You're amazing. But now you can let go." And within seconds, her heart monitor went beep . . . beeeep . . . beeeeeeep . . . beeeeeeeeeeeep . . . flatline. And she was gone.

How did my mom's heart keep beating for twelve hours after doctors disconnected life support? How did she know I was on the way? How did she know I had arrived in her hospital room? How did she know I gave her permission to let go?

My mother had heart. *Lots of it.* Her story proves nothing is impossible. Her story proves if your heart is big enough, it doesn't even matter if your brain is dead. Heart is what determines your level of success in life, not your brain, not your fancy college degree, not your connections, not your wealth.

That's the power of heart, that's the power of human spirit, that's the power of RELENTLESS! That, ladies and gentlemen, is how you fight to win. With every fiber in your body, with every ounce of courage, with heart and will and spirit. We must fight with the power of RELENTLESS. We must never ever, ever give up, or give in. We must fight to the end to save this country—the greatest nation in world history. It's time to relentlessly defend America and American exceptionalism—before it's gone *forever.*

The next president, Donald J. Trump, has a historic opportunity to reset and rebuild. Hopefully, he will look to implement some of the solutions I have laid out in this book.

By giving the power back to the American people, and getting government out of the way, we can enjoy another Ronald Reagan–like turnaround, expansion, and American renaissance. Then America can be proud to stand again as that shining city on a hill.

Always turn to the American people, the taxpayers, and small business to save America. They've never failed us, and they never will.

The battle is far from over. As a matter of fact, it's just beginning. And there is only one choice: VICTORY. The middle class can come back from death. The battle is not over. As a matter of fact, it is just beginning. It's time to be relentless.

It's time to fight like cornered wolverines. It's time to fight like America's existence depends on it. It's time to fight like your children's future depends on it. *Because it does.*

Now let's go take back America!

Thank you for listening. God bless you, and God bless America.

Acknowledgments

L et me start with God. God is my foundation, my moti-vation, and my source of inspiration. I pray to God to start every day. I prayed to God for the creativity and wisdom to write this book. I now pray that this book will empower, educate, enrich, and elevate the lives of every reader. I hope (and pray) that this book encourages Americans to fight for smaller government, reduced spending, lower taxes, more economic and personal freedom, and more respect for the Constitution. I pray that the taxpayers, capitalists, and patri-ots are able to take back this country from those looking to destroy it.

Now I want thank a few friends and family who were instrumental in my ability to write this book.

First, I want to thank my publisher, including Tony Lyons, Joe Craig, and my editor, Mike Lewis. I am forever grateful for all of your faith, professionalism, work ethic, and teamwork.

Doug Miller is my best friend and mentor of the past thirty-three years. Doug is a Nebraska farm boy turned Stan-ford MBA who specialized in turning around companies. We desperately need people like Doug to turn around the US economy. Unfortunately, we have the Obamas of the world instead. What a tragedy.

All those many years ago (1983), Doug was the first adult to ever believe in me and my talents. He saw tremendous potential and then helped turn that potential into real achievements over the next three decades. I can never repay my debt of gratitude. Everyone needs a friend and mentor like Doug Miller. Doug reviewed and edited every word I wrote in this book. His talents and creative ideas can be found throughout.

"Team Root" is fueled by the world's greatest publicist, Sandy Frazier; my personal attorney and great friend of twenty-five years, Lee Sacks; and my accountant of twenty-six years, Allyn Moskowitz. All of your friendship, advice, and counsel have made all the hard work and struggles worthwhile.

Thanks to a few personal friends who gave me great inspiration for this book. Lee Lipton, whose friendship, counsel, and daily rants about politics inspire and motivate me! Lee's ideas can be found in so much of what I write.

Special thanks to Doug Fleming, my high school principal, who saw the light in me in 1977 and changed my life; Arnie Rosenthal, who saw the raw potential in me and hired me at the age of twenty-six to become an anchorman at CNBC (then known as Financial News Network); and more recently, Edward Stolz took a chance and gave me my start as a conservative talk radio host on his great KBET (790 Talk) radio station in Las Vegas. Thank you all for your friendship, mentorship, and vision.

Thanks to my political heroes who inspired me from a young age: Barry Goldwater, Ronald Reagan, Ron Paul, and Jack Kemp. Thank you for your heroism and inspiration.

I hope and pray for President Donald Trump to carry on your conservative-capitalist traditions in 2016.

I saved the best for last—my family. Thank you to Debra for giving me the four most perfect children in the world. Thank you to my children Dakota (twenty-four), Hudson (sixteen), Remington (twelve), and Contessa (eight). Hudson gets special kudos for directing, producing, and editing all of my videos since the age of nine. This kid will be a superstar producer and director of TV and movies someday. My amazing children make my life worth living, make all the work seem effortless, and all the struggles seem like a walk in the park. You are the lights of my life. Everything I do, I do for you.

Wayne Allyn Root,
Las Vegas, Nevada
June 2016

W.A.R. Story

The Bio of Wayne Allyn Root

Wayne has been branded by media across the globe as "Mr. Relentless" and "the Capitalist Evangelist." Starting out as a blue-collar S.O.B. (son of a butcher) and small businessman, this real-life Renaissance man has achieved remarkable levels of success in the fields of business, politics, media, television, sports, and publishing. He is a CEO, serial entrepreneur, national media personality, bestselling author, international business speaker, television producer, syndicated columnist and popular talk radio host. His show "WAR Now: The Wayne Allyn Root Show" is the leading conservative talk show in Las Vegas, with plans to syndicate nationwide in the coming months. Wayne is a former Libertarian vice presidential nominee, Fox News regular, and political commentator.

Wayne is the author of eleven books, including three national bestsellers, and five Amazon bestsellers. His book, *The Ultimate Obama Survival Guide* was the number one political bestseller in bookstores, and finished 2013 as one of the Top Ten hardcover political bestsellers in America. *The Power of Relentless* hit number one on the CEO-READ business bestseller list in 2015. Steve Forbes named it as one of the eight best business books of the year in the November issue of *Forbes*.

Wayne is one of the most popular syndicated columnists in the political world, with millions of readers at sites like FoxNews, Breitbart, The Blaze, TownHall, WorldNetDaily, *Forbes,* and the *Washington Times.*

On the business side, Wayne is an international speaker, keynoting business conferences in places like New York, Chicago, Los Angeles, Vancouver, Honolulu, Maui, London, Amsterdam, Milan, Rome, Singapore, Costa Rica, Jamaica, Puerto Rico, and South Africa. He has spoken to business audiences as large as ten thousand, as well as political audiences as large as forty thousand.

Wayne serves as spokesman and "chief rainmaker" for multiple national and international companies. He is recognized as one of the world's foremost authorities on entrepreneurship, salesmanship, leadership, sales, marketing, promotion, celebrity branding, networking, and media credibility.

As a prolific television producer, Wayne has created and executive produced many hit television series, including the number one hit show on Travel Channel and his latest reality TV show *Las Vegas Law* on Investigation Discovery.

Wayne resides in the suburbs of Las Vegas, Nevada, and is the father of four beautiful children, including his oldest, Dakota Root, a recent Magna cum Laude graduate of Harvard and Oxford Universities.

CONTACTING WAYNE:

- Wayne is in the national and international media 24/7/364 (he takes off for Christmas).

- Wayne is a spokesman for many companies, both big and small. He is the face, voice, and host of their TV, radio, and Internet advertising campaigns.
- Wayne is a speaker at business conferences, personal development events, and corporate conventions, as well as presenting all-day branding, marketing, and sales seminars across the globe.
- Wayne is a speaker at GOP, conservative, Tea Party, and college Republican events.
- Wayne is always looking for unique deals and opportunities.

To contact Wayne:

Wayne Allyn Root

ROOTforAmerica.com

WayneRoot.com

RelentlessROOT.com

PHONE: 702-407-5548

Toll Free (888) 444-ROOT (7668)

EMAIL:

Wayne@ROOTforAmerica.com

or

WayneRoot@gmail.com

MAILING ADDRESS:

2505 Anthem Village Drive Ste 318

Henderson, NV 89052

Endnotes

Introduction

1. http://legalinsurrection.com/2014/10/hillary-clinton-businesses-dont-create-jobs-gubmint-does/
2. http://www.cnbc.com/2014/05/12/minorities-the-force-fueling-small-business-growth.html

Chapter 1

1. https://www.atr.org/obama-has-proposed-442-tax-hikes-taking-office
2. http://www.heritage.org/federalbudget/top10-percent-income-earners
3. http://www.cnbc.com/id/101264757

Chapter 2

1. http://www.pewsocialtrends.org/files/2010/10/Four-middle-classes.pdf

Chapter 3

1. http://nypost.com/2016/06/03/ugly-jobs-report-is-even-worse-than-it-looks/
2. http://www.zerohedge.com/news/2016-06-03/payrolls-huge-miss-only-38000-jobs-added-may-worst-september-2010
3. http://www.bizjournals.com/washington/breaking_ground/2014/12/districts-population-booming-approaches-660-000.html
4. http://www.breitbart.com/big-government/2015/05/08/all-net-employment-gains-among-women-went-to-foreign-born-since-recession/
5. http://theeconomiccollapseblog.com/archives/undeniable-evidence-that-the-real-economy-is-already-in-recession-mode

6. http://www.zerohedge.com/news/2015-09-16/obamas-recovery-just-9-charts; http://www.zerohedge.com/news/2016-06-03/these-are-9-zero-hedge-charts-showing-obamas-recovery-angered-washington-post

7. http://www.thegatewaypundit.com/2016/04/simply-worst-obama-first-president-ever-not-see-single-year-3-gdp/

8. http://www.thegatewaypundit.com/2016/04/simply-worst-obama-first-president-ever-not-see-single-year-3-gdp/

9. http://www.realclearmarkets.com/articles/2016/02/01/barack_obamas_sad_record_on_economic_growth_101987.html

10. http://www.realclearmarkets.com/articles/2016/02/01/barack_obamas_sad_record_on_economic_growth_101987.html

11. http://www.washingtonpost.com/blogs/wonkblog/wp/2014/05/05/u-s-businesses-are-being-destroyed-faster-than-theyre-being-created/?hpid=z5

12. http://personalliberty.com/2013/10/25/more-americans-on-government-entitlement-than-working-full-time/

13. http://www.zerohedge.com/news/2016-06-03/13-23-co-ops-created-under-obamacare-have-failed

14. http://www.zerohedge.com/news/2013-08-05/40-us-workers-now-earn-less-1968-minimum-wage

15. http://endoftheamericandream.com/archives/the-real-unemployment-rate-in-20-of-american-families-everyone-is-unemployed

16. http://www.zerohedge.com/news/2016-06-03/payrolls-huge-miss-only-38000-jobs-added-may-worst-september-2010

17. http://www.zerohedge.com/news/2016-05-24/more-young-americans-live-their-parents-any-time-great-depression

18. http://www.zerohedge.com/news/2016-04-07/shocking-statistic-over-40-student-borrowers-dont-make-payments

19. http://www.cbsnews.com/news/most-americans-cant-handle-a-500-surprise-bill/

20. http://www.factcheck.org/2016/01/obamas-numbers-january-2016-update/

21. http://www.politifact.com/truth-o-meter/statements/2014/may/28/facebook-posts/social-media-meme-says-75-have-joined-food-stamp-r/

22. http://www.foxnews.com/politics/2016/01/18/clinton-embraces-obama-in-final-stretch-fueling-gop-claims-seeking-3rd-term.html

Chapter 4

1. https://www.youtube.com/watch?v=yefOzZrHqBk&feature=youtu.be

2. http://nypost.com/2016/06/03/ugly-jobs-report-is-even-worse-than-it-looks/

3. https://en.wikipedia.org/wiki/Vast_right-wing_conspiracy

4. http://www.breitbart.com/2016-presidential-race/2016/06/05/scott-adams-hillary-campaign-signaling-its-morally-justified-to-assassinate-trump-likely-to-trigger-a-race-war/

5. http://www.washingtonexaminer.com/harry-reid-is-proud-he-lied-about-mitt-romneys-taxes/article/2562300

6. https://www.youtube.com/watch?v=9FnO3igOkOk

Chapter 5

1. https://en.wikipedia.org/wiki/Cloward–Piven_strategy

2. http://www.fairus.org/DocServer/ObamaTimeline_2016.pdf

3. http://www.dailywire.com/news/3186/obama-tells-border-agents-stand-down-hank-berrien

4. http://www.amren.com/news/2015/02/homeland-security-sets-up-obama-amnesty-complaint-hotlines-for-illegals

5. http://www.usatoday.com/story/news/politics/2014/06/06/obama-immigration-lawyers-children-border/10060725/

6. http://www.breitbart.com/big-government/2015/11/20/report-obama-80-percent-illegals-shielded-deportation

7. http://www.breitbart.com/big-government/2014/01/14/omnibus-spending-bill-continues-funding-food-stamp-ads-in-mexico-despite-appropriations-committee-claims-of-prohibition/

8. http://www.usnews.com/opinion/articles/2015/02/20/rudy-giuliani-says-obama-doesnt-love-america

9. http://townhall.com/columnists/dennisprager/2015/03/17/why-uc-students-voted-to-remove-american-flag-n1971676

10. http://www.dailymail.co.uk/news/article-2269938/France-totally-bankrupt-jobs-minister-admits-concerns-grow-Hollandes-tax-spend-policies.html

11. https://en.wikipedia.org/wiki/Decline_of_Detroit

12. http://www.conservativeusa.net/10planksofcommunism.htm

13. http://www.theblaze.com/stories/2015/02/18/obama-we-have-to-address-grievances-terrorists-exploit/

14. http://www.forbes.com/sites/robertwood/2015/03/09/tax-refunds-to-illegals-under-obama-immigration-action-would-be-stopped-by-bill/

15. https://grabien.com/story.php?id=22077

Chapter 6

1. http://www.thegatewaypundit.com/2013/05/breaking-obama-irs-scandal-widens-conservative-activists-and-businesses-targeted-too/

2. http://www.theblaze.com/contributions/there-is-no-more-doubt-i-have-the-proof-that-ties-obama-and-the-democratic-party-to-the-irs-scandal/

3. http://bernardgoldberg.com/traffic-jam-important-irs-scandal/

4. http://www.cfr.org/financial-crises/credit-rating-controversy/p22328

Chapter 8

1. http://www.pewsocialtrends.org/2016/05/11/americas-shrinking-middle-class-a-close-look-at-changes-within-metropolitan-areas/

2. https://www.washingtonpost.com/news/wonk/wp/2016/05/22/a-very-bad-sign-for-all-but-americas-biggest-cities

3. https://www.washingtonpost.com/news/wonk/wp/2016/05/22/a-very-bad-sign-for-all-but-americas-biggest-cities

4. http://www.washingtonexaminer.com/illegal-immigrant-households-get-5692-in-welfare-1261-more-than-american-families/article/2590744

Chapter 10

1. http://www.zerohedge.com/news/2016-06-03/13-23-co-ops-created-under-obamacare-have-failed
2. http://www.atr.org/failed-obamacare-state-exchanges-may-cost-taxpayers-millions-more
3. https://pjmedia.com/blog/doctors-abandoning-private-practice-in-droves-to-work-at-hospitals
4. http://cnsnews.com/news/article/uk-s-national-health-service-going-broke-british-docs-say-it-s-worse-communist-china

Chapter 11

1. https://www.psychologytoday.com/blog/reading-between-the-headlines/201305/white-middle-age-suicide-in-america-skyrockets
2. http://www.cato.org/blog/venezuela-reaches-final-stage-socialism-no-toilet-paper
3. http://www.forbes.com/sites/maggiemcgrath/2016/01/06/63-of-americans-dont-have-enough-savings-to-cover-a-500-emergency/#188613536dde
4. http://www.pbs.org/newshour/making-sense/todays-racial-wealth-gap-is-wider-than-in-the-1960s/
5. http://www.rasmussenreports.com/public_content/politics/general_politics/august_2015/has_obama_widened_the_racial_divide
6. http://www.usatoday.com/story/news/politics/2015/11/02/obama-tells-federal-agencies-ban-box-federal-job-applications/75050792/
7. http://www.breitbart.com/big-government/2016/04/05/obama-racist-for-landlords-not-to-rent-to-criminals/
8. http://www.westernjournalism.com/muslim-immigration-u-s-staggering-evidence-obama-attempting-change-america/
9. https://muslimstatistics.wordpress.com/2015/09/14/usa-muslim-refugees-91-4-on-food-stamps-68-3-on-cash-welfare/
10. http://www.washingtontimes.com/news/2016/apr/22/illegal-immigrant-families-set-record-pace-2016/
11. http://themostimportantnews.com/archives/the-number-of-illegal-immigrants-entering-texas-is-greater-than-the-number-of-babies-born

12. http://donaldtrumpnews.co/news/obama-cuts-2-6-billion-veterans-allocating-4-5-billion-syrian-migrants-moving-america/

13. https://thehornnews.com/obama-18000-set-aside-illegals/

14. http://theeconomiccollapseblog.com/archives/illegal-immigration-and-gangs-someday-our-cities-will-burn-because-we-didnt-protect-our-borders_

15. http://theeconomiccollapseblog.com/archives/illegal-immigration-and-gangs-someday-our-cities-will-burn-because-we-didnt-protect-our-borders

16. http://cnsnews.com/commentary/terence-p-jeffrey/obama-claims-power-make-illegal-immigrants-eligible-social-security

17. http://www.breitbart.com/big-government/2016/04/07/chart-u-s-admits-twice-number-migrants-muslim-world-europe/

18. http://www.washingtonexaminer.com/bienvenido-cubans-handed-cash-social-security-card-food-stamps-medicaid-at-u.s.-border/article/2587097

19. http://www.breitbart.com/tech/2016/05/28/zucked-silicon-valley-scared-death-trump-part-1/

20. http://www.foxnews.com/politics/2016/04/23/republicans-virginia-gov-mcauliffe-restored-felon-voting-rights-to-help-clinton-political-opportunism.html?intcmp=hpbt2

21. https://www.washingtonpost.com/news/post-nation/wp/2016/04/22/about-200000-convicted-felons-in-virginia-will-now-have-the-right-to-vote-in-november/

Chapter 12

1. http://www.nbcnewyork.com/news/local/First-Lady--381799061.html

2. http://www.reviewjournal.com/business/casinos-gaming/macau-sends-las-vegas-sands-revenue-profit-down-15

3. http://amigobulls.com/stocks/LVS/cash-flow/annual

4. http://www.fool.com/investing/general/2015/01/17/can-you-guess-which-las-vegas-casino-makes-the-mos.aspx

5. http://www.wsj.com/articles/wynn-resorts-reports-lower-profit-revenue-as-it-is-dragged-down-by-macau-1455230040

6. http://individual-contributors.insidegov.com/d/c/Gary-Loveman

7. http://fortune.com/2015/06/05/caesars-losing-las-vegas/

8. http://www.reviewjournal.com/business/casinos-gaming/caesars-cuts-net-loss-fourth-quarter

9. http://vegasinc.com/business/gaming/2016/may/05/caesars-entertainment-reports-revenue-increase-308/

10. http://nypost.com/2013/11/01/debt-ridden-caesars-buried-in-financial-woes/

11. http://vegasinc.com/business/gaming/2014/nov/21/sorting-out-caesars-how-company-slid-distress-and-/

12. https://www.thestreet.com/story/13227774/1/caesars-entertainment-czr-stock-plummeting-amid-debt-troubles.html

13. http://marketrealist.com/2014/09/caesars-entertainment-massive-24-billion-debt/

14. http://fortune.com/2015/06/05/caesars-losing-las-vegas/

Chapter 13

1. http://townhall.com/tipsheet/kevinglass/2014/06/15/chelsea-clinton-had-a-600000-salary-with-nbc-news-n1851370

2. http://hosted.ap.org/dynamic/stories/E/EU_REL_POPE_TRUMP? SITE=AP&SECTION=HOME&TEMPLATE=DEFAULTHi

3. http://www.theamericanmirror.com/photos-pope-calls-for-us-to-embrace-illegals-while-maintaining-massive-wall-around-vatican/

4. http://www.theblaze.com/stories/2013/11/11/does-a-border-fence-work-check-out-the-dramatic-change-after-israel-put-one-up/

5. https://en.wikipedia.org/wiki/Israeli_West_Bank_barrier

Chapter 14

1. https://www.washingtonpost.com/news/morning-mix/wp/2016/06/03/ugly-bloody-scenes-in-san-jose-as-protesters-attack-trump-supporters-outside-rally/

2. http://www.thegatewaypundit.com/2016/06/san-jose-police-chief-fire-allowing-attacks-trump-supporters-affiliated-la-raza/

3. http://www.wnd.com/2015/12/kill-trump-enraged-left-calls-for-trumps-assassination/

4. http://www.breitbart.com/big-journalism/2016/02/25/new-york-times-writer-jokes-trump-campaign-ends-with-assassination-attempt/

5. http://talkingpointsmemo.com/livewire/vox-editor-suspended-encouraging-riots-trump-rallies

6. http://www.thegatewaypundit.com/2016/04/media-cheers-rap-video-calls-assassination-donald-trump-video/

7. http://newsbusters.org/blogs/nb/kristine-marsh/2016/02/15/12-tweets-liberal-journalists-celebrating-scalias-death

8. http://www.zerohedge.com/news/2016-03-20/black-cop-exposes-anti-trump-protesters-most-hateful-evil-people-ever

9. http://www.infowars.com/soros-funded-moveon-org-takes-credit-for-violence-in-chicago/

10. http://www.breitbart.com/big-government/2016/03/16/anti-israel-black-lives-matter-activist-is-hell-bent-on-inciting-riots-over-trump/

11. http://www.campusreform.org/?ID=7174

12. http://heatst.com/uk/straight-white-men-banned-from-equality-conference/

13. http://www.armytimes.com/story/military/2016/05/10/west-point-cadet-photo-inappropriate-but-not-political/84196326/

Chapter 15

1. http://www.nbcnewyork.com/news/local/Eric-Garner-Manhattan-Dead-Cops-Video-Millions-March-Protest-285805731.html

2. http://www.bjs.gov/content/pub/pdf/htus8008.pdf

3. http://www.breitbart.com/big-government/2014/08/22/eric-holders-fair-investigation-in-ferguson/

4. http://topconservativenews.com/2014/11/black-teens-beat-white-motorist-to-death-with-a-hammer-in-st-louis/; http://topright-news.com/?p=7451

5. http://nypost.com/2014/04/12/sharpton-was-eager-to-sell-coke-in-the-80s-pal/;https://www.youtube.com/watch?v=imnAK0pV-7w...

6. http://time.com/53389/al-sharpton-informant-fbi-mafia

7. http://www.nytimes.com/2013/06/03/booming/revisiting-the-tawana-brawley-rape-scandal.html?_r=0

8. http://www.mediaite.com/online/ny-times-report-al-sharpton-owes-more-than-4-million-in-taxes/

9. http://www.rickwells.us/krauthammer-81-sharpton-white-house-visits-obama-agrees-with-using-him-as-spokesperson-a-mistake/

10. http://www.amren.com/news/2014/08/how-al-sharpton-became-obamas-go-to-man-on-race/

11. http://www.washingtonpost.com/blogs/the-fix/wp/2014/04/15/everything-you-need-to-know-about-the-long-fight-between-cliven-bundy-and-the-federal-government/

12. http://nypost.com/2015/01/04/how-sharpton-gets-paid-to-not-cry-racism-at-corporations/

13. http://www.reviewjournal.com/news/las-vegas/henderson-couple-describes-bombing-brussels-airport

14. http://www.washingtonexaminer.com/obama-does-the-wave-with-castro-in-cuba-after-brussels-terror-attacks/article/2586524

15. https://www.theguardian.com/world/2009/nov/18/political-repression-raul-castro

16. http://www.dailymail.co.uk/news/article-3504209/Obama-pressure-return-home-giving-40-minute-speech-Cuba-addressed-Brussels-terror-attack-just-one-minute.html

17. http://www.dailymail.co.uk/news/article-3506643/IS-trains-400-fighters-attack-Europe-wave-bloodshed.html

18. http://www.cnn.com/2016/03/23/politics/obama-dancing-tango-argentina/

19. https://pjmedia.com/trending/2016/03/25/obama-no-difference-between-capitalism-and-communism/

Chapter 17

1. http://abcnews.go.com/US/wireStory/north-carolina-governor-leads-lawsuit-lgbt-rights-38981667

2. http://thefederalist.com/2016/05/13/obama-threatens-schools-let-men-in-the-little-girls-room-or-else/

3. http://www.breitbart.com/tech/2015/12/27/nyc-will-fine-you-250000-for-misgendering-a-transsexual/
4. http://overpassesforamerica.com/?p=28738

Chapter 18
1. https://www.youtube.com/watch?v=wfl55GgHr5E
2. http://www.forbes.com/sites/theapothecary/2013/10/31/obama-officials-in-2010-93-million-americans-will-be-unable-to-keep-their-health-plans-under-obamacare/
3. http://www.washingtontimes.com/news/2014/oct/28/obamacare-sends-health-premiums-skyrocketing-by-as/?page=all
4. http://eaglerising.com/14513/smoking-gun-benghazi-documents-show-state-department-lied
5. https://www.youtube.com/watch?v=1kuTG19Cu_Q
6. http://spectator.org/articles/36529/gospel-according-wright
7. https://www.youtube.com/watch?v=UnlRrxXv-v8
8. http://www.cnsnews.com/news/article/barbara-boland/pew-study-christians-are-world-s-most-oppressed-religious-group
9. http://global.christianpost.com/news/obama-admin-criticized-for-joke-over-christians-attacked-in-egypt-103059
10. http://www.foxnews.com/opinion/2014/01/06/lawmakers-accuse-va-disrespecting-christians
11. http://www.usnews.com/opinion/articles/2015/02/19/obama-wont-link-islamic-state-extremism-to-religion
12. http://www.westernjournalism.com/obama-still-refuses-admit-isis-islamic/
13. http://nypost.com/2016/04/02/white-house-doctors-video-to-remove-islamic-terrorism-quote/
14. http://www.breitbart.com/big-government/2016/06/17/obama-admin-pace-issue-one-million-green-cards-migrants-majority-muslim-countries/
15. http://www.breitbart.com/big-government/2016/04/07/chart-u-s-admits-twice-number-migrants-muslim-world-europe/

16. http://www.breitbart.com/national-security/2015/06/24/shock-poll-51-of-american-muslims-want-sharia-25-okay-with-violence-against-americans/

17. http://www.breitbart.com/big-government/2015/09/10/more-than-90-percent-of-middle-eastern-refugees-on-food-stamps/

18. http://www.nationalinterest.org/blog/the-buzz/we're-losing-the-war-against-isis-iraq-13848

19. http://www.christiantoday.com/article/27.iraqi.christians.face.deportation.in.u.s.while.obama.offers.asylum.to.thousands.of.muslims.from.syria/71278.htm

20. http://www.bloomberg.com/news/articles/2015-11-22/russia-calls-for-un-brokered-moves-in-fighting-terror-ifx-says

21. http://conservativebyte.com/2015/11/u-s-pilots-obama-blocks-75-of-islamic-state-strikes/

22. http://www.breitbart.com/biggovernment/2015/11/18/report-8-syrians-caught-at-texas-border-in-laredo/

23. http://m.sandiegoreader.com/news/2015/nov/16/ticker-middle-easterners-baja-border-patrol/?templates=mobile

24. http://www.frontpagemag.com/fpm/260814/post-paris-obama-doubles-down-more-refugees-coming-robert-spencer

25. http://www.breitbart.com/big-government/2016/06/16/441-syrian-refugees-admitted-u-s-since-orlando-attack-dozens-fl/

26. http://www.cnsnews.com/news/article/patrick-goodenough/syria-refugee-surge-picks-steam-451-admitted-april-one-christian-440

27. http://www.express.co.uk/news/world/555434/Islamic-State-ISIS-Smuggler-THOUSANDS-Extremists-into-Europe-Refugees

28. http://www.jihadwatch.org/2015/10/dhs-confesses-no-databases-exist-to-vet-syrian-refugees

29. http://www.motherjones.com/mojo/2015/11/state-department-reminds-republican-governors-stop-refugees

30. http://www.foxnews.com/politics/2015/11/18/obama-threatens-to-veto-bill-strengthening-syrian-refugee-screening/?intcmp=hpbt2

31. http://www.cnn.com/2015/11/19/politics/house-democrats-refugee-hearings-obama/
32. http://www.dcclothesline.com/2015/09/18/obama-invites-clock-kid-to-white-house-ignores-students-suspended-for-u-s-flag-t-shirts-nerf-guns/
33. http://www.jihadwatch.org/2015/10/eeoc-wins-240000-damages-for-muslim-truckers-fired-for-not-delivering-beer
34. http://www.ibtimes.com/muslims-praise-obama-banning-non-halal-meat-122-federal-prisons-2137136
35. http://www.foxnews.com/politics/2011/07/26/texas-lawmaker-calls-for-congressional-probe-into-ban-christian-prayers-at
36. http://www.christianpost.com/news/military-chaplains-banned-from-using-jesus-name-reciting-bible-lawsuit-filed-in-calif-108734
37. http://skinnyreporter.com/clericsbanned.html
38. http://www.newsmax.com/InsideCover/graham-islam-pentagon-prayer/2010/04/26/id/356950
39. http://www.foxnews.com/opinion/2013/12/24/army-dont-say-christmas
40. http://www.usnews.com/news/politics/articles/2015/08/19/reaction-un-allowing-iran-to-inspect-alleged-nuke-work-site
41. http://www.gatestoneinstitute.org/6225/iran-150-billion-dollars
42. http://www.israelnationalnews.com/News/News.aspx/198164
43. http://directorblue.blogspot.com/2015/10/mission-accomplished-former-obama.html?utm_source=akdart
44. http://nypost.com/2015/09/08/spitting-on-the-constitution-to-pass-the-iran-deal
45. http://www.ijreview.com/2015/11/473634-oreilly-just-comes-right-out-and-asks-is-president-obama-delusional-about-isis/?utm_source=email&utm_medium=owned&utm_campaign=morning-newsletter
46. http://www.therebel.media/video_turkey_fans_boo_and_chant_allahu_akbar_during_moment_of_silence_for_paris_victims_at_soccer_game

Chapter 19

1. http://www.foxnews.com/politics/2015/02/21/mccaul-administra-tion-policy-allowing-syrians-onto-us-soil-is-dangerous

2. http://dcwhispers.com/obama-bringing-100-muslim-immigrants-u-s-per-day/#4IWyb3FTJ7rTTktb.99
3. http://www.frontpagemag.com/point/262449/us-giving-2x-more-green-cards-muslim-migrants-daniel-greenfield
4. http://donaldtrumpnews.co/news/obama-cuts-2-6-billion-veterans-allocating-4-5-billion-syrian-migrants-moving-america/
5. http://townhall.com/tipsheet/katiepavlich/2015/02/18/obama-extremists-have-legitimate-grievances-you-know-n1958902
6. http://nypost.com/2015/02/18/obama-refuses-to-acknowledge-muslim-terrorists-at-summit
7. http://www.dcclothesline.com/2015/02/20/video-white-house-dawah-summit-on-countering-violent-extremism-opens-with-muslim-prayer-no-other-faiths-represented
8. http://www.theblaze.com/stories/2015/02/20/historian-david-barton-takes-apart-obamas-claim-that-islam-has-been-woven-into-the-fabric-of-our-country-since-its-founding
9. http://www.theblaze.com/stories/2015/02/22/obama-wont-meet-netanyahu-but-hes-meeting-this-week-with-the-head-of-this-jihadist-supporting-country

Chapter 20

1. http://www.redstate.com/paulkib/2012/08/21/the-hill-calls-obamas-clinging-to-their-guns-and-religion-comment-a-gaffe/

Chapter 21

1. http://townhall.com/tipsheet/katiepavlich/2016/05/18/censure-resolution-introduced-for-irs-commissioner-n2165087
2. http://thehill.com/policy/healthcare/223578-obamacare-architect-lack-of-transparency-helped-law-pass
3. http://nypost.com/2016/05/21/the-scandal-in-washington-no-one-is-talking-about/
4. http://www.therichest.com/celebnetworth/politician/democrat/harry-reid-net-worth/
5. http://www.nationalreview.com/article/314025/how-did-harry-reid-get-rich-betsy-woodruff

6. http://www.thedailybeast.com/articles/2011/04/26/donald-trump-takes-up-birthers-obama-college-conspiracy-theory.html

7. http://money.cnn.com/2015/06/30/media/donald-trump-mexico/

8. http://www.americanthinker.com/blog/2015/06/donald_trump_when_was_the_last_time_the_us_won_on_a_trade_agreement_.html

9. http://dailycaller.com/2013/10/25/michelle-obamas-princeton-classmate-is-executive-at-company-that-built-obamacare-website/

10. http://www.thefiscaltimes.com/Articles/2014/05/13/Over-5-Billion-and-Counting-Obamacare-Websites

11. https://www.youtube.com/watch?v=iGAdrQ2RpdM

12. http://nypost.com/2013/11/18/census-faked-2012-election-jobs-report/

Chapter 22

1. http://www.breitbart.com/2016-presidential-race/2016/06/07/report-trump-university-judge-linked-group-calls-boycott-trumps-businesses/

Chapter 24

1. https://www.youtube.com/watch?v=hV-05TLiiLU

2. http://www.cnn.com/2015/06/11/politics/trade-deal-secrecy-tpp

3. http://www.breitbart.com/big-government/2015/05/21/sen-hatch-defends-obamatrade-shuts-down-push-for-transparency/

4. http://www.breitbart.com/big-government/2015/06/04/two-members-of-boehners-leadership-team-openly-refuse-to-admit-if-theyve-read-obamatrade/

5. http://www.breitbart.com/big-government/2015/06/11/paul-ryans-pelosi-esque-obamatrade-moment-its-declassified-and-made-public-once-its-agreed-to/

6. http://www.cnn.com/2015/06/11/politics/trade-deal-secrecy-tpp

7. http://www.commondreams.org/views/2015/04/24/trans-pacific-partnership-and-death-republic

8. https://en.wikipedia.org/wiki/Trans-Pacific_Partnership

Chapter 26

1. http://www.usherald.com/maine-welfare-recipients-must-work-for-their-benefits/#.VSVy1M53tiA.facebook
2. http://cnsnews.com/news/article/ali-meyer/food-stamp-beneficiaries-exceed-46000000-40-straight-months
3. http://www.washingtontimes.com/news/2014/nov/25/obama-amnesty-obamacare-clash-businesses-have-3000/?page=all

Chapter 27

1. http://michellemalkin.com/2014/02/14/5-years-later-hows-that-wreckovery-working-out-for-ya/
2. http://nation.foxnews.com/president-obama/2011/06/13/obama-jokes-jobs-council-shovel-ready-was-not-shovel-ready-we-expected

Chapter 28

1. https://en.wikipedia.org/wiki/Tax_Reform_Act_of_1986
2. http://www.nytimes.com/1990/01/17/opinion/the-reagan-boom-greatest-ever.html
3. http://www.forbes.com/sites/peterferrara/2011/05/05/reaganomics-vs-obamanomics-facts-and-figures
4. http://www.washingtonexaminer.com/norquist-blesses-trumps-tax-plan-brings-jobs-jobs-jobs/article/2572929

Chapter 30

1. http://www.crossroad.to/Quotes/communism/alinsky.htm
2. http://www.washingtontimes.com/news/2013/apr/16/collecting-billions-in-a-loophole-fraudulent-tax-r/

Chapter 31

1. http://www.cnn.com/2013/06/07/politics/btn-congressional-tenure/
2. http://www.cnn.com/2013/06/07/politics/btn-congressional-tenure/

Chapter 32

1. http://www.businessdictionary.com/definition/fraud.html
2. http://www.foxnews.com/opinion/2013/12/16/is-president-obama-too-big-to-jail/
3. http://www.theblaze.com/contributions/heres-how-to-impeach-obama-for-consumer-fraud-2/
4. http://articles.chicagotribune.com/2014-03-17/business/chi-kevin-trudeau-sentenced-20140317_1_kevin-trudeau-global-information-network-guzman
5. http://dailycaller.com/2014/11/09/obamacare-architect-lack-of-transparency-was-key-because-stupidity-of-the-american-voter-would-have-killed-obamacare/
6. http://www.forbes.com/sites/theapothecary/2013/10/31/obama-officials-in-2010-93-million-americans-will-be-unable-to-keep-their-health-plans-under-obamacare/
7. http://nation.foxnews.com/2014/11/10/obamacare-architect-admits-deceiving-americans-pass-law
8. http://www.businessdictionary.com/definition/fraud.html

Chapter 33

1. https://www.washingtonpost.com/blogs/in-the-loop/wp/2015/04/16/agency-to-vote-for-spikes-on-the-white-house-fence-but-no-moat/
2. http://www.forbes.com/sites/ralphbenko/2013/03/11/1-6-billion-rounds-of-ammo-for-homeland-security-its-time-for-a-national-conversation/
3. http://www.infowars.com/video-democrat-admits-obama-agenda-is-total-gun-ban/
4. http://www.breitbart.com/big-government/2016/05/04/hillary-clintons-six-outrageous-gun-control-proposals/
5. http://www.rasmussenreports.com/public_content/politics/general_politics/december_2012/following_school_shooting_86_want_more_action_to_identify_and_treat_mental_illness

6. http://www.zerohedge.com/news/2012-12-15/newtown-shooter-had-asperger-syndrome-and-some-us-gun-facts
7. https://www.gunowners.org/sk0802htm.htm
8. http://constitutionalistnc.tripod.com/hitler-leftist/id14.html
9. http://reason.com/blog/2013/03/13/communism-killed-94m-in-20th-century
10. http://www.washingtontimes.com/news/2016/mar/25/obama-on-capitalist-versus-communist-theory-just-c/
11. http://freedomoutpost.com/gun-control-dictator-style-tyrants-who-banned-firearms-before-slaughtering-the-people/

Chapter 36

1. http://www.washingtonsblog.com/2015/03/debt.html
2. https://www.treasurydirect.gov/govt/rates/pd/avg/2016/2016_01.htm
3. http://www.evansonasset.com/index.cfm?Page=161
4. http://www.zerohedge.com/news/2013-03-26/guest-post-whom-believe-gold-central-banks-or-bloomberg
5. http://www.forbes.com/sites/afontevecchia/2013/03/27/central-banks-bought-more-than-3-trillion-in-gold-in-2013-ubs/
6. http://www.zerohedge.com/news/2015-02-12/central-banks-buy-second-most-gold-50-years-look-whos-buying
7. http://www.ino.com/blog/2015/06/central-banks-keep-buying-gold-when-you-are-not/#.V2FvIFd_l7Y
8. http://www.prweb.com/releases/2010/11/prweb4795634.htm
9. http://www.abc.net.au/news/2014-01-11/brasher-doubloon-coin-sells-for-us-45-million/5195546
10. http://www.dailymail.co.uk/news/article-2268041/Rare-1794-silver-dollar-sells-record-10-million-U-S-auction.html
11. http://internationalhardasset.com/reports/IHAI_Report_ColoredDiamonds.pdf
12. http://www.cnbc.com/id/101196278
13. http://www.4cs.gia.edu/EN-US/